ge

# Spelling
## Teacher's Guide

- **Instructional Options**
- **Answers**

**HOLT, RINEHART AND WINSTON**

A Harcourt Classroom Education Company

**Austin** · New York · Orlando · Atlanta · San Francisco · Boston · Dallas · Toronto · London

## STAFF CREDITS

### EDITORIAL

*Director*

Mescal Evler

*Manager of Editorial Operations*

Bill Wahlgren

*Executive Editor*

Emily G. Shenk

*Project Editor*

James E. Eckel

### Writing and Editing

Karen S. Ellis, Michael Nassoiy, Peggy Ferrin, Steve Oelenberger, Jennifer R. Schwan, Stephanie Wenger

### Copyediting

Michael Neibergall, *Copyediting Manager;* Mary Malone, *Senior Copyeditor;* Joel Bourgeois, Elizabeth Dickson, Gabrielle Field, Julie A. Hill, Jane Kominek, Millicent Ondras, Theresa Reding, Dennis Scharnberg, Kathleen Scheiner, Laurie Schlesinger, *Copyeditors*

### Project Administration

Marie Price, *Managing Editor;* Lori De La Garza, *Editorial Operations Coordinator;* Thomas Browne, Heather Cheyne, Diane Hardin, Mark Holland, Marcus Johnson, Jill O'Neal, Joyce Rector, Janet Riley, Kelly Tankersley, *Project Administration;* Gail Coupland, Ruth Hooker, Margaret Sanchez, *Word Processing*

### Editorial Permissions

Janet Harrington, *Permissions Editor*

## ART, DESIGN, AND PHOTO

### Graphic Services

Kristen Darby, *Manager*

### Image Acquisitions

Joe London, *Director;* Tim Taylor, *Photo Research Supervisor;* Rick Benavides, *Assistant Photo Researcher;* Elaine Tate, *Supervisor;* Erin Cone, *Art Buyer*

### Cover Design

Sunday Patterson

## PRODUCTION

Belinda Barbosa Lopez, *Senior Production Coordinator*
Simira Davis, *Supervisor*
Nancy Hargis, *Media Production Supervisor*
Joan Lindsay, *Production Coordinator*
Beth Prevelige, *Senior Production Manager*
Gene Rumann, *Production Manager*

## MANUFACTURING

Shirley Cantrell, *Supervisor of Inventory and Manufacturing*

Printed in the United States of America

ISBN 0-03-064034-2

2  3  4  5      085      05  04  03  02

# Table of Contents

## Lessons

**UNIT 1**
Lessons, Tests, Activities

**UNIT 2**
Lessons, Tests, Activities

# Table of Contents *(continued)*

# Table of Contents *(continued)*

## Management Charts

## Student Worksheets and Answer Key

## Teacher Resources

# Philosophy of *Spelling*

*Spelling* presents spelling and vocabulary instruction that is developmental in sequence and comprehensive in scope. Based on extensive research, the program offers teachers useful and practical strategies for maximizing students' learning of spelling and provides numerous opportunities for students to learn and apply a variety of spelling strategies to all of their writing.

**INTRODUCTION**

*Spelling* is based upon these beliefs:

**BELIEFS**

- Use of an organized, developmental spelling curriculum and purposeful activities promotes spelling growth.
- A diagnostic tool that gives teachers insight into each student's stage of development is an integral part of an effective spelling program.
- A spelling program should help students develop a spelling consciousness—an ability to examine their own writing and identify misspelled words.
- Allowing students to invent or use temporary spelling in their writing, while gradually helping them arrive at more standard spellings, reflects the natural developmental process for learning spelling.
- Knowledge of the history and heritage of the English language, along with language play, is an essential component of a spelling program.

*Spelling* provides instruction and practice for every day of the week. Each core lesson, which can be combined with a Pretest and a Posttest, includes

**CONCEPT LESSONS**

- a spelling generalization
- a corresponding list of Spelling Words gathered from research
- activities that incorporate one or more graphophonic, visual, or morphemic spelling strategies that students practice and apply to learn to be strategic spellers

The last lesson of each unit in *Spelling* is a review lesson that connects to language skills. By reviewing spelling and vocabulary in the context of these activities, students reinforce spelling in a natural way.

**REVIEW LESSONS**

# Planning Instruction

The instructional plan of the developmental lessons is both consistent and flexible.

- Skill development takes place in the context of reading, writing, listening, and speaking.
- Students progress through the following stages in each lesson: discovery of spelling patterns through sorting, consideration of relevant rules and strategies, application of these rules and strategies, and confirmation of understanding.
- Suggestions for meeting individual needs help ensure that every student benefits from every lesson.
- Each developmental lesson has two parts that may be taught in 3–5 days.
- Opportunities for teacher choice allow instruction to be tailored to fit the various developmental levels of students.

**◀ INSTRUCTIONAL PLAN**

The first page of each Teacher's Guide lesson provides tools for making instruction appropriate for students and includes objectives and lesson-planning information as well as second-language support guidance. The Pretest/Posttest and answers to the Pupil's Edition sorting activity also appear on this page.

**◀ LESSON PREPARATION**

The first page of each lesson also offers a Pretest and a Self-Check procedure. Introducing the Lesson offers two options—Open Sort and Modeling. The open-sort activity allows students to use their own sorting criterion. The modeling activity allows teachers to introduce the lesson skill in context. Teaching the Lesson offers a closed-sort activity that walks through the various patterns represented in the list of Spelling Words.

**◀ INTRODUCING AND TEACHING STRATEGIES**

This page presents useful strategies and structural information about the Spelling Words. Students immediately put this new knowledge to use in the activities.

Students also have the opportunity to demonstrate proficiency by taking a Posttest. Answers to Spelling Clues, Proofreading, Fun with Words, and Working with Meaning are also included. Reteaching the Lesson provides help for students with learning differences.

**◀ PRACTICE AND REINFORCEMENT STRATEGIES**

The Unit Review Lesson gives students opportunities to work with the words, review strategies and rules, and apply accumulated knowledge.

**◀ UNIT REVIEW LESSONS**

# Meeting Individual Needs

Each lesson in the Teacher's Guide provides research-based support and teaching strategies to help meet the individual needs of students.

Many features of *Spelling* encourage application of different learning modalities:

- Reteaching the Lesson is designated for visual, auditory, or kinesthetic learners.
- The Self-Check activities and the open- and closed-sort activities in each lesson also address varying modalities.

**◄ LEARNING DIFFERENCES**

Each Teacher's Guide lesson includes Second-Language Support notes. These notes

- identify patterns and spelling skills that are transferable from certain languages to English
- describe phonemic elements that differ between some students' first language and English
- suggest ways to reinforce and convey the meaning of unfamiliar words and phrases
- encourage students acquiring English to work with peer tutors who can model correct usage and answer questions

The many oral language activities in *Spelling* are also of great benefit to students who are acquiring English.

**◄ SECOND-LANGUAGE SUPPORT**

*Spelling* recognizes that today's classroom includes students at different developmental levels. The Spelling Placement Inventory and the Pretests/Posttests provide insight into each student's developmental level, and each lesson includes suggestions for adapting instruction. See also page ix for help in determining your students' developmental levels.

**◄ DEVELOPMENTAL LEVELS**

# Developmental Levels of Spellers

Students benefit most from instruction that is appropriate to their developmental levels. The developmental levels of most students may be determined by using the Spelling Placement Inventory on pages xii–xiv of this Teacher's Guide.

◄ **TRANSITIONAL SPELLERS**
(Below Level)

- These students move from concrete to more abstract representation, one that requires greater reliance on visual memory—spelling words the way they look rather than the way they sound.
- Transitional spellers may include all the appropriate letters in a word, but they may reverse some letters, such as in *TAOD* for *toad* or *FETE* for *feet*.
- Students may still invent spellings, but they have learned many of the conventions of English spelling. They put vowels in every syllable, use vowel digraph patterns, spell inflectional endings correctly, and use English letter sequences that occur frequently.
- By reading, writing, and thinking about spelling, these students develop a sense of when a particular spelling looks correct.

◄ **SYNTACTIC-SEMANTIC SPELLERS**
(On Level)

- These students are competent and correct spellers. They understand the English spelling system and its basic rules.
- Students understand the accurate spelling of prefixes, suffixes, contractions, compound words, and many irregular spellings; they usually use silent letters and double consonants correctly; they are able to distinguish homophones.
- Through understanding the principles of syllable juncture and applying what they know about one-syllable words, students are able to spell multisyllabic words accurately.
- When spelling a new word, students think of alternative spellings and visualize the word.
- Students begin to recognize word origins and use this information to make meaningful associations as they accumulate a large body of known spellings.

◄ **STRATEGIC SPELLERS**
(Above Level)

- These students have already mastered basic spelling patterns and are able to apply them automatically.
- Students have developed a spelling consciousness that allows them to adapt and integrate spelling strategies as a natural part of the writing process.
- Their understanding of meaning relationships enables students to be confident language users and serves as a powerful spelling resource.

# Assessment

### Error Analysis Chart for Writing Activities

The chart on page 90 of this Teacher's Guide enables you to record and analyze the words students misspell as they complete writing activities in each unit. It is designed to help you analyze the nature of students' spelling errors and thereby customize instruction to meet individual needs.

### Portfolio Conference

Periodic conferences give students, teachers, and family members a chance to reflect on each student's writing and developing knowledge of spelling. An evaluation portfolio should be created for each student. See Guidelines for Portfolio Conferences on pages xv–xvii for suggestions of items to include in each evaluation portfolio.

### Spelling Placement Inventory

See pages xii–xiv for administering and interpreting the Spelling Placement Inventory. The Spelling Placement Inventory will help you devise an instructional plan for each student by assessing his or her developmental level.

### Pretest/Posttest/Practice Test

The Pretest/Posttest for each lesson provides a set of numbered context sentences for the Spelling Words. Students are asked to write each Spelling Word after hearing the word and its context sentence read aloud.

The Pretest given at the beginning of each lesson encourages students to draw on their prior knowledge. It determines which spelling patterns or generalizations have been mastered and which areas need improvement. The Self-Check activities encourage students to play an active role in evaluating their work. Assign or have students choose partners for assessing students' own words.

The Posttest given at the end of each lesson is an effective diagnostic tool for determining if extra practice is needed. In addition, the Practice Test at the end of each unit may be used to assess student progress.

◄ INFORMAL ASSESSMENT
OPTIONS

◄ FORMAL ASSESSMENT
OPTIONS

# Assessment *(continued)*

Research has shown that spelling instruction is most effective when it is linked to authentic writing tasks. For students to develop the skills and habits of proficient spellers, they need to view correct spelling within the broader context of reading, writing, and the communication of ideas. Therefore, the natural starting point for the assessment of spelling awareness is the written work that students complete in all subject areas as part of their daily assignments.

◀ **RESEARCH FINDINGS**

*Spelling* supports you in the ongoing informal assessment of each student's developing spelling skills. The Error Analysis Chart on page 90 provides space for recording the misspellings that appear in students' writing. Use the chart to help you identify recurring spelling errors, analyze the nature of the misspellings, and determine which lessons in *Spelling* will be of greatest benefit.

◀ **ERROR ANALYSIS CHART**

As students work through each lesson, mastering spelling and acquiring skills, update the charts. This process will enable you to identify areas of achievement and informally assess areas that need improvement.

The lessons in *Spelling* are designed to engage students actively in integrated listening, speaking, reading, and writing activities and to help them develop a spelling consciousness. All of the activities provide excellent opportunities for on-going performance-based assessment. Clues to students' developing word knowledge and attitudes toward spelling may also be revealed in oral summarizing activities. Throughout the lesson, students are encouraged to assess their progress and to help their classmates evaluate their work.

◀ **INTEGRATED ACTIVITIES**

To develop independent spelling awareness, *Spelling* teaches spelling as part of the writing process. Writing samples, including unfinished work and proofread drafts, should be included in an evaluation portfolio and reviewed periodically. The proofreading phase provides important clues to students' progress. For informal assessment during this stage, students can work independently, in pairs, or in small groups.

◀ **PORTFOLIO ASSESSMENT**

You may want to monitor students' performances, observing how effectively they edit their work and how successfully they select resources to confirm spellings. Students' Personal Word Logs are another useful measure of their growth as independent, competent spellers.

# Spelling Placement Inventory

## Administering the Spelling Placement Inventory

Administer the Spelling Placement Inventory on page xiv at the beginning of the school year.

1. Dictate the 25 words to students by pronouncing each word, using it in a sentence, and then pronouncing the word again.

2. Collect students' papers and score each Spelling Placement Inventory by writing the correct spelling beside each incorrect spelling. An example follows.

| ▶ STUDENT 1 | | ▶ STUDENT 2 | |
|---|---|---|---|
| duplicate | ✓ | dooplacate | duplicate |
| barbecue | ✓ | barbecue | ✓ |
| automaticly | automatically | automatickly | automatically |
| permanently | ✓ | permenetly | permanently |
| ocupant | occupant | ockupint | occupant |
| pennyless | penniless | penneless | penniless |
| debre | debris | dibree | debris |
| embarassment | embarrassment | imbaresment | embarrassment |
| tranciant | transient | transhant | transient |
| architecture | ✓ | arcitechure | architecture |

3. Assign a numerical score to each student's Spelling Placement Inventory (0 percent to 100 percent range, with 4 points taken off for each incorrect spelling). At the beginning of the school year, a student should be able to spell at least 30 percent of the list words correctly if he or she is to benefit fully from working in this grade level of *Spelling*.

Students who spell 30 percent or more of the pretest words correctly will likely produce misspellings that show adequate knowledge of eighth-grade spelling patterns. Student 1, in this example, spelled four of the ten words correctly (40 percent of this sample). Note, however, that each of the misspellings was off by only one feature (e.g., *automaticly* for *automatically*, *ocupant* for *occupant*, and *embarassment* for *embarrassment*). Student 1 should benefit from eighth-grade spelling instruction.

Student 2 spelled only one of the ten words correctly (10 percent of this sample). Note further that this student's misspellings, although interpretable, were often considerably off the mark (e.g., *automatickly* for *automatically*, *ockupint* for *occupant*, and *imbaresment* for *embarrassment*). Student 2 lacks spelling-pattern knowledge at the eighth-grade level and could benefit from studying spelling words at a lower grade or difficulty level.

4. By administering the same 25-word Spelling Placement Inventory at the end of this grade level and scoring it in the manner described, you will be able to document for each student pretest/posttest gains in the number of correct spellings and also corresponding pretest-to-posttest change in the quality of the student's misspellings. The Spelling Placement Inventory may also be administered periodically to determine growth over shorter periods.

By the end of the year, an achieving student should score at least 70 percent accuracy on the Spelling Placement Inventory, and the student's errors on the Spelling Placement Inventory should reflect grade-level spelling-pattern knowledge.

# Grade 8 Spelling Placement Inventory

Follow the directions on pages xii–xiii for administering this Spelling Placement Inventory.

| WORDS | STAGES Errors indicating instructional-level knowledge of the spelling system | Errors indicating below-grade-level knowledge of the spelling system |
|---|---|---|
| 1. duplicate | duplecate, douplicate | doplagate |
| 2. barbecue (*or* barbeque) | barbacue (*or* barbaque) | bobbacue (*or* bobbaque) |
| 3. automatically | automaticly | automatickly |
| 4. permanently | permenantly | permanetly |
| 5. occupant | ocupant | ockupint |
| 6. penniless | pennyless | penneless |
| 7. debris | debre | dibree, dobere |
| 8. embarrassment | embaressment | imberessment |
| 9. transient | trancient, transhant | trantiant |
| 10. architecture | archetecture | arcitecture |
| 11. irrigated | irigated, irregated | iragated |
| 12. combination | combanasion | combonashun |
| 13. medicine | medecin, medecine | medeicne |
| 14. advocate | advicate | addfocate |
| 15. criticism | critisism, critisizm | cretasesm |
| 16. obscure | abscure | upscure |
| 17. odyssey | oddesy | oddisee |
| 18. icicle | iceicle | icecicle |
| 19. circuit | curcuit, circut | serkut, sercet |
| 20. sensory | sensery | sensurey |
| 21. infinite | infanite, infanete | infinit |
| 22. persimmon | pursimmon, persimmin | persemen |
| 23. terrace | terace, terice | teress, terris |
| 24. satellite | satelite, satilite | sadelight |
| 25. occasionally | ocassionally, occaisionally | ocasianely |

**Note:** At Grades 6–8, the instructional level is the syntactic-semantic level. Below-level students spell at the transitional level. If students achieve higher than 70 percent accuracy on the Spelling Placement Inventory, they may be able to work at the strategic level of instruction.

# Guidelines for Portfolio Conferences

Since spelling occurs naturally within the context of writing, a portfolio provides an effective way of illustrating students' development as spellers. This section provides suggestions for including indicators of spelling progress in students' portfolios. It also offers guidelines for discussing spelling progress in conferences with students and with family members.

Each student should organize the contents of the portfolio according to a system with which he or she feels comfortable. After students have decided on a method, suggest that they think about ways to include examples of their spelling work. Ask them to decide how their spelling work best fits in with other categories in the portfolio.

◀ **INCORPORATING SPELLING SAMPLES INTO THE PORTFOLIO**

If a student has organized a portfolio by topic, he or she may want to place topic-related Spelling Words in the appropriate sections of the portfolio. If a student's portfolio is organized chronologically, spelling-related work might be placed in the portfolio according to when the work was done. Some students may prefer to create a separate section just for spelling work.

In addition to selecting several examples of completed spelling assignments, students might choose to include the following items in their portfolios:

◀ **ITEMS TO INCLUDE IN A PORTFOLIO**

**WRITING SAMPLES** Encourage students to add writing samples that show spelling corrections they have made. Drafts showing errors that students have discovered and corrected while proofreading are good indicators of their spelling progress.

**PRETEST AND POSTTEST** You may want to have students include Pretests and Posttests in their portfolios to show the progress they have made with particular groups of words. Such items should not be included as part of a formal assessment or as a means of judging students' weaknesses. Rather, the tests should be used as a method of demonstrating progress and as a way for students to assess their own achievements.

**PERSONAL WORD LOGS** If students are keeping Personal Word Logs of unusual and interesting words, encourage them to photocopy some of these pages and add them to the portfolio. These pages provide insight into a student's interests.

Learning about a word's origin by studying its root, such as the Latin root *aqua,* may help a student understand and spell a variety of unfamiliar words that share this root, such as *aqua-*

# Guidelines for Portfolio Conferences *(continued)*

*marine, aquatic,* and *aquarium.* Encourage students to record the root in their Personal Word Logs and add the sheet to their portfolios.

◄ **CONFERENCES BETWEEN A FAMILY MEMBER AND A TEACHER**

Discuss with the family member how the student has chosen to incorporate indicators of his or her spelling progress into the portfolio. Then share examples of the student's work that reveal spelling development, such as writing activities, Personal Word Log pages, and Pretest/Posttest pages. The following checklist may be used to help you emphasize the progress individual students have made and point out areas that need improvement:

- awareness of spelling patterns
- ability to apply knowledge of known words to unfamiliar words that share a similar pattern or origin
- developmental level of the student

◄ **CONFERENCES BETWEEN A TEACHER AND A STUDENT**

Try to conduct the conferences so that the student does most of the talking. Prompts such as these will help generate discussion:

- Tell me how you organized your spelling work in your portfolio.
- Let's look at a piece of writing that shows some corrections you made in spelling. How did you find the mistakes? How did you figure out how to spell the words correctly?
- What spelling strategies are most helpful to you when you are trying to spell new words?
- How often do you use a dictionary? How is a dictionary helpful?
- What kind of progress do you think you have made in spelling?

The student's responses to questions such as these will provide valuable insight into his or her attitudes, habits, and strengths. Help the student set goals that will develop increased proficiency in spelling. These goals might include using a dictionary more often when proofreading, consulting with peers when troublesome words are encountered, or referring to spelling strategies more often.

◄ **CONFERENCES BETWEEN TWO STUDENTS**

Peer portfolio conferences offer a valuable opportunity for students to discuss their progress, share the things they find most challenging, and compare problem-solving strategies with one another. The questions on page xvii can help students get their peer conferences off the ground. You might want to duplicate a set of questions for each pair of students to use as a guide during the conference.

# Guidelines for Portfolio Conferences *(continued)*

- How did you organize your portfolio?
- Where did you put your spelling work? What kinds of things did you include?
- What do you like about spelling? What is hard about spelling for you?
- What do you do when you want to write a word but don't know how to spell it?
- What are some difficult words you can spell? How did you learn to spell them?

Encourage students to share the strategies they have discovered that are the most useful for spelling new words and remembering the spelling of troublesome words. Ask students to try to be as specific as they can. For example, a student who has trouble with *ie/ei* spellings may have developed a mnemonic device for remembering which spelling to use.

Also, encourage students to become resources for one another in sharing their solutions and strategies. Encourage them to take notes during their peer conferences and add them to the portfolio. Each student's name, his or her partner's name, the date of the conference, and any valuable information learned during the conference should be included.

# How to Study a Word

The strategy described in How to Study a Word on Pupil's Edition page v will help students become successful, independent spellers. The strategy utilizes visual, auditory, and kinesthetic modalities.

- The first step has students say the word aloud and think about its meaning, reinforcing the meaning basis for spelling.
- The second step asks students to look at the word, think about words that are related in meaning or resemble the word, and visualize the word. (This step develops the use of analogy as a spelling cue.)
- The third step has students spell the word silently and think about sound-letter relationships, reinforcing sound-letter relationships and sound-letter cues.
- The fourth step utilizes a kinesthetic mode—writing—to develop students' visual memory of the word. Students write the word, check the clarity of the letters, and then rewrite the word if necessary. (This step reminds students to write legibly to avoid spelling errors.)
- The fifth step strengthens students' visual memory of the word by having them cover the word they wrote and check its spelling.

Before students begin their work in the Pupil's Edition, introduce them to How to Study a Word. Have students read page v silently. Ask volunteers to re-read the five steps aloud. Guide students through the steps, using an example.

◀ **INTRODUCING THE STUDY STEPS**

Discuss with students how they might use How to Study a Word. Here are some suggestions:

◀ **WAYS TO USE THE STEPS**

- when they encounter unfamiliar words or words they are unsure of how to spell
- when they misspell words in their writing
- when they misspell words on the pretest or posttest

# Spelling and Proofreading Strategies

The lessons in *Spelling* are designed around and utilize two major strategies of instruction: (a) phonology—consistent spelling patterns based on sound-letter relationships and (b) analogy—common characteristics of words as the basis for predicting the spelling of unfamiliar words.

To aid students in developing the tools to become competent, independent spellers, spelling and proofreading strategies are provided to maximize their learning. The strategies help students think about spelling as a skill they can develop through a variety of processes such as these:

- Utilizing a five-step strategy can help them learn the spelling of new words.
- Using a variety of spelling strategies can help them remember the spelling of troublesome words.
- Using possible spellings, thinking about word families, and using a dictionary can help them figure out how to spell new words.
- Proofreading will help them identify spelling errors in their own writing.

These specific strategies and others are presented in *Spelling:*

◀ **SPELLING STRATEGIES**

- *How to Study a Word* Students are encouraged to use the five study steps to help them learn the spelling of new words.
- *Picture/Sound Out a Word* In this strategy, students picture a word they want to write and think about the sound a letter stands for.
- *Try Different Spellings* Students think about the vowel sound in a word, consider different ways this sound can be represented by letters, and try different spellings until the word looks right.
- *Guess and Check* Students guess the spelling of a word and then check its spelling in a dictionary.
- *Rhyming Words/Word Families* By thinking about word families or rhyming words that share the same spelling pattern and sound-letter relationship, students often figure out the spelling of a word.
- *Use a Dictionary* Students can simply look up the spelling of a word in a dictionary.
- *Homophones* Students pay particular attention to context clues and make sure homophones are spelled correctly.
- *Compound Words* Students break compound words into two smaller words and check the spelling of each word.
- *Mnemonic Devices/Memory Clues* Good spellers develop and use memory clues, including mnemonic devices, to help them remember the spelling of words.

# Spelling and Proofreading Strategies *(continued)*

These particular strategies are helpful to students as they proofread:

- *Proofread Twice* By proofreading their writing twice, students identify spelling errors they know they have made as well as possible misspellings.
- *Proofread with a Partner* Using this strategy, students work with a partner to check and discuss each other's spelling.
- *Proofread Backward* By beginning with the last word in a paragraph and reading each word in isolation, students are apt to notice misspellings because the words are not in context.

Ask students to name some strategies they can use to help them figure out how to spell a word that is new to them and to remember the spelling of words they know. List their suggestions on the board. Explain that students will learn about some additional spelling strategies they can use as they write and proofread. Have students read pages vi and vii silently. Then, invite volunteers to read aloud the strategies.

Encourage students to summarize the strategies by asking questions such as these:

- Which strategies might you use when you are trying to figure out how to spell a word you don't know?
- Imagine that you want to spell the word *light*. How can thinking about the words *might* and *bright* help you?
- Imagine that you need to spell the compound word *firehouse*. What strategy could you use to help you?
- How can proofreading your written work two times help you find spelling errors?

Invite students to share mnemonic devices they have heard or made up themselves that help them remember the spellings of new words.

Discuss with students when to use spelling and proofreading strategies. Point out that these strategies are also useful as students are writing. Encourage students to refer to pages vi and vii as they write.

**◄ PROOFREADING STRATEGIES**

**◄ INTRODUCING THE STRATEGIES**

# Word Logs

A Word Log provides an excellent opportunity for students to record new words they learn, keep an ongoing record of words they have misspelled on pretests or in other writing, and note troublesome words as an aid to writing and proofreading. A Word Log also encourages students to record words that are of special interest to them, such as words having to do with a favorite activity, place, or topic. The Pupil's Edition of *Spelling* includes Word Logs in which students may record words from the spelling lessons, words they have misspelled in pretests and posttests, and words they acquire from other sources.

Ask students to name some different ways they learn new words *(reading books, signs, menus; listening to the radio; watching TV; talking with friends)*. To introduce the idea of a Word Log, ask students to name some ways they can remember new words they learn. Explain that there is a special section of their spelling book that they can use for recording new words. Have students read page viii of the Pupil's Edition silently.

Invite students to examine the Word Logs in their books.

**◀ INTRODUCING THE WORD LOGS**

You might also have students create additional or separate individual Word Logs. Encourage students to use sheets of lined paper that they can keep in a notebook. To be useful, each Word Log should be organized so that students can easily find words they have written and systematically add new words. Students might organize their logs alphabetically, with one page for each letter of the alphabet.

**◀ CREATING WORD LOGS**

Encourage students to include these items in their logs:

- troublesome words such as *there, their,* and *they're,* along with context sentences or definitions that help students remember which word to use
- words that share a spelling pattern or common structure
- interesting word facts about word origins and history

Set aside some time for students to create or decorate the covers for their Word Logs.

# Lesson 1: Compound Words

## OBJECTIVE
To spell words that are formed by joining two different words

## HOME ACTIVITY
The home activity is on page 94.

## SECOND-LANGUAGE SUPPORT
The concept of compound words should be familiar to most of your second-language students, as many languages have compound words. Write these words on the board: *overexcited*, *coat hanger*, *white-haired*, *doorstep*, *Central Park*, and *horse-drawn*. Have students brainstorm other English words that are compound words, and write those words on the board, too. Have volunteers draw a vertical line between the two parts of each word and explain the meaning of the word based on the meanings of the word parts. DETERMINING MEANING

## PRETEST/ POSTTEST
1. Susan gets **homesick** whenever she goes away on vacation.
2. We decorate several types of **evergreen** trees in December.
3. A **well-wisher** waved to his friend as the train left the station.
4. Wendy carried the **picnic basket** from the car to the beach.
5. Carl likes **homemade** bread, so he bakes it once a week.
6. Our **long-term** plans include adding a second story to our house.
7. The **underground** tunnels in our city need some repairs.
8. Aunt Doris always carries a white **handkerchief.**
9. Building the new gym is a **large-scale** project.
10. Henry made a huge batch of **gingerbread** cookies.
11. It was a long movie; **furthermore,** it was boring!

*(continued on next page)*

## Pretest
Administer the test on this page as a pretest. Say each word, use it in the sentence, and then repeat the word. ACCESSING PRIOR KNOWLEDGE

**SELF-CHECK** Have students check their own pretests against the list of Spelling Words. Remind students to write misspelled words in their Lesson Word Logs. STUDENT SELF-ASSESSMENT

## Introducing the Lesson

### Option A (Open Sort)
Distribute the word cards (page 93) to individuals or small groups, and guide them in an open-sort activity. In open sort, students group the word cards according to a criterion they select themselves. They might group words that share the same beginning or middle sound, words that are related by topic, or words that have a similar shape.

### Option B (Modeling)
Read aloud with students the lesson title and the Spelling Words. Use this model sentence to introduce the lesson skill in a context.

*Let's get a **root beer** and **something** to eat.*

## Teaching the Lesson

- Ask volunteers to name the Spelling Words that are spelled with two words joined together. As students name words, list the words on the board. *(homesick, evergreen, homemade, underground, handkerchief, gingerbread, furthermore, stagecoach, headquarters, loudspeaker)*
- Follow the same procedure for the words that are spelled with a hyphen and then for the compounds that are written as two separate words. (**hyphenated:** *well-wisher, long-term, large-scale, good-natured;* **open:** *picnic basket, heart attack*)
- After students have named words in all these categories, have them decide which heading—*Closed, Hyphenated,* or *Open*—belongs above each column.
- Have students add their own examples to the columns.

**IN SUMMARY** Ask students to summarize the lesson in their own words. Elicit from students the response that some compounds are closed, some are hyphenated, and some are open.

**ASSIGNMENT** Students can complete the first page of the lesson as a follow-up to the group activity, either in class or as homework.

# Lesson 1: Compound Words (continued)

## Practicing the Lesson

### Spelling Clues: Compound Words

Suggest to students that when they encounter a compound word whose spelling they are unsure of, they find the two smaller words that it is made of. They should try using various spellings for the words and various ways of combining them as compounds and then choose the spelling that looks correct. If they are still unsure, they should look up the word in a dictionary. Point out that most compound words are two words that are joined together. Most compound words in English start out as two separate words, evolve into a hyphenated form, and finally become one word. Explain that a few compound words may be written two ways; *vice president*, for example, may be open or hyphenated.   APPLYING SPELLING STRATEGIES

### Proofreading

You may wish to have students review Spelling Clues: Compound Words before proofreading the note.

### Fun with Words

Students may complete this activity individually or with a partner. Tell students to look for clues in the silly definitions and to choose the correct Spelling Word based on that clue.

## Posttest

Administer the test on page xxii as a posttest, or administer one of your own. Say each word, use it in a sentence, and then repeat the word.

## Reteaching the Lesson

Have students draw a row of connected boxes for each Spelling Word, with one box for each letter. Instruct students to fill in each word's first letter and to leave the other boxes empty. For example, the row of boxes for *long-term* would be drawn as follows:

The row of boxes for *heart attack* would be drawn as follows:

After students have drawn the boxes, dictate the Spelling Words in random order, and ask students to write each word in the appropriate row of boxes. Then have students check their spellings, highlight any word parts that they misspelled, and rewrite the words correctly.   VISUAL MODALITY

*(Pretest/Posttest, continued)*

12. Eating less fat can help prevent a **heart attack.**
13. Our local history museum has a **stagecoach** on display.
14. Allan has a **good-natured** dog.
15. The **headquarters** for our catering business is Carol's house.
16. You'll need a **loudspeaker** to amplify your voice.

### PRACTICE ACTIVITY

The practice activity is on page 95.

### Answers: Spelling Clues

1. well-wisher
2. large-scale
3. heart attack
4. furthermore
5. handkerchief
6. headquarters

### Answers: Proofreading

7. evergreen
8. good-natured
9. long-term
10. picnic basket
11. homemade
12. underground

### Answers: Fun with Words

13. loudspeaker
14. stagecoach
15. gingerbread
16. homesick

# Lesson 2: Homophones

## OBJECTIVE
To recognize and spell homophones

## HOME ACTIVITY
The home activity is on page 97.

## SECOND-LANGUAGE SUPPORT
To provide practice with homophones, prepare flashcards of homophone pairs. On one side of the card, write one of the words, and include an illustration that demonstrates its meaning. Do the same for the other word on the other side of the card. Have a volunteer pick a card. Make up a sentence containing context clues to the meaning of one of the words. Have students write the correct spelling of the word for the sentence you have given. Then repeat these steps for the other word in the pair. Some homophone pairs that you might use in addition to the Spelling Words are *air—heir, ball—bawl, hear—here,* and *chilly—chili.* DETERMINING MEANING

## PRETEST/POSTTEST
1. Janet lives near the **border** of California and Nevada.
2. Although he was innocent, Don was accused of a **capital** crime.
3. Many kinds of wild **fowl** fly over our neighborhood on their way south.
4. The **principal** of our school used to be a teacher here.
5. As a **boarder** in our home, you will need a key to the door.
6  Sam might have been a **bard,** had he lived in medieval times.
7. Meg's favorite exercise machine is the **stationary** bicycle.
8. An important **principle** in sports is fair play.
9. The artist's **palette** held many shades of blue.
10  Paul ordered a thousand sheets of **stationery.**

*(continued on next page)*

## Pretest
Administer the test on this page as a pretest. Say each word, use it in the sentence, and then repeat the word.   ACCESSING PRIOR KNOWLEDGE

**SELF-CHECK**   Have students check their own pretests against the list of Spelling Words. Remind students to write misspelled words in their Lesson Word Logs.   STUDENT SELF-ASSESSMENT

## Introducing the Lesson

### Option A (Open Sort)
Distribute the word cards (page 96) to individuals or small groups, and guide them in an open-sort activity. In open sort, students group the word cards according to a criterion they select themselves. Then guide students in comparing and discussing the criteria they selected.

### Option B (Modeling)
Read aloud with students the lesson title and the Spelling Words. Use this model sentence to introduce the lesson skill in a context.

*The **sun shone** brightly in the window.*

## Teaching the Lesson

- Ask volunteers to name and spell the homophone pairs in which the middle parts of the words are spelled differently. List the words on the board. *(border, boarder; fowl, foul; bard, barred; pallette, pallet)*
- Ask volunteers to name and spell the homophone pairs in which the endings of the words are spelled differently. List the words on the board. *(capital, Capitol; principle, principal; stationary, stationery; burro, burrow)*
- Invite students to name and spell other words that follow these patterns. Add the words to the lists.
- Have volunteers read aloud and define all the words.

**IN SUMMARY**   Have students summarize the lesson in their own words. Elicit the information that knowing the definitions of homophones and noting the context in which they are used can help determine which spelling to use. Lead students to understand that recognizing word structure and using memory clues are other ways to choose the correct spelling.

**ASSIGNMENT**   Students can complete the first page of the lesson as a follow-up to the group activity, either in class or as homework.

# Lesson 2: Homophones (continued)

## Practicing the Lesson

### Spelling Clues: Homophones

Suggest to students that when they get ready to proofread their work, they think about the meanings of the words. Remind them of the importance of using context clues to determine meaning. Once the meaning is determined, they can better judge whether the spelling of the homophone is correct. APPLYING SPELLING STRATEGIES

### Proofreading

You may wish to have students review Spelling Clues: Homophones before proofreading the report.

### Working with Meaning

Students may complete this activity individually or with a partner. After students have completed this activity, you may wish to expand it. Have students write sentences using the words that were incorrectly used in the cartoon. As an additional challenge, have them write sentences that tell a story.

**SECOND-LANGUAGE SUPPORT** Encourage second-language students to pay close attention to the context in which each word is used. Picture clues in the cartoon will help them figure out the intended meaning. USING PICTURE CLUES

## Posttest

Administer the test on page 2 as a posttest, or administer one of your own. Say each word, use it in a sentence, and then repeat the word.

## Reteaching the Lesson

Students with attention deficits are at a disadvantage in spelling homophones. The following activities give the students practice in spelling words in context and provide additional sensory input.

Gather a small group of students around a writing surface. Tell them about homophones and about the two different spellings for words that sound the same. Say a homophone, such as *principal*, and have one student dictate a sentence to you. Write the sentence on a blank copy master, leaving a space for the Spelling Word (for example: *The name of our _____ is Ms. Baxter*). Ask the students to think of a way in which the homophone *principle* can be used, and have one student dictate another sentence. Write the sentence, leaving a blank space for the homophone. Photocopy enough copies for all students. The goal is to have the students write the correctly spelled word in the blank. VISUAL MODALITY

*(Pretest/Posttest, continued)*

11. We each rode a **burro** to the bottom of the Grand Canyon.
12. Al bought a new bed to replace his **pallet** on the floor.
13. The **Capitol** in Washington is a large domed building.
14. The rabbit found safety from the hunter in its **burrow.**
15. A **foul** odor came from the garbage dump.
16. The castle door was **barred** to keep strangers out.

### PRACTICE ACTIVITY

The practice activity is on page 98.

### Answers: Spelling Clues

1. burro        4. palette
2. stationary   5. fowl
3. bard         6. capital

### Answers: Proofreading

7. Capitol      10. stationery
8. principal    11. border
9. burrow

### Answers: Working with Meaning

12. barred      15. pallet
13. boarder     16. principle
14. foul

# Lesson 3: Adding Endings to Words

## OBJECTIVE

To spell inflected forms of words by adding -s, -es, -ed, or -ing

## HOME ACTIVITY

The home activity is on page 100.

## SECOND-LANGUAGE SUPPORT

To provide students with practice in forming the plural by adding -s to a noun, draw a chart on the board. On one side of the chart, draw pictures for the words *boys, girls, shoes,* and *shirts.* Talk about the pictures with students, using the singular form of the words. For example, say *This is a boy; this is a shoe.* Then have students count how many boys, girls, shoes, and shirts there are in the classroom. Place the number next to the words. Review your findings, putting emphasis on the plural forms of the words. RECOGNIZING PLURAL ENDINGS

## PRETEST/POSTTEST

1. Would you rather have rice or **potatoes** with your dinner?
2. I had trouble **separating** the egg yolks from the egg whites.
3. My favorite part of having a garden is **harvesting** the tomatoes.
4. The envelope **contained** directions and a map to the treasure.
5. The **programming** at the radio station is always changing.
6. Mikey **refused** to eat any cereal that contained raisins.
7. Why was my name **omitted** from the guest list?
8. The trees **produced** a lot of oranges this year.
9. Bryan has **acquired** a library of more than two hundred books.
10. Her **abilities** on the ice are well above average.
11. Cindy **submitted** all the proper forms to enter the contest.

*(continued on next page)*

## Pretest

Administer the test on this page as a pretest. Say each word, use it in the sentence, and then repeat the word.    ACCESSING PRIOR KNOWLEDGE

**SELF-CHECK**    Have students check their own pretests against the list of Spelling Words. Remind students to write misspelled words in their Lesson Word Logs.    STUDENT SELF-ASSESSMENT

## Introducing the Lesson

### Option A (Open Sort)

Distribute the word cards (page 99) to individuals or small groups, and guide them in an open-sort activity. In open sort, students group the word cards according to a criterion they select themselves. Then guide students in comparing and discussing the criteria they selected.

### Option B (Modeling)

Read aloud with students the lesson title and the Spelling Words. Use this model sentence to introduce the lesson skill in a context.

*We **tried** to grow **tomatoes** in our garden.*

## Teaching the Lesson

- Ask students to name the base word of each Spelling Word. Then ask volunteers to name the words in which the addition of the ending has not changed the spelling of the base word. List the words on the board. *(refused, produced, acquired, harvesting, contained, nutrients, resources)*
- Ask volunteers to name and spell the words whose spelling changes when endings are added. List the words on the board. *(programming, omitted, submitted, forbidding, separating, potatoes, abilities, justified, petrified)*
- Guide students in grouping the words in the second list according to the kinds of spelling changes they require.
- Invite students to add words from their own writing to the columns. Have volunteers read all the words aloud and underline the endings.

**IN SUMMARY**    Ask students to summarize the lesson in their own words. Have students explain the kinds of spelling changes some words require when an ending is added.

**ASSIGNMENT**    Students can complete the first page of the lesson as a follow-up to the group activity, either in class or as homework.

# Lesson 3: Adding Endings to Words *(continued)*

## Practicing the Lesson

### Spelling Clues: Word Endings

Suggest to students that when they write words that end in *-s*, *-es*, *-ed*, or *-ing*, they consider whether any changes need to be made to the base word. Remind them that in multisyllabic words, when the stress is on the last syllable, the final consonant is often doubled before *-ed* or *-ing* is added. Then students should try a few different spellings until they find one that looks right. If they are still not sure, they should look the word up in the dictionary.    APPLYING SPELLING STRATEGIES

### Proofreading

You may wish to have students review Spelling Clues: Word Endings before proofreading the story.

### Fun with Words

To extend this activity, you might wish to have students write sentences using each word. Have them leave blanks in sentences and exchange sentences with a partner. Then have them complete the sentences written by their partners.

## Posttest

Administer the test on page 4 as a posttest, or administer one of your own. Say each word, use it in a sentence, and then repeat the word.

## Reteaching the Lesson

One hypothesis about students with learning difficulties is that they are inactive learners; they do not become engaged in the learning process. Encourage active participation on the student's part by using the discovery method (inductive reasoning) of arriving at a generalization.

Write the Spelling Words that exemplify a spelling generalization on the board or on chart paper. Beside each Spelling Word, write the base word. Ask one student at a time to underline the letters that have been added to the base word as you and the other students read the Spelling Word aloud. Ask a student to formulate a hypothesis about what happens to the spelling of the word when an ending is added. Guide the students into discovering the principle of changing the *y*. Evaluate students' grasp of the generalization by asking them to spell several words that follow the same pattern. Follow the same procedure for the other generalization in this lesson. VISUAL MODALITY

*(Pretest/Posttest, continued)*

12. Winning the scholarship **justified** the long hours of studying.
13. Didn't you see the sign **forbidding** fishing in this pond?
14. Alex has a collection of **petrified** wood.
15. This salad dressing has many **nutrients** and few calories.
16. Paula used all her **resources** to fix up that old house.

### PRACTICE ACTIVITY
The practice activity is on page 101.

### Answers: Spelling Clues
1. contained
2. harvesting
3. produced
4. nutrients
5. petrified
6. separating
7. omitted
8. abilities

### Answers: Proofreading
9. acquired
10. programming
11. refused
12. submitted
13. justified
14. resources

### Answers : Fun with Words
15. potatoes
16. forbidding

# Lesson 4: Related Words

## OBJECTIVE
To spell words that are formed from the same base word

## HOME ACTIVITY
The home activity is on page 103.

## SECOND-LANGUAGE SUPPORT
Students acquiring English may find related words confusing. Provide extra practice by writing these words on the board: *beauty—beautiful—beautify, care—carefully—careless, duty—dutiful—dutifully, forget—forgetful—forgetting, grace—graceful—gracious,* and *rest—restful—resting.* Have volunteers pronounce the words orally. Direct students' attention to the similarities in each set. RECOGNIZING RELATED WORDS

## PRETEST/POSTTEST
1. The alarm made an **awful** noise.
2. Tim would like to take a **drama** class next year.
3. The **strain** was showing on Jim's face as he lifted the heavy weights.
4. Stan was **awfully** glad to see his friend Carol after all those years.
5. The party will **continue** even after Hank leaves.
6. One day Dora will enter the medical **profession** as a doctor.
7. The next scene is the most **dramatic** one in the play.
8. A feeling of **despair** suddenly came over her.
9. I was in **awe** of such a talented writer.
10. Glen always behaves very **professionally** at work.
11. A **continuous** flow of conversation kept the party interesting.
12. That kind of work is too **strenuous** for a young child.
13. Jane talked **continuously,** but no one listened.

*(continued on next page)*

## Pretest
Administer the test on this page as a pretest. Say each word, use it in the sentence, and then repeat the word.   ACCESSING PRIOR KNOWLEDGE

**SELF-CHECK**   Have students check their own pretests against the list of Spelling Words. Remind students to write misspelled words in their Lesson Word Logs.   STUDENT SELF-ASSESSMENT

## Introducing the Lesson

### Option A (Open Sort)
Distribute the word cards (page 102) to individuals or small groups, and guide them in an open-sort activity. In open sort, students group the word cards according to a criterion they select themselves. Then guide students in comparing and discussing the criteria they selected.

### Option B (Modeling)
Read aloud with students the lesson title and the Spelling Words. Use this model sentence to introduce the lesson skill in a context.

*Please tell your aunt what a **pleasure** it was to see her.*

## Teaching the Lesson

- Write the headings *Base Word Changes* and *Base Word Stays the Same* on the board.
- Ask volunteers to name related Spelling Words in which the spelling of the base word stays the same. As students name words, list the words on the board. *(profession/professionally, drama/dramatic/dramatically)*
- Ask volunteers to name some related words in which the spelling of the base word changes. List the words on the board. *(awe/awful/awfully, continue/continuous/continuously, strain/strenuous/strenuously, despair/desperately)*
- Have students add words from their own writing to the columns. Then have volunteers read all the words aloud and underline the base words.

**IN SUMMARY**   Have the students summarize the lesson in their own words. Elicit from students the fact that knowing how to spell one word in a word family can help them spell other words that are related to it. Sometimes the base word may require spelling changes before a word ending is added.

**ASSIGNMENT**   Students can complete the first page of the lesson as a follow-up to the activity, either in class or as homework.

# Lesson 4: Related Words (continued)

## Practicing the Lesson

### Spelling Clues: Base Words

Suggest to students that when they consider how to spell a word that has a suffix, they think about its parts, making sure that the suffix is spelled correctly. Then they should decide if the base word needs to be changed before the suffix is added. If they are still not sure of the spelling, they should look the word up in a dictionary.   APPLYING SPELLING STRATEGIES

### Proofreading

You may wish to have students review Spelling Clues: Base Words before proofreading the sentences.

### Fun with Words

Students may complete this activity individually or with a partner. To extend the activity, you may wish to have students write sentences with each of the Spelling Words used in the cartoon.

SECOND-LANGUAGE SUPPORT   Have students work together in small groups. They can help one another by sharing knowledge as they try to determine the correct spelling of the words in the cartoon.

## Posttest

Administer the test on page 6 as a posttest, or administer one of your own. Say each word, use it in a sentence, and then repeat the word.

## Reteaching the Lesson

Have individual students who need additional practice follow a four-step sequence.

1. Write the word plus the prefix. For example: *awful + ly = awfully.*

2. Trace the word, using a felt-tip pen.

3. In pencil, copy the word underneath the model, saying the name of each letter as it is written.

4. Cover the model and write the word from recall.

   Since some base words change their spellings when suffixes are added, have students study those Spelling Words separately. Have students follow a three-step process: write the word and the ending, cross out the letter that is to be dropped or changed, and then write the word with the ending. VISUAL/KINESTHETIC MODALITIES

*(Pretest/Posttest, continued)*

14. When sales go up **dramatically,** everyone is happy.
15. We tried **desperately** to clean the house before the guests arrived.
16. As a fitness trainer, Glenda works out **strenuously** every day.

### PRACTICE ACTIVITY
The practice activity is on page 104.

### Answers: Spelling Clues
1. dramatically
2. strenuous
3. continuous
4. professionally

### Answers: Proofreading
| | |
|---|---|
| 5. awe | 7. drama |
| 6. despair | 8. strain |

### Answers: Fun with Words
| | |
|---|---|
| 9. continuously | 13. strenuously |
| 10. awful | 14. continue |
| 11. desperately | 15. dramatic |
| 12. awfully | 16. profession |

# Lesson 5: Easily Confused Words

## OBJECTIVE
To spell words that have similar pronunciations and that are easily confused with one another

## HOME ACTIVITY
The home activity is on page 106.

## SECOND-LANGUAGE SUPPORT
Since even native speakers of English have difficulties with these words, students acquiring English will certainly find them confusing. Provide extra practice by making flashcards with a Spelling Word on one side and a simple sentence using the word on the other side. Read the sentences aloud, and have volunteers pronounce and define each word as you display it. RECOGNIZING EASILY CONFUSED WORDS

## PRETEST/POSTTEST
1. After running a mile, Mark could hardly catch his **breath.**
2. The concert was **finally** over.
3. We bought many interesting items at the **bazaar.**
4. Jerry took an **antidote** after being bitten by a snake.
5. "I think he's becoming **conscious**," said the doctor as Ray opened his eyes.
6. Pete made pillow covers from the **excess** fabric.
7. Grace's dinosaur costume is quite **bizarre.**
8. The recipe calls for **finely** chopped onions to be added to the mix.
9. The **breadth** of the barn is twice as much as its height.
10. If you are **persecuted**, you are mistreated for no good reason.
11. Sally's **conscience** was clear because she was telling the truth.
12. He will be **prosecuted** for breaking the law.

*(continued on next page)*

## Pretest
Administer the test on this page as a pretest. Say each word, use it in the sentence, and then repeat the word.   ACCESSING PRIOR KNOWLEDGE

**SELF-CHECK**   Have students check their own pretests against the list of Spelling Words. Remind students to write misspelled words in their Lesson Word Logs.   STUDENT SELF-ASSESSMENT

## Introducing the Lesson

### Option A (Open Sort)
Distribute the word cards (page 105) to individuals or small groups, and guide them in an open-sort activity. In open sort, students group the word cards according to a criterion they select themselves. Then guide students in comparing and discussing the criteria they selected.

### Option B (Modeling)
Read aloud with students the lesson title and the Spelling Words. Use this model sentence to introduce the lesson skill in a context.

*Do you think this **costume** is too **casual** for the publicity **picture?***

## Teaching the Lesson

- Ask volunteers to name a pair of one-syllable Spelling Words that are easily confused. As students name the words, list them on the board under the heading *One Syllable.* (*breath/breadth*)
- Follow the same procedure for two- and three-syllable words that are easily confused. List the words on the board under the appropriate headings. (*bazaar/bizarre, futile/feudal, conscious/conscience, excess/access, persecuted/prosecuted, antidote/anecdote*)
- Ask volunteers to name a pair of words that have a different number of syllables and that are easily confused. List the words on the board under the heading *Differing Number of Syllables. (finally, finely)*
- Have students add their own examples to the columns. Then have volunteers read all the words aloud and define them.

**IN SUMMARY**   Ask students to summarize the lesson in their own words. Elicit the response that some words are easily confused and that it helps to be aware of them.

**ASSIGNMENT**   Students can complete the first page of the lesson as a follow-up to the activity, either in class or as homework.

# Lesson 5: Easily Confused Words (continued)

## Practicing the Lesson

### Spelling Clues: Correct Pronunciation
Suggest to students that when they encounter a word that is very similar to another word, they take care to pronounce it correctly before trying to spell it. Correct pronunciation is a good clue to the correct spelling of easily confused words. APPLYING SPELLING STRATEGIES

**TRANSITIONAL SPELLERS** Have students complete this activity cooperatively with a partner or in a small group. You may wish to have students use the words in sentences.

### Proofreading
You may wish to have students review Spelling Clues: Correct Pronunciation before proofreading the sentences.

### Working with Meaning
Students may complete this activity individually or with a partner. Suggest to students that they use picture clues to help them figure out the word that best matches each picture. After students have completed the activity, you may wish to provide more practice by having students write sentences for a partner, using the rest of the Spelling Words. Then they can exchange papers, complete each other's sentences, and exchange again to check each other's work.

## Posttest
Administer the test on page 8 as a posttest, or administer one of your own. Say each word, use it in a sentence, and then repeat the word.

## Reteaching the Lesson
Prepare a copy master with pairs of similar words, leaving sufficient space underneath each pair for the students to write four sentences. With a copy of the copy master in front of each of them, ask the students to listen carefully as you say one of the two words that sound similar. Have one student look up the meaning of the word, and have two other students give examples of the word used in a sentence. Discussing the meaning of the word will help students remember something about the word that may be useful when they attempt to spell the word independently. Leave the other word of the similar word pair for the next day so that the students will not have problems in remembering which spelling applies to which word.   AUDITORY MODALITY

*(Pretest/Posttest, continued)*

13. In a **futile** attempt to remove the stain, Wendy bleached the shirt.
14. These stairs provide **access** to the attic.
15. Karen entertained us with an **anecdote** about her trip to Canada.
16. Under the **feudal** system, only the lords could own land.

### PRACTICE ACTIVITY
The practice activity is on page 107.

#### Answers: Spelling Clues
1. futile  4. breath
2. persecuted  5. prosecuted
3. anecdote  6. feudal

#### Answers: Proofreading
7. excess  10. finely
8. finally  11. breadth
9. Bizarre  12. conscious

#### Answers: Working with Meaning
13. bazaar  15. conscience
14. antidote  16. access

# Lesson 6: Prefixes *ad-*, *in-*

## OBJECTIVE
To spell words that contain a form of the prefix *ad-* or *in-*

## HOME ACTIVITY
The home activity is on page 109.

## SECOND-LANGUAGE SUPPORT
The concept of prefixes should be familiar to most of your second-language students, as many languages use them. Write these words on the board: *incision, illusion, imprint, adapt, account, affair, aggressive, announce, appearance,* and *arrive.* Have volunteers draw a vertical line between the two parts of the word and explain the meaning of the word based on the meanings of the word parts. DETERMINING MEANING

## PRETEST/POSTTEST
1. We saw a shoplifter get **arrested** by the police at the mall.
2. Planting those flowers really **improved** the appearance of the yard.
3. A free drink is **included** in the price of the movie ticket.
4. The farmer **irrigated** his crops with water from the river.
5. We had to stop for an **inspection** by the border patrol.
6. Chet wanted to pay his own way, but Jo **insisted** on paying for him.
7. This book was **illustrated** by a famous artist.
8. The best **advice** I can give you is to choose your friends wisely.
9. All members of the club **approved** the plans for the parade.
10. Sonny has a very **agreeable** smile.
11. The chemist **investigated** the pollutants in rain water.

*(continued on next page)*

## Pretest
Administer the test on this page as a pretest. Say each word, use it in the sentence, and then repeat the word.   ACCESSING PRIOR KNOWLEDGE

**SELF-CHECK**   Have students check their own pretests against the list of Spelling Words. Remind students to write misspelled words in their Lesson Word Logs.   STUDENT SELF-ASSESSMENT

## Introducing the Lesson

### Option A (Open Sort)
Distribute the word cards (page 108) to individuals or small groups, and guide them in an open-sort activity. In open sort, students group the word cards according to a criterion they select themselves. Then guide students in comparing and discussing the criteria they selected.

### Option B (Modeling)
Read aloud with students the lesson title and the Spelling Words. Use this model sentence to introduce the lesson skill in a context.

*This shot will* ***increase*** *your* ***immunity*** *to the flu.*

## Teaching the Lesson

- Ask volunteers to name words that begin with the prefix forms *ad-, ac-, af-, ag-, an-, ap-,* and *ar-.* List words on the board under the corresponding headings. (*advice, accomplished, affectionate, agreeable, announcement, approved, arrested*)
- Follow the same procedure for Spelling Words that begin with the prefix forms *in-, il-, im-,* and *ir-.* (***in-:*** *included, inspection, insisted, investigated;* ***il-:*** *illustrated;* ***im-:*** *improved, impressed;* ***ir-:*** *irrigated, irresponsible*)
- Have students add their own examples to the columns. Then have volunteer read all the words aloud and underline the prefixes.

**IN SUMMARY**   Have students summarize the lesson in their own words. Elicit from students the information that some prefixes, like *tri-* in *tricycle* and *re-* in *regain,* are added to a root word without spelling changes. Others, like *ad-* and *in-,* change form, or spelling, to match the beginning letter of the word part to which they are being added. This type of prefix is called an *absorbed prefix.*

**ASSIGNMENT**   Students can complete the first page of the lesson as a follow-up to the activity, either in class or as homework.

# Lesson 6: Prefixes *ad-*, *in-* (continued)

## Practicing the Lesson

### Spelling Clues: Doubling Consonants
Suggest to students that when they write a word that has a prefix, they make sure that the base word is spelled correctly. If they are still unsure of the spelling of the word when the prefix is added, they should look up the word in a dictionary.

Point out that a prefix usually does not change the spelling of the base word. A common mistake is made when a prefix is added to a base word that begins with the same letter as the last letter of the prefix. That common mistake is to drop the first letter of the base word. Thus, a word like *approved* is often misspelled by people who use one *p* instead of two. APPLYING SPELLING STRATEGIES

### Proofreading
You may wish to have students review Spelling Clues: Doubling Consonants before proofreading the paragraph.

### Fun with Words
Students may complete this activity individually or with a partner. You might wish to expand the activity by having students write sentences that include misspellings of Spelling Words other than those used in the activity. Then have students trade papers with partners, find the misspelled words, and write the correct spellings.

## Posttest
Administer the test on page 10 as a posttest, or administer one of your own. Say each word, use it in a sentence, and then repeat the word.

## Reteaching the Lesson
Some students with special needs are impulsive rather than reflective in their behavior. As a result, they do what first comes to mind instead of considering any options, and are often incorrect in their impulsive choices. One strategy that has been very successful for getting students to consider several options is to teach them a metacognitive strategy of "self-talk," a method that requires the student to take time to consider the possibilities.

Teach one type of "self-talk," self-interrogation, by having the student ask himself or herself questions while spelling a word: *Can I divide this word into syllables? What sound do I hear in each syllable? What letter or letter combinations are represented by that sound?* After they spell a word, have students look at the word to see if it looks right. Encourage them to make corrections if it doesn't.   AUDITORY MODALITY

---

*(Pretest/Posttest, continued)*

12. The **announcement** was made over the loudspeaker.
13. Ms. Parker was very **impressed** with David's good manners.
14. Allan has **accomplished** a lot in just four years.
15. The best thing about my dog is its **affectionate** nature.
16. It was **irresponsible** of you to leave your coat outside.

## PRACTICE ACTIVITY
The practice activity is on page 110.

### Answers: Spelling Clues
1. irrigated        4. advice
2. approved        5. accomplished
3. improved        6. irresponsible

### Answers: Proofreading
7. illustrated
8. announcement
9. affectionate
10. investigated
11. inspection
12. agreeable

### Answers: Fun with Words
13. impressed      15. included
14. arrested       16. insisted

# Unit 1 Review

## OBJECTIVES

- To review spelling patterns and strategies in Lessons 1–6
- To give students the opportunity to recognize and use these spelling patterns and Spelling Words in their writing

## UNIT 1 WORDS

The following words are reviewed in Practice Test, Parts A and B.

### Lesson 1: Compound Words
handkerchief    homesick
gingerbread

### Lesson 2: Homophones
stationary    border
barred    burro

### Lesson 3: Adding Endings to Words
abilities    potatoes
acquired

### Lesson 4: Related Words
desperately    continue
strenuous

### Lesson 5: Easily Confused Words
conscience    finally
bazaar    access

### Lesson 6: Prefixes *ad-, in-*
irrigated    approved
investigated

## Review Strategies

Review with students the following spelling-clue strategies for Lessons 1–6.

### Lesson 1    Spelling Clues: Compound Words

Write the word *head* on the board. Then have a student spell *quarters*. Ask students how the two words would be joined to make a compound word *(headquarters)*. Do the same with *heart* and *attack (heart attack)*, and *long* and *term (long-term)*.

### Lesson 2    Spelling Clues: Homophones

Write this sentence on the board: *The stationary bikes were two aisles away from stationary and other office supplies.* Ask students to find the misspelled word (the second *stationary*) and to spell the word correctly. Ask them to state a mnemonic device that helps them remember the spelling of these homophones (for example: stationary bikes stay in the same place; stationery goes into envelopes).

### Lesson 3    Spelling Clues: Word Endings

Write the words *potato, separate, ability,* and *omit* on the board. Then write the inflectional endings *-s, -es, -ed,* and *-ing,* and have students add the appropriate endings to the words. Discuss the possible spelling changes in base words when such endings are added.

### Lesson 4    Spelling Clues: Base Words

Write these adverbs on the board: *dramatically, professionally,* and *continuously.* Ask a student to name the base word and the related adjective in each *(drama, dramatic; profess, profession, professional;* and *continue, continuous).* Then ask whether the base word changes when a suffix or suffixes are added.

### Lesson 5    Spelling Clues: Correct Pronunciation

Write the words *breath* and *breadth* on the board, and have a volunteer pronounce them. Remind students that paying special attention to the pronunciation of commonly confused words can help them spell the word correctly. Review how to check the pronunciation of a word in the dictionary.

### Lesson 6    Spelling Clues: Doubling Consonants

Write on the board *irresponsible—iresponsible* and *acomplished—accomplished.* Ask a volunteer to underline the words that are spelled correctly. Then remind students that the prefixes *ad-* and *in-* can take on different spellings depending upon the spelling of the root to which they are being added. Point out that the first consonant is usually doubled when the prefix being added ends with the same letter that begins the root.

# Unit 1 Review *(continued)*

## Practice Test

The Practice Test provides an opportunity to review Spelling Words and spelling generalizations in a standardized test format, complete with a sample answer card.

### Option 1

Use Practice Test: Part A as a pretest. Later, use Practice Test: Part B as a posttest.

### Option 2

Have students review their Lesson Word Log for this unit. If they need extra help, you may wish to review the spelling generalizations discussed in the individual lessons. Then administer both parts of the Practice Test to determine whether students have mastered the spelling generalizations.

### Practice Test: Part A

1. (D) handkercheif [handkerchief]
2. (D) strenous [strenuous]
3. (B) ginger bread [gingerbread]
4. (A) desparately [desperately]
5. (C) statonary [stationary]
6. (C) irigated [irrigated]
7. (A) abillities [abilities]
8. (D) concience [conscience]
9. (B) aquired [acquired]
10. (A) investagated [investigated]

### Practice Test: Part B

1. (B) barred
2. (C) border
3. (A) homesick
4. (D) potatoes
5. (C) burro
6. (A) bazaar
7. (D) finally
8. (C) continue
9. (B) access
10. (C) approved

## Options for Evaluation

- Have students check their own Practice Tests against their lists of Spelling Words. The list on the opposite page provides references to the lessons where they can find words they misspelled.
- You may prefer to assign partners and have students check each other's Practice Tests, using their own list of Spelling Words.

## REVIEW ACTIVITIES

### Activity 1

Make flashcards using words from Unit 1. On one side of each card, spell the word correctly. On the other, spell it incorrectly. Shuffle the cards, and spread them out on a table in such a way that about half of the cards show misspelled words. Have students turn over the ones that display incorrect spellings, so that only the correct spellings show.

### Activity 2

Write the words from this review lesson on cards, making two for each word. Have students use them to play a matching game. All cards are placed facedown on a table, arranged eight across and five down. Players take turns trying to find pairs by turning two cards over, one at a time. If the cards match, the player keeps them and takes another turn. If they do not match, the player flips them back over, and the next player takes a turn. The player with the most pairs at the end of the game wins.

### Activity 3

Have students make up sentences using the words from this review lesson or other words from the unit, but tell them to leave blanks where the words would go. Then they can exchange papers and write the correct word in each blank.

# Unit 1 Review *(continued)*

## WHAT'S IN A WORD?

### ◆ *bard*

To extend the activity, have students write the names of two favorite bards. Suggest to students that they play the role of bard by writing a short poem or rhyme using a pair of homophones. Then have students share their poems with others in a small group and record in their Word Logs any new or interesting words they hear in one another's work.

### ◆ *bazaar*

Provide pictures of various bazaars. You might find some in travel books, especially in those about the Middle East, where bazaars are more common than they are here. As students consider the kinds of stories they would set in a bazaar, encourage them to describe the events in their stories that would be enhanced by a bazaar setting. Ask them why a bazaar would work better for certain stories than for others.

## Unit Activity Options

### Game of Combinations

Have students make their own set of cards for the Spelling Words. Then have them use the words in sentences as they find word combinations.

### Just a Reminder

Here are some other examples you might wish to give:

At the end of a <u>row</u> of carrots, the rabbit dug a bur<u>row</u>.

When he was bar<u>red</u> from entering the house, the man saw <u>red</u>.

On the third strike, a <u>fou</u>l ball doesn't <u>count</u> as an <u>out</u>.

Capit<u>ol</u>s often have d<u>o</u>mes.

### Put It Together

Another twist on this game would be to require that the sentences go together to tell a story.

### Extended Family

You might wish to have students read their paragraphs to the class. As students read their paragraphs, write their new words on the board so that others can add them to their own Word Logs.

### The Match Game

To extend the activity, play it with all sixteen of the Spelling Words and have each player choose eight instead of four cards. When partners have finished playing the game using their own eight cards, they can exchange cards and write new sentences for the other eight words. Remind students to provide context clues in their sentences, so that the other player will be able to tell which Spelling Word goes in each sentence.

**SECOND-LANGUAGE SUPPORT**   To help students who have limited proficiency in English, have them work with a partner to write context sentences using the Spelling Words.

### Building with Prefixes

When students have finished this activity, you might want to list on the board all the words they named for each prefix. Then have students add the words to their Word Logs.

◆ This indicates a Unit Spelling Word.

# Unit 1 Review (continued)

## Curriculum Options

### Language Arts: Concentration

Make two cards for each Spelling Word. Spread the cards out facedown. Players take turns turning over two cards, trying to make matches. If the player makes a match, he or she keeps the pair of cards and takes another turn. If the player fails to make a match, he or she turns the cards back over, and play passes to the next player. When all the cards are gone, the player with the most pairs is the winner.

### Mathematics: Letter Addition

This game may be played by a large or small group of students. First, assign each letter of the alphabet a number, such as 1 for *a*, 2 for *b*, 3 for *c*, and so on. Then ask each student to choose a Spelling Word and compute the "value" of the word by adding the numbers that stand for each letter.

$$
\begin{aligned}
r &= 18 \\
e &= 5 \\
a &= 1 \\
l &= 12 \\
i &= 9 \\
s &= 19 \\
m &= 13 \\
\hline
&= 77
\end{aligned}
$$

A volunteer challenger begins the game by giving the value of his or her word and challenging the other players to guess the word. (For example, "My word is worth 77 points. What is it?" Answer: *realism*) The first student to guess correctly is the next to give the value of a word and challenge others to figure out what it is. Continue the game until all students have had a turn to be the challenger.

### Social Studies: Questions and Answers

Ask students to imagine that they are reporters interviewing candidates in a national or local election. Discuss the kinds of issues that reporters would want to raise with candidates, such as trade, the environment, immigration, crime, technology, and the treatment of minority groups. Have students list several issues and questions in the following format:

| Issues | Questions to Ask |
|--------|------------------|

Begin by calling on a student to ask one of his or her questions. The other students should imagine that they are candidates and should formulate an answer. Their answers must include one of the Spelling Words. If the student chosen to answer uses and spells the word correctly, he or she asks the next "reporter's" question, and another "candidate" answers it.

## WHAT'S IN A WORD?

### ◆ *gingerbread*

Remind students that when bakers make gingerbread cookies, they often cut them in the shape of human figures. These figures are then decorated with raisins, candies, marshmallows, and other items. Lead a class discussion designed to get students to come to the conclusion that there is a relationship between all this trimming on the cookies and the gingerbread style of architecture, in which trimming and decoration might be excessive. If possible, show students pictures of gingerbread architecture or furniture.

### ◆ *principal* and *principle*

Divide the class into two teams and ask one team to write two or three sentences using the word *principal* and the other to write sentences using the word *principle*. Collect the sentences and read them to the class, having students guess the correct spelling in each case. You may want to make it a team game, giving one point for correct guesses and taking two points away for incorrect guesses.

◆ This indicates a Unit Spelling Word.

# Lesson 8: Words from French

**OBJECTIVE**

To spell words that have French origins

**HOME ACTIVITY**

The home activity is on page 112.

**SECOND-LANGUAGE SUPPORT**

To provide students with extra practice recognizing words with French origins, make illustrated flashcards. Write a word on one side of each card, and provide an illustration of the word on the other side. Some words you might want to use are *brunette, castle, entree, fruit, juggler, letter, mirror, prince, question, ravine, soldier,* and *village.* Have students choose a card at random, read and define the word, and use the illustration to check their answer.    USING PICTURE CLUES

**PRETEST/POSTTEST**

1. That **pigeon** is the only one that is afraid to eat from my hand.
2. **Perfume** bottles come in all sizes and shapes.
3. Judy met John at the train **depot** downtown.
4. I can't afford the clothes in that **elite** shop.
5. The family of four took a **suite** at the hotel for their vacation.
6. After the **matinee,** we talked about the movie for an hour.
7. My new **blouse** was ruined in the washing machine.
8. The gardeners forgot to pick up all the **debris** in the backyard.
9. A **surgeon** must have very steady hands.
10. Sam was **embarrassed** when he forgot his mom's birthday.
11. When she could no longer drive, Marla hired a **chauffeur.**
12. One of my favorite outdoor games is **croquet.**

*(continued on next page)*

## Pretest

Administer the test on this page as a pretest. Say each word, use it in the sentence, and then repeat the word.    ACCESSING PRIOR KNOWLEDGE

**SELF-CHECK**    Have students check their own pretests against the list of Spelling Words. Remind students to write misspelled words in their Lesson Word Logs.    STUDENT SELF-ASSESSMENT

## Introducing the Lesson

### Option A (Open Sort)

Distribute the word cards (page 111) to individuals or small groups, and guide them in an open-sort activity. In open sort, students group the word cards according to a criterion they select themselves. Then guide students in comparing and discussing the criteria they selected.

### Option B (Modeling)

Read aloud with students the lesson title and the Spelling Words. Use this model sentence to introduce the lesson skill in a context.

*The **menu** was posted on the door of the **restaurant**.*

## Teaching the Lesson

- Ask volunteers to name the Spelling Words that are spelled with a VC ending. List the words on the board. (*depot, debris, coup, crochet, croquet, amateur, chauffeur, surgeon, pigeon*)
- Follow the same procedure for words that are spelled with a VV pattern and for words that have other patterns. (*perfume, elite, suite, matinee, blouse, embarrassed, plateau*)
- Invite students to add words from their own writing to the columns. Then have volunteers read all the words aloud and underline the different patterns found in the words.

**IN SUMMARY**    Have students summarize the lesson in their own words. Elicit the information that when words are borrowed from other languages, parts of the words may still sound the way they do in the original languages. Lead students to the understanding that knowing the spellings of these sounds can help them spell the borrowed words.

**ASSIGNMENT**    Students can complete the first page of the lesson as a follow-up to the group activity, either in class or as homework.

# Lesson 8: Words from French (continued)

## Practicing the Lesson

### Spelling Clues: French Spelling Patterns

Suggest to students that when they encounter a word from the French language whose spelling they are unsure of, they think of other words they know that have the same pronunciation for the difficult part. If they are still unsure, they should look up the word in a dictionary.   APPLYING SPELLING STRATEGIES

### Proofreading

You may wish to have students review Spelling Clues: French Spelling Patterns before proofreading the diary entry.

### Fun with Words

After students have completed the activity, you may wish to provide more practice by having students make up their own conversations, using as many of the words on the list as they can. They might then wish to draw cartoons that illustrate their conversations.

## Posttest

Administer the test on page 16 as a posttest, or administer one of your own. Say each word, use it in a sentence, and then repeat the word.

## Reteaching the Lesson

Students with visual processing deficits often rely on auditory analysis when they spell words. Words with silent letters, such as many of these Spelling Words, cause persistent problems because the letters represent no sounds.

   Have students make a list of the Spelling Words that contain silent letters on the left-hand side of their papers. On the right-hand side, have them write each word, leaving a space where the silent letter(s) belongs. Have them fold their papers in half lengthwise. Dictate the words with silent letters. Have students fill in on the right-hand side the letters they don't hear. Then have students unfold their papers and compare their two lists of words. Any misspelled words should be crossed out and written correctly.

   During a spelling test, you may wish to cue students to each word with silent letters by placing a finger to your lips after dictating the word.   VISUAL/AUDITORY MODALITIES

*(Pretest/Posttest, continued)*

13. The Olympics used to be open only to **amateur** athletes.
14. Phil plans to **crochet** a blanket for the new baby.
15. The view from the **plateau** was spectacular.
16. It was quite a **coup** for David and Diane when they won the election.

## PRACTICE ACTIVITY

The practice activity is on page 113.

### Answers: Spelling Clues

| | |
|---|---|
| 1. croquet | 4. crochet |
| 2. depot | 5. debris |
| 3. plateau | 6. surgeon |

### Answers: Proofreading

| | |
|---|---|
| 7. blouse | 10. pigeon |
| 8. suite | 11. perfume |
| 9. matinee | |

### Answers: Fun with Words

| | |
|---|---|
| 12. amateur | 15. chauffeur |
| 13. coup | 16. embarrassed |
| 14. elite | |

# Lesson 9: Adjective Endings

## OBJECTIVE
To spell words that have adjective endings

## HOME ACTIVITY
The home activity is on page 115.

## SECOND-LANGUAGE SUPPORT
Some students may have difficulty differentiating the final sound of *crooked* from the final sound of *confederate*. To provide practice in differentiating between these sounds, write the words *cod* and *cot* on the board and read the words aloud. Ask students how the words are different. Have a student underline the letter that stands for the ending sound of *cod*, identify the letter, and say the word with you. Do the same for *cot*. Then have students listen to and repeat the words *bed—bet, fad—fat, had—hat, mad—mat, rod—rot*. Explain that the ending sound/t/ is sometimes spelled *te*, with a silent *e*, as in some of the Spelling Words. DIFFERENTIATING BETWEEN ENDING SOUNDS

## PRETEST/POSTTEST
1. I refuse to ride on that **horrid** roller coaster ever again!
2. John felt **stupid** when he realized he had forgotten his keys.
3. Driving on such a **crooked** road could be dangerous.
4. Mario is working on a new **electronic** invention.
5. Abraham Lincoln made a **historic** speech at Gettysburg.
6. We used old, **ragged** towels to wash the car.
7. Compass needles point to the **magnetic** north, not to true north.
8. They couldn't enter the store because they were **barefooted.**

*(continued on next page)*

## Pretest
Administer the test on this page as a pretest. Say each word, use it in the sentence, and then repeat the word.   ACCESSING PRIOR KNOWLEDGE

**SELF-CHECK**   Have students check their own pretests against the list of Spelling Words. Remind students to write misspelled words in their Lesson Word Logs.   STUDENT SELF-ASSESSMENT

## Introducing the Lesson

### Option A (Open Sort)
Distribute the word cards (page 114) to individuals or small groups, and guide them in an open-sort activity. In open sort, students group the word cards according to a criterion they select themselves. Then guide students in comparing and discussing the criteria they selected.

### Option B (Modeling)
Read aloud with students the lesson title and the Spelling Words. Use this model sentence to introduce the lesson skill in a context.

*We were **fortunate** to have a **splendid** view of the ocean.*

## Teaching the Lesson

- Ask volunteers to name and spell the Spelling Words with the adjective ending *-ate*. List the words on the board. *(passionate, confederate)*
- Follow the same procedure for words with the adjective endings *-ic, -ed,* and *-id*. List the words on the board. (*-ic: electronic, historic, magnetic, democratic, poetic, metallic; -ed: crooked, ragged, barefooted, contented, undersized; -id: horrid, stupid, rigid*)
- Then have students name and spell other words that have these adjective endings, including words from their own writing. Add the words to the appropriate lists on the board.

**IN SUMMARY**   Ask students to summarize the lesson in their own words. Elicit the information that knowing the meaning of common adjective endings can help students understand the words that contain them. Elicit also that the endings *-ate*, *-id*, and often *-ic* mean "relating to" and that *-ed* means "state or quality of."

**ASSIGNMENT**   Students can complete the first page of the lesson as a follow-up to the group activity, either in class or as homework.

# Lesson 9: Adjective Endings *(continued)*

## Practicing the Lesson

### Spelling Clues: Adjective Endings

Suggest to students that whenever they add an adjective ending to a word, they consider whether the base word needs any spelling changes before the ending is added. Point out that in this activity, the spelling changes have already been made and the ending simply needs to be added.    APPLYING SPELLING STRATEGIES

### Proofreading

You may wish to have students review Spelling Clues: Adjective Endings before proofreading the paragraph.

### Working with Meaning

Students may complete this activity individually or with a partner. After students have completed this activity, you may wish to expand it by having students write sentences using the words. As an additional challenge, suggest that they write sentences that tell a story.

**SECOND-LANGUAGE SUPPORT**    To help students complete this activity, suggest that they concentrate on the activity or item that is described by each phrase. Then have them look at the list of Spelling Words and think about the meanings of the words. This will help them make a connection between the phrases and the words.    USING CONTEXT CLUES

## Posttest

Administer the test on page 18 as a posttest, or administer one of your own. Say each word, use it in a sentence, and then repeat the word.

## Reteaching the Lesson

Have students who need additional practice follow a four-step sequence:

1. Write the word plus the suffix.

2. Trace the word, using a colored marker or felt-tip pen.

3. In pencil, copy the word underneath the model, saying the name of each letter.

4. Cover the model, and write the word from recall.
   VISUAL/KINESTHETIC MODALITIES

*(Pretest/Posttest, continued)*

9. We follow **democratic** principles in our club.

10. Barbara is quite **passionate** about the piano.

11. The deer stood **rigid** with fear, staring at the bright light.

12. My cat is most **contented** when curled up in my lap.

13. The words to that song are really **poetic.**

14. That **undersized** basketball player is not even six feet tall.

15. We used a **metallic** gold paint for the trim on the cabinets.

16. John's speech proved he was a **confederate** in our cause.

### PRACTICE ACTIVITY

The practice activity is on page 116.

### Answers: Spelling Clues

| | |
|---|---|
| 1. democratic | 5. electronic |
| 2. crooked | 6. historic |
| 3. poetic | 7. magnetic |
| 4. passionate | |

### Answers: Proofreading

| | |
|---|---|
| 8. rigid | 11. ragged |
| 9. horrid | 12. metallic |
| 10. stupid | |

### Answers: Working with Meaning

| | |
|---|---|
| 13. barefooted | 15. confederate |
| 14. undersized | 16. contented |

# Lesson 10: Greek Word Parts

## OBJECTIVE
To recognize and spell words that have Greek word parts

## HOME ACTIVITY
The home activity is on page 118.

## SECOND-LANGUAGE SUPPORT
Write the five Greek word parts and their meanings on the board. Then write a Spelling Word representing each Greek word part. Discuss the meaning of each word and ask students to name words from their first languages that are cognates of the Spelling Words. For example, in Spanish the word *teléfonos* is similar to *telephones*, *ciclo* to *cycle*, *fonografía* to *phonograph*, and *simpático* to *sympathetic*.   RECOGNIZING SIMILARITIES IN WORDS

## PRETEST/POSTTEST
1. We have four **telephones** in our three-bedroom house.
2. The formation of clouds is part of the water **cycle.**
3. We **recycle** our aluminum cans, newspapers, and glass bottles.
4. This old **phonograph** is a real collector's item now.
5. Waving the flag is a **symbolic** act.
6. Please speak into the **microphone** so that we can hear you.
7. Every **generation** creates its own type of music.
8. The **cyclone** that came through here lifted our boat off the lake.
9. One of the **symptoms** of measles is red spots on the body.
10. Albert Einstein was a scientific **genius.**
11. How many **synonyms** can you think of for the word *large*?
12. When the electricity went out, the emergency **generator** took over.

*(continued on next page)*

## Pretest
Administer the test on this page as a pretest. Say each word, use it in the sentence, and then repeat the word.   ACCESSING PRIOR KNOWLEDGE

**SELF-CHECK**   Have students check their own pretests against the list of Spelling Words. Remind students to write misspelled words in their Lesson Word Logs.   STUDENT SELF-ASSESSMENT

## Introducing the Lesson

### Option A (Open Sort)
Distribute the word cards (page 117) to individuals or small groups, and guide them in an open-sort activity. In open sort, students group the word cards according to a criterion they select themselves. Then guide students in comparing and discussing the criteria they selected.

### Option B (Modeling)
Read aloud with students the lesson title and the Spelling Words. Use this model sentence to introduce the lesson skill in a context.

*The **xylophone** duets **generated** some excitement at the party.*

## Teaching the Lesson

- Ask volunteers to name and spell the Spelling Words that have the Greek word part *-cycl-*. List the words on the board. *(cycle, recycle, cyclone)*
- Ask volunteers to name and spell the words that have the Greek word part *sym-* or *syn-*. List the words on the board. *(symbolic, symptoms, synonyms, synthetic, sympathetic, symphony)*
- Follow the same procedure for words with the Greek word part *-phon-* and for words with the word part *gen-*. (**-phon-:** *telephones, phonograph, microphone;* **gen-:** *generation, genius, generator, genes)*
- Invite students to add other words to the columns, including words from their own writing.

**IN SUMMARY**   Ask students to summarize the lesson. Elicit the information that many English words have word parts that come from Greek. Knowing those Greek word parts can help students understand the English words.

**ASSIGNMENT**   Students can complete the first page of the lesson as a follow-up to the group activity, either in class or as homework.

# Lesson 10: Greek Word Parts *(continued)*

## Practicing the Lesson

### Spelling Clues: Greek Word Parts

Suggest to students that when they write a word that has the Greek word part *-cycl-, sym-, syn-, -phon-,* or *gen-,* they recall that the spelling of the word part seldom changes. If they are still not sure of a word's spelling, they should look it up in a dictionary.   APPLYING SPELLING STRATEGIES

**TRANSITIONAL SPELLERS**   Have students complete this activity cooperatively with a partner or in a small group. To give additional practice, have students draw pictures that illustrate the words. Another possibility is to have students act out the words.

### Proofreading

You may wish to have students review Spelling Clues: Greek Word Parts before proofreading the paragraph.

### Working with Meaning

Students may complete this activity individually or with a partner. To extend the activity, you might have students write a sentence using each word. Have them leave blanks in sentences and exchange sentences with a partner. Then have them complete the sentences written by their partners.

**SECOND-LANGUAGE SUPPORT**   Have students work together in small groups. They can help one another by sharing knowledge about word definitions. Then they can discuss each phrase and decide which Spelling Word is described.

## Posttest

Administer the test on page 20 as a posttest, or administer one of your own. Say each word, use it in a sentence, and then repeat the word.

## Reteaching the Lesson

Many students with memory deficits have persistent difficulties in recalling the correct spelling of multisyllabic words. To assist students in learning multisyllabic words, teach one word root at a time until you are certain that students have learned it. Following this strategy, select one of the Greek roots in the lesson. At the end of the week, ask students to spell aloud words selected at random from their individual sets of word cards. This activity may be done in peer pairs, with each student taking the role of teacher and asking the other to spell the word. Allow "think time" before the student begins spelling. KINESTHETIC MODALITY

*(Pretest/Posttest, continued)*

13. I'd rather wear cotton than any **synthetic** fabric.
14. Both of Sarah's parents have **genes** for brown eyes.
15. When I told Dad about my problem, he was **sympathetic.**
16. The Danish **symphony** will play first tonight.

### PRACTICE ACTIVITY

The practice activity is on page 119.

### Answers: Spelling Clues
1. symptoms
2. generation
3. sympathetic
4. generator
5. symbolic
6. synthetic

### Answers: Proofreading
7. cyclone
8. microphone
9. recycle
10. phonograph
11. telephones
12. cycle

### Answers: Working with Meaning
13. synonyms
14. symphony
15. genius
16. genes

# Lesson 11: Words from Greek

## OBJECTIVE
To spell words that have Greek origins

## HOME ACTIVITY
The home activity is on page 121.

## SECOND-LANGUAGE SUPPORT
Students acquiring English may find words from Greek difficult to spell and understand. Provide extra practice by having students work together with English-speaking partners. For each Spelling Word, have students discuss the definitions, looking them up if necessary. Then, have each second-language student provide the word's equivalent, if possible, in his or her first language; write both words, and underline any parts that are similar. RECOGNIZING RELATED WORDS

## PRETEST/POSTTEST
1. The English **alphabet** has twenty-six letters.
2. Bob's favorite part of **arithmetic** is long division.
3. The players on the winning team were treated like **heroes.**
4. The **stadium** was packed for the playoff game.
5. Anita does not get enough **physical** exercise.
6. The **aroma** of the freshly baked apple pie filled the whole apartment.
7. In the last **episode** of our story, the car had just run out of gas.
8. Mark was very thirsty after running the **marathon.**
9. After the star sang her solo, the **chorus** came in.
10. Betty was in the hospital with **pneumonia** for a week.
11. The sound of the falling rain has a soothing **rhythm.**
12. We could hardly get through the **labyrinth** at the Fun Zone.

*(continued on next page)*

## Pretest
Administer the test on this page as a pretest. Say each word, use it in the sentence, and then repeat the word.   ACCESSING PRIOR KNOWLEDGE

**SELF-CHECK**   Have students check their own pretests against the list of Spelling Words. Remind students to write misspelled words in their Lesson Word Logs.   STUDENT SELF-ASSESSMENT

## Introducing the Lesson

### Option A (Open Sort)
Distribute the word cards (page 120) to individuals or small groups, and guide them in an open-sort activity. In open sort, students group the word cards according to a criterion they select themselves. Then guide students in comparing and discussing the criteria they selected.

### Option B (Modeling)
Read aloud with students the lesson title and the Spelling Words. Use this model sentence to introduce the lesson skill in a context.

*The **astronaut** showed us a **photograph** of the star.*

## Teaching the Lesson

■ Ask volunteers to name Spelling Words that use the letter combination *ph* to stand for the sound /f/. List the words on the board. (*alphabet, physical, philosophy, phenomenon*)
■ Follow the same procedure, asking for words that use the letter combination *ch* to stand for the sound /k/ and words that use *pn* to stand for the sound /n/. (*/k/: chorus, melancholy, architecture; /n/: pneumonia*)
■ Ask volunteers to name other Spelling Words that come from Greek. List the words on the board. (*arithmetic, heroes, stadium, aroma, episode, marathon, rhythm, labyrinth*)
■ Invite students to add words from their own writing to the columns. Then have volunteers read all the words aloud and underline the troublesome areas.

**IN SUMMARY**   Have students summarize the lesson in their own words. Elicit the information that knowing the sound/letter correspondence of such letter combinations as *ph, ch,* and *pn* can help students spell words that come from Greek.

**ASSIGNMENT**   Students can complete the first page of the lesson as a follow-up to the group activity, either in class or as homework.

# Lesson 11: Words from Greek *(continued)*

## Practicing the Lesson

### Spelling Clues: Recognizing Correct Spellings

Suggest to students that when they consider how to spell a word that has the sound /k/, /f/, or /n/, they should consider using the Greek spelling for the sound. Explain that the *pn* spelling is rare in English and that it occurs only at the beginning of a word.   APPLYING SPELLING STRATEGIES

### Proofreading

You may wish to have students review Spelling Clues: Recognizing Correct Spellings before proofreading the paragraph.

### Fun with Words

Students may complete this activity individually or with a partner. To extend the activity, you might have students write sentences of their own, using the Spelling Words from the cartoons.

**TRANSITIONAL SPELLERS**   Have students complete this activity cooperatively with a partner or in a small group. Suggest that they read the dialogue aloud.

**SECOND-LANGUAGE SUPPORT**   Have students work together in small groups. They can help one another by sharing knowledge as they try to determine what context clues are given in the art.   USING PICTURE CLUES

## Posttest

Administer the test on page 22 as a posttest, or administer one of your own. Say each word, use it in a sentence, and then repeat the word.

## Reteaching the Lesson

Students with learning difficulties often have trouble modifying their behavior to the demand of the task and situation. Give students a strategy for analyzing multisyllabic words. Use a combination of auditory and visual approaches.

   Prepare a written list of the Spelling Words. Say a word aloud, and have students repeat it. Have students divide the words into their component parts by making slash marks between the syllables (for example: al/pha/bet). Encourage students to whisper each word to themselves several times so that they can analyze it. Finally, have students write the word from dictation.   VISUAL/AUDITORY MODALITIES

*(Pretest/Posttest, continued)*

13. Frank told ten jokes to try to get Sue out of her **melancholy** mood.
14. What is your **philosophy** about finding happiness?
15. An eclipse is an exciting **phenomenon** of nature.
16. Ron is studying **architecture** at the university.

### PRACTICE ACTIVITY

The practice activity is on page 122.

### Answers: Spelling Clues
1. pneumonia
2. philosophy
3. aroma
4. melancholy
5. architecture
6. episode
7. rhythm
8. phenomenon

### Answers: Proofreading
9. labyrinth
10. stadium
11. chorus
12. heroes

### Answers: Fun with Words
13. alphabet
14. marathon
15. physical
16. arithmetic

# Lesson 12: Science/Technology Words

## OBJECTIVE
To spell words that come from science and technology

## HOME ACTIVITY
The home activity is on page 124.

## SECOND-LANGUAGE SUPPORT
Some students may find these words confusing. Provide extra practice by writing and illustrating the Spelling Words on flashcards and having volunteers pronounce and define each one as you display it. Have students brainstorm other words that come from science and technology. Write those words on the board, and continue having volunteers pronounce and define them.   RECOGNIZING SPECIALIZED VOCABULARY

## PRETEST/POSTTEST
1. The police officer used **radar** to determine the speed of the car.
2. The **electrical** storm was quite a spectacular sight.
3. **Scuba** divers carry compressed air in tanks on their backs.
4. Our knowledge of the **universe** is rapidly increasing.
5. The only **chemical** we use in our garden is one designed to fight snails.
6. The **scientists** discovered a cure for the disease.
7. Bats use a special kind of **sonar** to judge distance.
8. A surgeon's **instruments** have to be sterile.
9. Gravity helps keep our **atmosphere** from drifting into space.
10. Our **experiments** with the plants were successful.
11. In which **hemisphere** is the United States located?
12. In a polluted **environment,** living things suffer.

*(continued on next page)*

## Pretest
Administer the test on this page as a pretest. Say each word, use it in the sentence, and then repeat the word.   ACCESSING PRIOR KNOWLEDGE

**SELF-CHECK**   Have students check their own pretests against the list of Spelling Words. Remind students to write misspelled words in their Lesson Word Logs.   STUDENT SELF-ASSESSMENT

## Introducing the Lesson

### Option A (Open Sort)
Distribute the word cards (page 123) to individuals or small groups, and guide them in an open-sort activity. In open sort, students group the word cards according to a criterion they select themselves. Then guide students in comparing and discussing the criteria they selected.

### Option B (Modeling)
Read aloud with students the lesson title and the Spelling Words. Use this model sentence to introduce the lesson skill in a context.

*We were flying at a high **altitude** when we saw something moving **vertically** toward us.*

## Teaching the Lesson

- Ask volunteers to name the Spelling Words that are acronyms. As students name words, list the words on the board. *(radar, scuba, sonar, laser)*
- Follow the same procedure for words that are nouns and words that are adjectives. List the words on the board. (**nouns:** *universe, scientists, instruments, atmosphere, experiments, hemisphere, environment, probability, molecules;* **adjectives:** *chemical, electrical, technological)*
- Have students add words from their own writing to the columns. Then have volunteers read all the words aloud and define them.

**IN SUMMARY**   Ask students to summarize the lesson in their own words. Elicit the information that knowing how to spell science and technology words is important, because they are so widely used today. Also elicit the fact that many of these words have common suffixes, such as *-ment, -al, -ity,* and *-ist.*

**ASSIGNMENT**   Students can complete the first page of the lesson as a follow-up to the group activity, either in class or as homework.

# Lesson 12: Science/Technology Words *(continued)*

## Practicing the Lesson

### Spelling Clues: Working Together

Suggest to students that when they are working together, they take care to pronounce the words accurately. Correct pronunciation is a good clue to the correct spelling of a word. If students are still unsure of the spelling of a word, they should consult a dictionary.   APPLYING SPELLING STRATEGIES

### Proofreading

You may wish to have students review Spelling Clues: Working Together before proofreading the sentences.

### Fun with Words

Students may complete this activity individually or with a partner. Suggest to students that they use the picture clues to help them figure out the words that best complete the dialogue in the cartoons.

**TRANSITIONAL SPELLERS**   Have students complete this activity cooperatively with a partner or in a small group.

## Posttest

Administer the test on page 24 as a posttest, or administer one of your own. Say each word, use it in a sentence, and then repeat the word.

## Reteaching the Lesson

Students with learning difficulties may have trouble both remembering what words look like and analyzing the sounds they hear.

Provide students with a list of the Spelling Words for visual recognition. You may write the words on the board for a group activity, or you may write them on copy masters for individual use.

As a recognition strategy, ask students to select from three or four choices the correct spelling of a word. In making the decoy words, you can control the skills that will be emphasized. For students with visual memory deficits, write decoys that have the same sound but are written with a different letter. To help students focus on auditory analysis, omit syllables or write incorrect but easily heard vowels. Have students cross out any misspelled words and write them correctly, using the model.   VISUAL MODALITY

*(Pretest/Posttest, continued)*

13. A **laser** was used to perform the eye surgery.
14. The **probability** of winning the game is slim.
15. Because of **technological** advances, riding in a car is safer now.
16. Water **molecules** consist of two parts hydrogen and one part oxygen.

### PRACTICE ACTIVITY

The practice activity is on page 125.

### Answers: Spelling Clues

1. instruments
2. molecules
3. environment
4. electrical
5. chemical
6. probability
7. technological
8. experiments

### Answers: Proofreading

9. sonar
10. laser
11. radar
12. scuba

### Answers: Fun with Words

13. scientists
14. hemisphere
15. atmosphere
16. universe

# Unit 2 Review

## OBJECTIVES

- To review spelling patterns and strategies in Lessons 8–12
- To give students the opportunity to recognize and use these spelling patterns and Spelling Words in their writing

## UNIT 2 WORDS

The following words are reviewed in Practice Test, Parts A and B.

### Lesson 8: Words from French

chauffeur     debris

embarrassed     depot

pigeon

### Lesson 9: Adjective Endings

democratic     horrid

passionate     rigid

magnetic

### Lesson 10: Greek Word Parts

synthetic     genius

recycle

### Lesson 11: Words from Greek

marathon     heroes

chorus     episode

aroma

### Lesson 12: Science/Technology Words

environment     instruments

## Review Strategies

Review with students the following spelling-clue strategies for Lessons 8–12.

### Lesson 8  Spelling Clues: French Spelling Patterns

Write the words *beau* and *nouveau* on the board. Then have a volunteer spell *chauffeur*. Ask students to tell how the spelling patterns of the three words are related. (The long *o* sound is spelled *eau* or *au*.) Do the same with some other words from Lesson 8. For example, for *passionate*, you might give the examples *impression* and *discussion* (/sh/ is spelled *ss*). Review with students the spelling patterns found in words with French origins.

### Lesson 9  Spelling Clues: Adjective Endings

Write these words on the board: *passionate, magnetic,* and *democratic.* Ask a student to name the base word in each (*passion, magnet,* and *democracy*). Then ask students if the base word changes when an adjective ending is added. Remind students that breaking a word into its parts can help them determine the correct spelling.

### Lesson 10  Spelling Clues: Greek Word Parts

Have volunteers spell the Greek word parts *-cycl-* and *-gen-* and the Greek prefix *syn-*. Then write the following words on the board, asking volunteers to supply the missing letters:

_ _ _thetic     re_ _ _ _e     _ _ _ius
(synthetic)     (recycle)     (genius)

Ask students to name other English words that use these Greek word parts (for example, *generate, genealogy, generation, bicycle, encyclopedia, Cyclops, synchronize, syndrome,* and *synonym*). Demonstrate that the spelling of the Greek word part remains intact.

### Lesson 11  Spelling Clues: Recognizing Correct Spellings

Write the words *telephone* and *photograph* on the board. Then have a volunteer spell *physical*. Ask students to tell how the spelling patterns of the three words are related. (The /f/ sound is spelled *ph*.) Do the same with some other words from Lesson 11. For example, for *chorus*, you might give the examples *echo* and *ache* (/k/ is spelled *ch*). Review with students the spelling patterns found in words with Greek origins.

### Lesson 12  Spelling Clues: Working Together

Ask volunteers to explain the advantages of proofreading with a partner. Have them explain why it is easier to see an error if you are listening to a partner as well as looking at your writing.

# Unit 2 Review (continued)

## Practice Test

The Practice Test provides an opportunity to review Spelling Words and spelling generalizations in a standardized test format, complete with a sample answer card.

### Option 1

Use Practice Test: Part A as a pretest. Later, use Practice Test: Part B as a posttest.

### Option 2

Have students review their Lesson Word Log for this unit. If they need extra help, you may wish to review the spelling generalizations discussed in the individual lessons. Then administer both parts of the Practice Test to determine whether students have mastered the spelling generalizations.

### Practice Test: Part A

1. correct [chauffeur]
2. incorrect [embarrassed]
3. correct [synthetic]
4. incorrect [pigeon]
5. incorrect [debris]
6. incorrect [environment]
7. correct [democratic]
8. incorrect [passionate]
9. incorrect [marathon]
10. incorrect [magnetic]

### Practice Test: Part B

1. (B) recycle
2. (D) genius
3. (A) chorus
4. (C) aroma
5. (D) heroes
6. (B) depot
7. (D) instruments
8. (A) horrid
9. (B) episode
10. (B) rigid

### Options for Evaluation

- Have students check their own Practice Tests against their lists of Spelling Words. The list on the opposite page provides references to the lessons where they can find words they misspelled.
- You may prefer to assign partners and have students check each other's Practice Tests, using their own list of Spelling Words.

## REVIEW ACTIVITIES

### Activity 1

Have students who need a reteaching activity copy these headings: *French, Greek, Adjective Endings,* and *Science and Technology.* Then have them list each word from this review lesson.

### Activity 2

Distribute blank forms for bingo-type cards, with five columns and four rows. Have students write, in random order, the words from this review lesson, one word per blank. Have students use their cards to play a game of bingo. Call out the words, in random order. Students can check off each word as it is called, or they can cover it with a button or a scrap of paper. The first one to check off or cover a complete row (horizontal, vertical, or diagonal) and call out the word *bingo* is the winner.

### Activity 3

Play "Thumbs Up, Thumbs Down!" with Spelling Words from Unit 2. Write the words on the board, spelling some correctly and some incorrectly. As you do so, have students give a thumbs-up or thumbs-down sign to indicate whether the spelling is correct.

### Activity 4

Have partners write letters to each other, using as many of the words in this review lesson as possible. Then have them proofread each other's letters, correcting any errors in spelling, punctuation, capitalization, or letter form.

# Unit 2 Review *(continued)*

## WHAT'S IN A WORD?

### ◆ *alphabet*

Have students research different kinds of alphabets (for example, sign language, Arabic, Hebrew, Cyrillic) and report to the class about their findings. You may also wish to have them find out about the history of the Roman alphabet.

### ◆ *coup*

Ask students to use the dictionary to find expressions beginning with the word *coup* (for example, *coup de grâce, coup de théâtre*). Have them write the expressions and their meanings.

### ◆ *croquet*

You may wish to extend this activity by discussing Lewis Carroll's book *Alice's Adventures in Wonderland*. Read aloud Chapter 8 from the book. This chapter describes a very strange croquet ground: "It was all ridges and furrows: the croquet balls were live hedgehogs, and the mallets live flamingoes, and the soldiers had to double themselves up and to stand upon their hands and feet, to make arches." Discuss the meaning of the French word *croquer,* "to crack." Why is this word appropriate for the game? If you wish, show students pictures of croquet equipment, diagram the playing area, and discuss the rules and strategy of the game. Have students add to their Word Logs any new words they learn.

### ◆ *environment*

You may wish to have students discuss their own environment and to compare it to that of other parts of their state, the United States, or other countries. To prepare them for this activity, ask them to make a chart listing the various factors in each environment.

## Unit Activity Options

### Competing for Adjectives

You may wish to extend the game by having students match their adjectives with nouns in order to get the points. For example, they might pair *classical* with *music, historical* with *monument,* and *discontented* with *workers.*

### Say It Quickly

A variation on the game is to have the word parts written on cards, which are then shuffled and placed face down on the table. Players choose cards rather than call out word parts.

**Working Together**   Have each group appoint one member to check students' spellings after each round.

### Homophone Fun

Remind students to be sure that they have given adequate context clues so that a classmate can identify the pair of homophones.

### Expanding Vocabularies

Have students use each of their new words in a sentence. Other words they might list include the following: *alphabetical, alphabetically, alphabetize, alphabetizing,* and *alphabetization; heroic, heroically, heroics, heroine,* and *heroism.*

### A Detective Game

To extend the activity, suggest to students that they include related words in their speeches. For example, in addition to *electrical,* they might use *electricity, electric,* and *electrically.* Award points for each appearance of a related word as well.

### Proofreading Partners

Have students read the instructions for the activity, and answer any questions they may have. Remind students to review the list carefully and to select the Spelling Words they find most troublesome; this approach will make the activity a useful tool for improving their spelling skills. Then have students select their own partners and complete the activity.

◆ This indicates a Unit Spelling Word.

# Unit 2 Review *(continued)*

## Curriculum Options

### Cross-Curriculum: In a Class by Yourself

Organize students into several groups. Tell them that in this game every group can win if the members try hard enough. The object of the game is to list as many compound words as they can for the subject area you assign to them. Their group wins if they list at least twenty words. Suggested subject areas are given below. Remind students that compound words may be written as one word, may be hyphenated, or may be written as two words. Allow them to consult any books you have in the classroom to help them find words.

### Categories and Examples:

**Science:** thunderstorm, black hole, quarter moon, seashell
**Physical education:** baseball, track meet, touchdown, goal post, fleet-footed
**History:** cave dwellers, right to vote, women's liberation, hiding place
**Geography:** southeast, capital city, superhighway, subway, train track, right of way
**Literature:** newspaper, storyteller, songwriter, ghost stories, typewritten, bookcase
**Art:** performance art, cutout, wallpaper, real-life, deckle-edged, brush stroke

### Health: First-Aid Posters

Organize students into small groups. Assign each group a particular first-aid technique to research (for example, how to bandage a cut, how to treat a burn, or how to administer mouth-to-mouth resuscitation). Group members should find out the exact step-by-step procedure to follow in that type of emergency. Then have students create posters that inform readers what to do in case of emergencies. Use as many Spelling Words as possible on the posters. Later, hang the posters around the classroom so that others can benefit from the information.

### Language Arts: Play a Board Game

To prepare for this activity, trace a path on poster board. Mark off one-inch spaces. Write a Spelling Word in each space. Students advance from Start by tossing dice or using a spinner. As they land on a space, they must pronounce the word and use it in a sentence that shows they know the meaning. If they do this, they can remain on the space. If not, they must go back to where they were before the turn began. The first player to reach the finish line wins.

## WHAT'S IN A WORD?

### ♦ *labyrinth*

To extend this activity, you may want to have students design their own labyrinth-like puzzle (or maze). Tell them to create a design in which many paths seem to lead somewhere, but only one path leads to the destination (a treasure, a letter X, a sticker). Then have students exchange papers and try to figure out which is the true path in the other student's labyrinth.

### ♦ *laser*

Ask students to research the different kinds of lasers in use (for example, solid-state lasers, gas lasers, semiconductor lasers, and dye lasers). What are the various uses of lasers?

### ♦ *synonym*

Divide the class into groups of three or four and provide a list of words (for example, *share, awkward, lawyer, practice*) for each group to look up in the dictionary. Ask them to write the synonyms and the definitions for each word and to read their results to the class. You may also wish to have them list the antonyms.

♦ This indicates a Unit Spelling Word.

# Lesson 14: Latin Roots, I

## OBJECTIVE
To recognize the Latin roots *-serv-*, *-port-*, *-dict-*, and *-migr-* and spell words that contain these roots

## HOME ACTIVITY
The home activity is on page 127.

## SECOND-LANGUAGE SUPPORT
Many English words with Latin roots are similar to or the same as words in Spanish. Call on volunteers to name the Spanish equivalents of the Spelling Words. Compare the pronunciations and meanings of the Spanish and the English words. Then have students name other Spanish and English words with these Latin roots. COMPARING AND CONTRASTING

## PRETEST/ POSTTEST
1. Most of the oil in Saudi Arabia is **exported** to other countries.
2. The thirteen colonies **imported** many goods from England.
3. Some birds **migrate** thousands of miles when the seasons change.
4. Many people bring **portable** radios to parks and beaches.
5. Scientists are **predicting** a large growth in the world's population.
6. A **dictator** seized control of the country.
7. The roofs of ancient Greek buildings were **supported** by columns.
8. The jury returned to the courtroom to announce its **verdict.**
9. Many **dictionaries** give histories as well as definitions of words.
10. My Native American friend lives on a **reservation.**
11. People keep photographs to ensure the **preservation** of family history.
12. The city issued guidelines for water **conservation.**

*(continued on next page)*

## Pretest
Administer the test on this page as a pretest. Say each word, use it in the sentence, and then repeat the word.   ACCESSING PRIOR KNOWLEDGE

**SELF-CHECK**   Have students check their own pretests against the list of Spelling Words. Remind students to write misspelled words in their Lesson Word Logs.   STUDENT SELF-ASSESSMENT

## Introducing the Lesson

### Option A (Open Sort)
Distribute the word cards (page 126) to individuals or small groups, and guide them in an open-sort activity. In open sort, students group the word cards according to a criterion they select themselves. Then guide students in comparing and discussing the criteria they selected.

### Option B (Modeling)
Read aloud with students the lesson title and the Spelling Words. Use this model sentence to introduce the lesson skill in a context.

*Taking public* **transportation** *is one way to* **conserve** *energy supplies.*

## Teaching the Lesson

- For each of the four roots, ask volunteers to name Spelling Words that include that root. List the words on the board and discuss their meanings. Then call students' attention to the positions that the roots can occupy (beginning, middle, or end of a word). (*-serv-: reservation, preservation, conservation, observatory;* *-port-: exported, imported, portable, supported;* *-dict-: predicting, dictator, verdict, dictionaries, indictment;* *-migr-: migrate, emigrate, immigration*)
- After students have added words from their own writing to the columns, have volunteers read all the words aloud and underline the root in each word.

**IN SUMMARY**   Have students summarize the lesson in their own words. Elicit the response that recognition of word roots can enable students to predict the spelling and the meaning of a word.

**ASSIGNMENT**   Students can complete the first page of the lesson as a follow-up to the group activity, either in class or as homework.

# Lesson 14: Latin Roots, I *(continued)*

## Practicing the Lesson

### Spelling Clues: Checking Roots

Suggest to students that when they proofread their work, they first check for words with familiar roots and other word parts. If students are still unsure how to spell a word, they should check the spelling in a dictionary.

You might point out that many English words are made up of Latin roots with suffixes and prefixes attached to them. If students think about the meanings of words of Latin origin, they will often be able to identify spelling errors in prefixes, suffixes, and roots. The *im-* in *immigration,* for example, means "within" or "toward." The *pre-* in *predicting* means "before." APPLYING SPELLING STRATEGIES

### Proofreading

You may wish to have students review Spelling Clues: Checking Roots before proofreading the letter.

**TRANSITIONAL SPELLERS**　Have students work in pairs to complete items 7–12. Suggest that they use pronunciation as well as their knowledge of roots to help them identify the misspelled words.

### Working with Meaning

Students may complete this activity individually or with a partner.

**SECOND-LANGUAGE SUPPORT**　Have students discuss the illustrations before they complete the items in Working with Meaning.　USING PICTURE CLUES

## Posttest

Administer the test on page 30 as a posttest, or administer one of your own. Say each word, use it in a sentence, and then repeat the word.

## Reteaching the Lesson

You might want to use this strategy to help students with learning difficulties develop a technique for learning new words. Review the meanings of the Latin roots in this lesson. Write the Spelling Words on the board. Have volunteers underline all the Spelling Words that contain one of the Latin roots, such as *-serv-*. Then, ask students to copy each of the words containing that root onto a sheet of paper. Finally, have students underline the root in each of the words with a colored marker, read the word aloud, and spell it from memory. VISUAL MODALITY

*(Pretest/Posttest, continued)*

**13.** We went to the **observatory** to study the stars.

**14.** The **indictment** charged the company with violating safety laws.

**15.** A famine forced thousands of people to **emigrate.**

**16.** This book is about a family's **immigration** to the United States.

### PRACTICE ACTIVITY

The practice activity is on page 128.

### Answers: Spelling Clues

1. emigrate
2. indictment
3. verdict
4. dictator
5. immigration
6. dictionaries

### Answers: Proofreading

7. preservation
8. conservation
9. reservation
10. migrate
11. observatory
12. predicting

### Answers: Working with Meaning

13. imported
14. exported
15. portable
16. supported

# Lesson 15: More Related Words

## OBJECTIVE

To determine the correct spelling of a word by applying one's knowledge of a related form of the word

## HOME ACTIVITY

The home activity is on page 130.

## SECOND-LANGUAGE SUPPORT

Students learning English as a second language may have difficulty distinguishing short vowel sounds. Have students listen to and repeat several one-syllable words with short vowel sounds. Then, have them pronounce the Spelling Words and identify the short vowel sound they hear in a particular syllable.  IDENTIFYING VOWEL SOUNDS

## PRETEST/POSTTEST

1. The mayor of our city will **propose** a new program for summer jobs.
2. Voters defeated the **proposition** to ban sidewalk vendors.
3. Factories **disposed** of dangerous chemicals in special locations.
4. Jenny is known for her smile and sunny **disposition.**
5. To make pancake batter, **combine** flour, eggs, and shortening.
6. We used a **combination** of dark and bright colors in the mural.
7. The **patriots** defended their country's independence.
8. That is a **patriotic** song.
9. We helped **distribute** food and clothing to hurricane victims.
10. We hired extra workers to assist in the **distribution** of food.
11. I **repeated** my instructions, since no one had heard me the first time.
12. The **repetition** made the song easy to memorize.
13. Traffic safety laws **oblige** us to wear seat belts.

*(continued on next page)*

## Pretest

Administer the test on this page as a pretest. Say each word, use it in the sentence, and then repeat the word.   ACCESSING PRIOR KNOWLEDGE

**SELF-CHECK**   Have students check their own pretests against the list of Spelling Words. Remind students to write misspelled words in their Lesson Word Logs.   STUDENT SELF-ASSESSMENT

## Introducing the Lesson

### Option A (Open Sort)

Distribute the word cards (page 129) to individuals or small groups, and guide them in an open-sort activity. In open sort, students group the word cards according to a criterion they select themselves. Then guide students in comparing and discussing the criteria they selected.

### Option B (Modeling)

Read aloud with students the lesson title and the Spelling Words. Use this model sentence to introduce the lesson skill in a context.

*Take the **medicine** only if it has a true **medicinal** value.*

## Teaching the Lesson

- Review the three kinds of vowel-sound changes illustrated in the sorting activity. For example, in the pair *preside/president,* have students identify the vowel sound in the second syllable in each word. *(propose/proposition, disposed/disposition, combine/combination, repeated/repetition, oblige/obligation)*

- Have volunteers read the remaining Spelling Words, one pair at a time, and identify the vowel sound that is clearly heard in one word but not in the other. Then have students place the words in the correct category. *(fat̲al/fat̲ality: patriots/patriotic, ac̲ademy/ac̲ademic: distribute/distribution, medicine/medicinal)*

- After students have added their own words to the columns, have volunteers read all the word pairs aloud and identify the vowel-sound changes.

**IN SUMMARY**   Have students summarize the lesson. Elicit the information that if students are not sure how to spell the schwa sound in an unstressed syllable, they can use their knowledge of a related word.

**ASSIGNMENT**   Students can complete the first page of the lesson as a follow-up activity, either in class or as homework.

# Lesson 15: More Related Words *(continued)*

## Practicing the Lesson

### Spelling Clues: Pronouncing Other Forms

To illustrate the strategy presented in the Pupil's Edition, use pairs of words such as *fatal/fatality, academy/academic,* and *preside/president.* Point out that the first word in each pair has an indistinct vowel sound that may cause spelling problems. In each related word, the vowel sound is in a stressed syllable, making it easier to identify the vowel.   APPLYING SPELLING STRATEGIES

### Proofreading

You may wish to have students review Spelling Clues: Pronouncing Other Forms before proofreading the paragraphs.

### Fun with Words

After students have completed the activity, you may wish to point out the relationship of the words *patriots* and *rebels* in item 15. You can extend the activity by having students think of a sentence using an antonym of one of the Spelling Words and having the rest of the class supply the missing word. An example might be, *I wanted to separate the drawings from the photographs in the display, but my friend decided to _____ them.* (combine)

## Posttest

Administer the test on page 32 as a posttest, or administer one of your own. Say each word, use it in a sentence, and then repeat the word.

## Reteaching the Lesson

Students with language difficulties may experience trouble with auditory analysis. Help students practice by using this combined visual and auditory strategy.

Prepare a copy master with the pairs of Spelling Words. Omit the schwa vowel from the word with the weak vowel sound (for example: *oblige, obl__gation*). Direct the students' attention to one Spelling Word pair, and pronounce the word with the strong vowel. Have the students underline the strong vowel sound and write that same vowel in the second word pair, which contains the weak vowel.

When students have correctly completed two sets in succession, have them read the word with the strong vowel themselves and try to identify the strong vowel. This activity should be done on a one-to-one basis.   VISUAL / AUDITORY MODALITIES

*(Pretest/Posttest, continued)*

14. Bicycle riders have an **obligation** to observe traffic laws.
15. The cough **medicine** worked quickly.
16. Many herbs and plants have **medicinal** value.

### PRACTICE ACTIVITY

The practice activity is on page 131.

### Answers: Spelling Clues

1. medicine        4. combination
2. disposition     5. obligation
3. repetition      6. proposition

### Answers: Proofreading

7. disposed        11. combine
8. distribute      12. repeat
9. distribution    13. patriotic
10. medicinal      14. oblige

### Answers: Fun with Words

15. patriots       16. propose

# Lesson 16: Prefixes—Position, I

## OBJECTIVE

To spell words with the prefixes *pro-*, *tele-*, *under-*, and *inter-*

## HOME ACTIVITY

The home activity is on page 133.

## SECOND-LANGUAGE SUPPORT

Help students read and analyze the words by having them look at smaller words within each word, such as *profit* in *profitable* and *nation* in *international*. When possible, write the base word first, and then ask students to copy it and add the prefixes and suffixes that are needed to form the Spelling Word. RECOGNIZING WORD PARTS

## PRETEST/POSTTEST

1. Colonists **protested** the tax on tea by dumping tea into the harbor.

2. He will **undertake** the responsibility of caring for a pet.

3. If your message is urgent, you can send a **telegram.**

4. Before the **telegraph** was invented, people relied on messengers.

5. The **provisions** for our camping trip were ready to be packed.

6. The United Nations is an **international** organization.

7. It's a good idea to arrive early for an **interview.**

8. Astronomers use **telescopes** to study stars and planets.

9. We searched for the **underlying** cause of the problem.

10. We found the house key **underneath** the doormat.

11. The owners worked hard to make their business **profitable.**

12. The **proceeds** from the car wash will be used to buy uniforms.

13. John joined the **intermediate** swimming class.

*(continued on next page)*

## Pretest

Administer the test on this page as a pretest. Say each word, use it in the sentence, and then repeat the word.   ACCESSING PRIOR KNOWLEDGE

**SELF-CHECK**   Have students check their own pretests against the list of Spelling Words. Remind students to write misspelled words in their Lesson Word Logs.   STUDENT SELF-ASSESSMENT

## Introducing the Lesson

### Option A (Open Sort)

Distribute the word cards (page 132) to individuals or small groups, and guide them in an open-sort activity. In open sort, students group the word cards according to a criterion they select themselves. Then guide students in comparing and discussing the criteria they selected.

### Option B (Modeling)

Read aloud with students the lesson title and the Spelling Words. Use this model sentence to introduce the lesson skill in a context.

*We hoped the **interaction** of older people and younger people would **promote** a stronger community spirit.*

## Teaching the Lesson

- Write the four prefix headings on the board. As students name Spelling Words with each prefix, list the words under the headings. Have students identify words in which the meaning of the prefix is evident to them. (**pro-:** *protested, provisions, profitable, proceeds, prosperity;* **tele-:** *telegram, telegraph, telescopes;* **under-:** *undertake, underlying, underneath;* **inter:** *international, interview, intermediate, interrupted, intercept*)

- Invite students to add words from their own writing to the columns. Then have volunteers read all the words aloud and discuss the meanings.

**IN SUMMARY**   You may want to have students summarize the lesson in their own words. Elicit from students a statement to the effect that they can use their knowledge of prefixes to spell and understand the meanings of words.

**ASSIGNMENT**   Students can complete the first page of the lesson as a follow-up to the group activity, either in class or as homework.

# Lesson 16: Prefixes—Position, I *(continued)*

## Practicing the Lesson

### Spelling Clues: Comparing Possible Spellings

Suggest to students that they look at several "clues" to help them spot words in their writing that may be misspelled. First they should check the spelling of any prefixes or suffixes in the word. Then they should look at the rest of the word, using pronunciation clues and their knowledge of related words to help them correct spelling errors.

Stress that the point at which a prefix joins a root or a base word sometimes causes spelling problems. A common spelling error, for example, is *interract,* which should be spelled with only one *r.* Recognition of a word as a combination of a prefix and a base word (in this case, *inter-* plus *act*) can help students spot errors such as this one.   APPLYING SPELLING STRATEGIES

### Proofreading

You may wish to have students review Spelling Clues: Comparing Possible Spellings before proofreading the fact file.

### Working with Meaning

After students have completed this activity, you may wish to have them discuss the relationships between the words in each pair. In item 13, for example, *profit* is a noun while *profitable* is an adjective. You may also wish to have students name other related forms of each word, such as *profiteer* and *prosper.*

## Posttest

Administer the test on page 34 as a posttest, or administer one of your own. Say each word, use it in a sentence, and then repeat the word.

## Reteaching the Lesson

Students with auditory difficulties may experience trouble both in segmenting and in blending the components of words.

Review the prefixes and their meanings with students. Have them write each Spelling Word in large, cursive writing on an index card. Have them draw lines between the prefixes and the root words. Then, have them cut the cards along the lines with a pair of scissors.

Make two boxes, one labeled *Prefixes* and the other *Root Words.* Have students place the card pieces in the appropriate boxes. Then, mix up the card pieces in each box.

For the auditory blending activity, have students pick one card from each box and decide whether they can blend the components to make a word.   KINESTHETIC MODALITY

*(Pretest/Posttest, continued)*

**14.** They wished us happiness and **prosperity** for the new year.

**15.** The director **interrupted** the actors in the middle of a scene.

**16.** Jamie tried to **intercept** the ball before the opposing team caught it.

## PRACTICE ACTIVITY

The practice activity is on page 134.

### Answers: Spelling Clues

1. underlying
2. protested
3. interrupted
4. interview
5. intercept
6. proceeds

### Answers: Proofreading

7. underneath
8. undertake
9. intermediate
10. telescopes
11. telegraph
12. telegram

### Answers: Working with Meaning

13. profitable
14. provisions
15. international
16. prosperity

# Lesson 17: Prefixes—Position, II

## OBJECTIVE
To spell words that begin with the prefixes *ab- (a- or abs-)*, *sub-*, *trans-*, and *extra-*

## HOME ACTIVITY
The home activity is on page 136.

## SECOND-LANGUAGE SUPPORT
Write the four prefixes and their meanings on the board. Below each prefix, draw a diagram to illustrate its meaning, using simple shapes such as squares and arrows. You might also invite students to use gestures to show the meanings of the prefixes. Then, list several Spelling Words below the diagrams, and discuss their meanings.   USING VISUAL CLUES

## PRETEST/POSTTEST
1. The **subway** in London is the longest underground railway in the world.
2. The coach **subjected** the players to long, hard practice sessions.
3. We practiced adding and **subtracting** two-digit numbers.
4. Airplanes provide one of the safest, fastest means of **transportation.**
5. Her illustration made the **abstract** idea easier to understand.
6. Each **transaction** at the bank took about five minutes.
7. Kathy was in **absolute** shock when she won the race.
8. Jackson is always **extravagant** with his money.
9. The speaker's calm words **subdued** the angry crowd.
10. The Thirteenth Amendment **abolished** slavery in the United States.
11. I looked for an English **translation** of the Japanese folktale.

*(continued on next page)*

## Pretest
Administer the test on this page as a pretest. Say each word, use it in the sentence, and then repeat the word.   ACCESSING PRIOR KNOWLEDGE

**SELF-CHECK**   Have students check their own pretests against the list of Spelling Words. Remind students to write misspelled words in their Lesson Word Logs.   STUDENT SELF-ASSESSMENT

## Introducing the Lesson
### Option A (Open Sort)
Distribute the word cards (page 135) to individuals or small groups, and guide them in an open-sort activity. In open sort, students group the word cards according to a criterion they select themselves. Then guide students in comparing and discussing the criteria they selected.

### Option B (Modeling)
Read aloud with students the lesson title and the Spelling Words. Use this model sentence to introduce the lesson skill in a context.

*A* **submarine** *can* **transmit** *radio signals.*

## Teaching the Lesson
- Ask volunteers to name Spelling Words that begin with the prefix *ab- (a-, abs-)*. As students name the words, list the words on the board and discuss their meanings. *(abstract, absolute, abolished)*
- Follow the same procedure for *sub-*, *trans-*, and *extra-*. Have students identify the base words to which a prefix has been added. Discuss how the addition of the prefix changes the meaning of the base word. (***sub-:*** *subway, subjected, subtracting, subdued, submerged;* ***trans-:*** *transportation, transaction, translation, transferred, transient;* ***extra-:*** *extravagant, extraordinary, extraterrestrial)*
- After students have added words from their own writing to the columns, have volunteers read all the words aloud and underline the prefixes.

**IN SUMMARY**   Have students summarize the lesson in their own words. Elicit from students the information that prefixes are word parts added to the beginning of roots or base words.

**ASSIGNMENT**   Students can complete the first page of the lesson as a follow-up to the group activity, either in class or as homework.

# Lesson 17: Prefixes—Position, II (continued)

## Practicing the Lesson

### Spelling Clues: Checking Syllables

Point out to students that the careful pronunciation of words, especially words of Latin or Greek origin, is often a good guide to spelling them correctly. Suggest to students that they look at the two spellings of each word and then say the word, using what they believe is the correct pronunciation. In most cases, students should be able to identify the correctly spelled word by counting syllables and pronouncing all the sounds in the syllables carefully.   APPLYING SPELLING STRATEGIES

### Proofreading

You may wish to have students review Spelling Clues: Checking Syllables before proofreading the paragraphs.

### Fun with Words

You may wish to have students complete this activity in pairs. Discuss with students how the speaker's choice of words reveals his attitude. (He calls the colonists' demands "extravagant.")

## Posttest

Administer the test on page 36 as a posttest, or administer one of your own. Say each word, use it in a sentence, and then repeat the word.

## Reteaching the Lesson

Have the students make a prefix chart showing the four lesson prefixes and their meanings. Then, provide a copy master with definitions of the Spelling Words, grouped by words having the same prefix. As you say each Spelling Word aloud, have students write it beside its definition, underlining the prefix. Encourage students to refer to their prefix charts. Help students remember the complete words by emphasizing the meanings of the prefixes and the root words.   VISUAL MODALITY

*(Pretest/Posttest, continued)*

12. The tidal wave completely **submerged** the village near the shore.
13. I **transferred** my books from the damaged locker to another one.
14. The hotels in this area are filled with **transient** guests.
15. A tightrope walker needs an **extraordinary** sense of balance.
16. Do you think **extraterrestrial** creatures may exist?

## PRACTICE ACTIVITY

The practice activity is on page 137.

### Answers: Spelling Clues

1. abstract
2. subtracting
3. submerged
4. extraterrestrial
5. transient
6. transaction

### Answers: Proofreading

7. subway
8. transportation
9. transferred
10. translation
11. subdued

### Answers: Fun with Words

12. extraordinary
13. extravagant
14. subjected
15. abolished
16. absolute

# Lesson 18: Noun and Verb Endings

## OBJECTIVE
To spell nouns and verbs ending with the suffix *-ate*

## HOME ACTIVITY
The home activity is on page 139.

## SECOND-LANGUAGE SUPPORT
In Spanish, the *-ate* ending for nouns is *-ato;* the *-ate* ending for verbs is usually *-ar.* You might ask Spanish-speaking students to give the Spanish equivalents of some of the Spelling Words. Students will recognize almost all of them as having the same origin as the English word.    COMPARING AND CONTRASTING

## PRETEST/POSTTEST
1. The **debate** was about the pros and cons of year-round schooling.
2. The city needed extra police officers to **regulate** traffic.
3. We used balloons to **decorate** the party room.
4. We **estimate** that the room is 14 feet long.
5. Steve didn't **hesitate** for a minute before diving into the icy water.
6. We watched the pilot **demonstrate** a perfect takeoff.
7. We hired a detective to **investigate** the cause of the accident.
8. Every **delegate** will have a chance to address the assembly.
9. With the radio on, Mark couldn't **concentrate** on his homework.
10. His sweeping victory gave the new leader a **mandate** for change.
11. It is not easy to **eliminate** sugar from your diet.
12. I **advocate** that we add a bicycle lane to the narrow road.
13. Our model will **simulate** conditions in a tropical rain forest.

*(continued on next page)*

## Pretest
Administer the test on this page as a pretest. Say each word, use it in the sentence, and then repeat the word.    ACCESSING PRIOR KNOWLEDGE

**SELF-CHECK**    Have students check their own pretests against the list of Spelling Words. Remind students to write misspelled words in their Lesson Word Logs.    STUDENT SELF-ASSESSMENT

## Introducing the Lesson
### Option A (Open Sort)
Distribute the word cards (page 138) to individuals or small groups, and guide them in an open-sort activity. In open sort, students group the word cards according to a criterion they select themselves. Then guide students in comparing and discussing the criteria they selected.

### Option B (Modeling)
Read aloud with students the lesson title and the Spelling Words. Use this model sentence to introduce the lesson skill in a context.

*The city needed to **evaluate** locations for the new **consulate**.*

## Teaching the Lesson
- Review with students the definitions of a noun and a verb.
- Write the headings *Nouns, Verbs,* and *Both* on the board. Have volunteers write the Spelling Words below the correct headings. You may need to help students with the word *mandate,* which is not listed as a verb in some student dictionaries. (**Noun:** *phosphate;* **Verbs:** *regulate, decorate, hesitate, demonstrate, investigate, eliminate, simulate, participate, negotiate;* **Both nouns and verbs:** *debate, estimate, delegate, concentrate, mandate, advocate*)
- After students have added their own words to the columns, have volunteers read all the words aloud.
- Discuss the pronunciation differences for words that can be used as both nouns and verbs.

**IN SUMMARY**    Ask students to summarize the lesson in their own words. Elicit from students the information that *-ate* can be used to form both nouns and verbs.

**ASSIGNMENT**    Students can complete the first page of the lesson as a follow-up to the group activity, either in class or as homework.

# Lesson 18: Noun and Verb Endings *(continued)*

## Practicing the Lesson

### Spelling Clues: Checking Short Vowel Sounds

Tell students that careful pronunciation of a word can some-times help them spot and correct spelling errors in their writing. For items 1–6, students should first try using pronunciation as a guide to determining correct spelling. If the word includes the schwa sound, advise students to use another strategy, such as thinking of a related word that has a strong vowel sound. (This strategy works for item 4, *decorate*, in which the schwa sound in the second syllable is heard as a strong /ô/ in the related word *decor.*    APPLYING SPELLING STRATEGIES

**TRANSITIONAL SPELLERS**    When students come across words they are unsure of, they should first count the number of syllables and then check the letters representing vowel sounds to help them determine the correct spelling.

### Proofreading

You may wish to have students review Spelling Clues: Checking Short Vowel Sounds before proofreading the paragraph.

### Working with Meaning

After students have supplied the missing words in items 12–16 and guessed the identity of the American leader (Ben Franklin), have them discuss his other accomplishments. (formed a fire department, a subscription library, and a college that became the University of Pennsylvania)

## Posttest

Administer the test on page 38 as a posttest, or administer one of your own. Say each word, use it in a sentence, and then repeat the word.

## Reteaching the Lesson

Have students make a series of flip cards with decreasing cues for spelling each Spelling Word. For example, you could have students make the following set of cards for the word *participate: part _ _ ipate, par _ _ _ _ _ate, par _ _ _ _ _ _ _ _* , and *_ _ _ _ _ _ _ _ _ _*. The lines on the cards provide clues for students who are uncertain how many letters there are in the word. Staple the cards together on one side so that after the student has completed one card, it can be folded back and the word on the new card can be completed from memory. VISUAL MODALITY

*(Pretest/Posttest, continued)*

14. Everyone was encouraged to **participate** in team sports.
15. The warring countries finally decided to **negotiate** a treaty.
16. Some cities and states ban the use of **phosphate** in detergents.

### PRACTICE ACTIVITY

The practice activity is on page 140.

### Answers: Spelling Clues

1. simulate
2. estimate
3. investigate
4. decorate
5. regulate
6. phosphate

### Answers: Proofreading

7. participate
8. delegate
9. mandate
10. eliminate
11. debate

### Answers: Working with Meaning

12. demonstrate
13. concentrate
14. hesitate
15. negotiate
16. advocate

# Unit 3 Review

## OBJECTIVES

- To review spelling patterns and strategies in Lessons 14–18

- To give students the opportunity to recognize and use these spelling patterns and Spelling Words in their writing

## UNIT 3 WORDS

The following words are reviewed in Practice Test, Parts A and B.

### Lesson 14: Latin Roots, I

| | |
|---|---|
| conservation | migrate |
| dictator | portable |

### Lesson 15: More Related Words

| | |
|---|---|
| disposition | patriotic |
| medicine | repetition |

### Lesson 16: Prefixes–Position, I

| | |
|---|---|
| interrupted | telegraph |
| prosperity | underlying |

### Lesson 17: Prefixes—Position, II

| | |
|---|---|
| extraordinary | submerged |
| extravagant | transaction |

### Lesson 18: Noun and Verb Endings

| | |
|---|---|
| eliminate | participate |
| negotiate | regulate |

## Review Strategies

Review with students the following spelling-clue strategies for Lessons 14–18.

### Lesson 14    Spelling Clues: Checking Roots

Write this sentence on the board: *I reported my obsirvations to the guard.* Ask students to find the misspelled word *(obsirvations)* and to spell it correctly *(observations)*. Have students identify the Latin root in *observations (-serv-)* and name other words with the same root (for example, *preserve, reserve,* and *conserve*). Remind students that recognizing a root in a word can help them spell the word correctly.

### Lesson 15    Spelling Clues: Pronouncing Other Forms

Write on the board *grammer, tolerent, tyrint,* and *histery.* Ask students which of these words are misspelled (all of them). Have them help you correct the words. Then ask them to suggest related forms of each word *(grammatical, tolerate, tyrannical,* and *historical).* In each case, discuss how the fully stressed vowel in the related word can help students decide which letter to use for the unstressed vowel in the original word.

### Lesson 16    Spelling Clues: Comparing Possible Spellings

Write this sentence on the board: *The interior of the house was not damaged.* Ask students to find the misspelled word *(interior)* and to tell you how to spell it correctly. Write all their responses on the board, and ask which spelling is correct. Remind students that writing a word in several ways can sometimes help them determine the correct spelling.

### Lesson 17    Spelling Clues: Checking Syllables

Write on the board *eletricity* and *govinment.* Ask students to pronounce each word as it should be pronounced and then write the correct spelling of the word *(electricity, government).* Discuss how careful pronunciation can help students spot and correct spelling errors.

### Lesson 18    Spelling Clues: Checking Short Vowel Sounds

Write on the board *dacorate* and *duplacate.* Ask students to correct the spellings and to identify the short vowel sound they hear in each (short *e* in the first syllable of *decorate,* short *i* in the second syllable of *duplicate*). Note the two pronunciations of *duplicate* (as noun and as a verb). Discuss with students how saying a word aloud and listening for short vowel sounds can help them spell the word.

# Unit 3 Review (continued)

## Practice Test

The Practice Test provides an opportunity to review Spelling Words and spelling generalizations in a standardized test format, complete with a sample answer card.

### Option 1

Use Practice Test: Part A as a pretest. Later, use Practice Test: Part B as a posttest.

### Option 2

Have students review their Lesson Word Log for this unit. If they need extra help, you may wish to review the spelling generalizations discussed in the individual lessons. Then administer both parts of the Practice Test to determine whether students have mastered the spelling generalizations.

| Practice Test: Part A | Practice Test: Part B |
|---|---|
| 1. (C) portable | 1. (D) prosperity |
| 2. (B) dictator | 2. (D) extravagant |
| 3. (A) migrate | 3. (C) underlying |
| 4. (B) transaction | 4. (C) participate |
| 5. (D) medicine | 5. (B) extraordinary |
| 6. (C) repetition | 6. (A) disposition |
| 7. (A) patriotic | 7. (C) conservation |
| 8. (B) regulate | 8. (C) negotiate |
| 9. (B) interrupted | 9. (A) submerged |
| 10. (C) telegraph | 10. (B) eliminate |

## Options for Evaluation

- Have students check their own Practice Tests against their lists of Spelling Words. The list on the opposite page provides references to the lessons where they can find words they misspelled.
- You may prefer to assign partners and have students check each other's Practice Tests, using their own list of Spelling Words.

## REVIEW ACTIVITIES

### Activity 1

For students who need a reteaching activity, write one of the prefixes, roots, or endings from the words in this review lesson. Ask students to list all the words they can think of with that word part, or give them clues and ask them to write the words that fit the clues. For the words in Lesson 15, write one word at a time, substituting a blank for the unstressed vowel. Ask students to spell a related form of the word, and then have them provide the missing vowel.

### Activity 2

Have students look back through their written work for this unit and pick out any words that they misspelled more than once. Ask them to write each word correctly on an index card and to put the cards in their own spelling boxes for future reference.

### Activity 3

The word *repetition* has the pattern 1 2 3 2 4 5 4 5 6 7, since the second and fourth letters are the same, the fifth and seventh letters are the same, and the sixth and eighth letters are the same. Choose some of the words from this review lesson, and write the numerical pattern for them on the board. Challenge students to identify the words represented by the patterns.

## WHAT'S IN A WORD?

### ♦ *abolish*

You may wish to point out to students that people who opposed slavery in the United States were called *abolitionists*. If students wish, they may write about laws or customs, as well as rules, that they think should be abolished.

### ♦ *immigration* and *emigration*

You may wish to ask students whether any of their family members or friends have come to the United States as immigrants. Have students discuss some of the reasons that people emigrate and the difficulties and challenges they face in adjusting to life in another country.

## Creating a Word Puzzle

If possible, provide graph paper for students to use in making their puzzles. Explain that words may be written horizontally, vertically, or diagonally.

## Spelling Clues

You may wish to extend the activity by having students use five Spelling Words in sentences or in a paragraph and reading their work aloud.

## Team Charades

You may wish to set a three-minute time limit for each word being acted out. The team with the shortest amount of guessing time is the winner.

## Abolish Spelling Problems

Have students make a running list of words they spelled incorrectly and review them at a later time.

## Looking for Spelling Words

Provide old magazines that contain many advertisements or other pictures of people. To extend the activity, you may want to have students write sentences using the pictured Spelling Words.

## Proofreading Partners

Have students read the instructions for the activity, and answer any questions they may have. Remind students to review the list carefully and to select the Spelling Words they find most troublesome; this approach will make the activity a useful tool for improving their spelling skills. Then have students select their own partners and complete the activity.

♦ This indicates a Unit Spelling Word.

# Unit 3 Review (continued)

## Curriculum Options

### Art: Picture This

Have students play "Picture This" together. One player goes to the board and sketches a picture clue for one of the Spelling Words. The clue must be in pictures only—words (spoken or written) and gestures are not permitted. The first player to guess the word correctly has the next turn to sketch a clue.

Students may want to extend the game to include words other than this lesson's Spelling Words.

### Language Arts: Bingo

To prepare for this activity, have students make bingo cards, on which they write words instead of numbers. There is no free space. There are five columns and five rows, as shown in the example below. The Spelling Words are used, in addition to some other words that are related to these word families. Each card should show the words in different order. A caller calls off words from a list at random, and players cover the squares with bits of paper, buttons, or pennies as words are called. The first player to get five covered spaces in a row (across, down, or diagonally) is the winner.

conservation  disposition  interrupted  extraordinary  eliminate

| | | | | |
|---|---|---|---|---|
| dictator | medicine | prosperity | extravagant | negotiate |
| migrate | patriotic | telegraph | submerged | participate |
| portable | repetition | underlying | transaction | regulate |
| exported | patriots | telescopes | transient | advocate |

### Social Studies: That's Debatable

Divide the class into four or five debating teams, with several students on each team. Choose a debate topic with the class, such as the construction of a new school stadium or gym, requirements for part-time jobs, or any issue of school or community interest. Give the students a few minutes to practice their debate. Ask them to incorporate as many as they can of the Spelling Words, or other words with the suffix -ate, in their remarks. Call on volunteers to present their debates, and have one member of the debate team record all -ate words on the board as they are used.

## WHAT'S IN A WORD?

**♦ investigate**

Discuss with students the methods used by some of their favorite fictional detectives to investigate mysteries. Have students consider the importance of investigating psychological evidence, such as a character's motive or state of mind, in addition to physical evidence.

**♦ patriot**

Discuss the meaning of patriot—"one who loves one's country and supports its interests"—and ask students to name figures in American history that they consider patriots. Have students look up the meanings of other words derived from the Latin word pater ("father"), such as patriarch, paternal, patrician, and patrimony.

**tablet**

After students have completed this activity, you may wish to extend it by having them write a paragraph using as many words as possible from their list. Have students read their paragraphs aloud. As they do so, have a volunteer keep track of appropriate words by writing them on the board. Students can then add these words to their Word Logs.

♦ This indicates a Unit Spelling Word.

# Lesson 20: Prefixes—Size and Amount

## OBJECTIVE
To spell words with prefixes that tell size and amount

## HOME ACTIVITY
The home activity is on page 142.

## SECOND-LANGUAGE SUPPORT
To provide extra practice, make illustrated flashcards. Write a word on one side of the card and provide an illustration on the other side. Some words you might want to use for this practice are *multicolored, multimedia,* and *multicultural.* Have students choose a card at random, read and define the word, and use the illustration to check their answer.   USING PICTURE CLUES

## PRETEST/POSTTEST
1. Wendy heats leftovers in her **microwave** oven.
2. Bob does his homework on a **microcomputer.**
3. The **multiplication** of those numbers will give you the answer.
4. Telescopes **magnify** images of stars and other celestial objects.
5. Flo's **multicolored** costume won the prize at the party.
6. We were surprised by the **magnitude** of the art collection.
7. One of the goals of the French Revolution was **equality** for all.
8. A **multitude** gathered to watch the parade.
9. He looked at the insect through a **microscope.**
10. One side of the **equation** was 4 + 6, and the other was 10.
11. A **multimedia** campaign was used to promote the new product.
12. The **equator** divides Earth into two hemispheres.

*(continued on next page)*

## Pretest
Administer the test on this page as a pretest. Say each word, use it in the sentence, and then repeat the word.   ACCESSING PRIOR KNOWLEDGE

**SELF-CHECK**   Have students check their own pretests against the list of Spelling Words. Remind students to write misspelled words in their Lesson Word Logs.   STUDENT SELF-ASSESSMENT

## Introducing the Lesson

### Option A (Open Sort)
Distribute the word cards (page 141) to individuals or small groups, and guide them in an open-sort activity. In open sort, students group the word cards according to a criterion they select themselves. Then guide students in comparing and discussing the criteria they selected.

### Option B (Modeling)
Read aloud with students the lesson title and the Spelling Words. Use this model sentence to introduce the lesson skill in a context.

*The **multimillionaire** was in favor of **equalizing** taxes.*

## Teaching the Lesson

- Ask volunteers to name and spell the words with the prefix *magni-*. List the words on the board. (*magnify, magnitude, magnificently*)
- Follow the same procedure for the prefixes *micro-, multi-,* and *equ(i)-*. As students name words, list the words on the board. (***micro-:*** *microwave, microcomputer, microscopic, microorganism;* ***multi-:*** *multiplication, multicolored, multitude, multimedia, multicultural;* ***equ(i)-:*** *equality, equation, equator, equivalent*)
- Have students add other words with these prefixes to the columns. Then have volunteers read all the words aloud and underline the prefixes.

**IN SUMMARY**   Have students summarize the lesson in their own words. Elicit from students the meanings of the four prefixes. Also elicit the fact that the spelling of the prefix *equ(i)-* may change when it is added to a word part that begins with a vowel.

**ASSIGNMENT**   Students can complete the first page of the lesson as a follow-up to the group activity, either in class or as homework.

# Lesson 20: Prefixes—Size and Amount (continued)

## Practicing the Lesson

### Spelling Clues: Visualization

Suggest to students that when they encounter a word whose spelling they are unsure of, they visualize the word spelled in several different ways. Then they should choose the spelling that looks correct. If they are still unsure, they can look up the word in a dictionary.    APPLYING SPELLING STRATEGIES

### Proofreading

You may wish to have students review Spelling Clues: Visualization before proofreading the sentences.

### Working with Meaning

Students may complete this activity individually or with a partner. Tell students to look for clues in the review and to choose the correct Spelling Word based on those clues. After students have completed the activity, you may wish to provide more practice by having students write their own paragraphs, using as many of the words on the list as they can.

**TRANSITIONAL SPELLERS**    Have students complete this activity cooperatively with a partner or in a small group. To extend the activity, have students write their own sentences, using the Spelling Words in the review.

## Posttest

Administer the test on page 44 as a posttest, or administer one of your own. Say each word, use it in a sentence, and then repeat the word.

## Reteaching the Lesson

For some students, spelling presents trouble because of its high demand on visual and auditory memory.

Praise is a powerful motivator for those students who are not intrinsically motivated. Have the students write the Spelling Words on cards, omitting the prefixes (for example: _____ wave). Place the cards facedown in a pile, and have the students draw a card from the pile and spell the prefix. For each word spelled correctly, sincerely praise the students.

You may want to chart the students' growth as a visual reminder of their success.    AUDITORY MODALITY

*(Pretest/Posttest, continued)*

13. The **microorganism** that causes that disease has been found.
14. The fair had an obvious **multicultural** theme.
15. The hall was **magnificently** decorated.
16. The bracelet and the necklace are **equivalent** in value.

### PRACTICE ACTIVITY

The practice activity is on page 143.

### Answers: Spelling Clues

1. equation
2. magnify
3. multiplication
4. microwave
5. magnitude or multitude
6. microcomputer

### Answers: Proofreading

7. microorganism
8. equator
9. multimedia
10. multicultural
11. microscopic
12. equality

### Answers: Working with Meaning

13. multitude
14. magnificently
15. multicolored
16. equivalent

# Lesson 21: Double Consonants

## OBJECTIVE
To spell words that have doubled consonants

## HOME ACTIVITY
The home activity is on page 145.

## SECOND-LANGUAGE SUPPORT
To demonstrate the relationship between short vowel sounds and doubled consonants, write the following words on the board: *bitter–biter, cutter–cuter, dinner–diner, flatter–flavor, hotter–hotel,* and *mopping–moping.* Read each pair of words aloud, stressing the first vowel sound in each word. Then, have students sort the words under the headings *Short Vowel Sounds* and *Long Vowel Sounds.*

Help students to see that each short vowel sound is followed by a doubled consonant. Point out, however, that not all words follow this generalization.    RECOGNIZING PATTERNS

## PRETEST/POSTTEST
1. Ted was so cold that his teeth were **chattering.**
2. When asked how he felt, James **uttered** just one word: "Great!"
3. The styles worn by Laura **triggered** a whole new fad at our school.
4. Stuart looked **terrific** when he returned from his vacation in Mexico.
5. The wind is **scattering** all the leaves that fell last week.
6. The water in this lake has been **polluted** with chemicals.
7. With a demanding cry, the cat **summoned** Christine to the door.
8. The moon is a natural **satellite** of the earth.
9. The baby wasn't feeling well after she received her **vaccination.**
10. Betty was involved in an **intellectual** discussion with Bert.

*(continued on next page)*

## Pretest
Administer the test on this page as a pretest. Say each word, use it in the sentence, and then repeat the word.    ACCESSING PRIOR KNOWLEDGE

**SELF-CHECK**    Have students check their own pretests against the list of Spelling Words. Remind students to write misspelled words in their Lesson Word Logs.    STUDENT SELF-ASSESSMENT

## Introducing the Lesson

### Option A (Open Sort)
Distribute the word cards (page 144) to individuals or small groups, and guide them in an open-sort activity. In open sort, students group the word cards according to a criterion they select themselves. Then guide students in comparing and discussing the criteria they selected.

### Option B (Modeling)
Read aloud with students the lesson title and the Spelling Words. Use this model sentence to introduce the lesson skill in a context.

*It was **necessary** for Paul to put his **luggage** on a **commercial** jet.*

## Teaching the Lesson

- Ask volunteers to name and spell the two-syllable words with doubled consonants in the middle. List the words on the board. *(uttered, triggered, summoned)*
- Follow the same procedure for three-, four-, and five-syllable words with doubled consonants. List the words on the board. *(**three-syllable words:** chattering, terrific, scattering, polluted, satellite, narrative, penniless, parallel, embassy, torrential; **four-syllable word:** vaccination; **five-syllable words:** intellectual, exaggerated)*
- Have students add other words that follow these patterns to the columns. Then, have volunteers read all the words aloud and define them.

**IN SUMMARY**    Ask students to summarize the lesson in their own words. Elicit the information that sometimes when a consonant follows a short vowel sound and there is another syllable after it, the consonant is doubled.

**ASSIGNMENT**    Students can complete the first page of the lesson as a follow-up to the group activity, either in class or as homework.

# Lesson 21: Double Consonants *(continued)*

## Practicing the Lesson

### Spelling Clues: Double Consonants

Suggest that when students encounter a word that they think might be spelled with a double consonant in the middle, they try spelling it with a single consonant and with a double consonant. Sometimes it is easy to choose the correct spelling if they see it written both ways. If they are still unsure of the spelling of the word, they should look up the word in a dictionary. APPLYING SPELLING STRATEGIES

### Proofreading

You may wish to have students review Spelling Clues: Double Consonants before proofreading the advertisement.

### Fun with Words

Students may complete this activity individually or with a partner. After students complete the activity, you may wish to expand it by having them write sentences using the words.

## Posttest

Administer the test on page 46 as a posttest, or administer one of your own. Say each word, use it in a sentence, and then repeat the word.

## Reteaching the Lesson

For students who have memory deficits, it is often easier to remember a generalization if they have arrived at it by inductive reasoning.

Write the Spelling Words in two lists on the board. In the first list, put the words that follow the generalization about doubling the consonant after a short vowel; in the second, put the exceptions to the generalization. Align the words so that the doubled letters are in a column. Ask one student at a time to underline the doubled letter and preceding vowel in each word as you and the other students read the word aloud. Ask a student to formulate a hypothesis about when a consonant should be doubled. Guide students to the generalization about doubling the consonant following a short vowel.

Then, direct students to the second list. Again, ask students to underline the double letter and preceding vowel in each word. Ask students whether there are any short vowels followed by single consonants. When students observe that these words do not follow the spelling generalization, ask volunteers to look up the etymology of each word in a dictionary. Elicit the information that each word in the second list comes from Latin or Greek. VISUAL MODALITY

*(Pretest/Posttest, continued)*

11. The **narrative** began with the traditional "Once upon a time."

12. A series of bad investments left the man **penniless.**

13. The yard lines on a football field are **parallel.**

14. The stranded travelers went to the American **embassy** to seek help.

15. It was obvious Phil had **exaggerated** his cooking ability.

16. The **torrential** rains caused great damage to the harbor.

### PRACTICE ACTIVITY

The practice activity is on page 146.

#### Answers: Spelling Clues

| | | | |
|---|---|---|---|
| 1. | chattering | 4. | vaccination |
| 2. | penniless | 5. | satellite |
| 3. | uttered | 6. | polluted |

#### Answers: Proofreading

| | | | |
|---|---|---|---|
| 7. | intellectual | 10. | narrative |
| 8. | summoned | 11. | terrific |
| 9. | parallel | 12. | embassy |

#### Answers: Fun with Words

| | | | |
|---|---|---|---|
| 13. | scattering | 15. | exaggerated |
| 14. | torrential | 16. | triggered |

# Lesson 22: Noun Endings

## OBJECTIVE
To spell words that have noun-forming suffixes

## HOME ACTIVITY
The home activity is on page 148.

## SECOND-LANGUAGE SUPPORT
Prepare a set of flashcards for the Spelling Words, and pair each student acquiring English with a student fluent in English. Have partners choose a card, read the word aloud, and use it in a sentence. Then, have students find words from another language that are cognates of the Spelling Words. For example, in Spanish *patriotismo* is similar to *patriotism, mecanismo* to *mechanism, pobreza* to *poverty, crueldad* to *cruelty, rivalidad* to *rivalry,* and *specialidad* to *specialty.* RECOGNIZING SIMILARITIES IN WORDS

## PRETEST/POSTTEST
1. Only by working at two jobs could he avoid living in **poverty.**
2. A crowd gathered to watch the queen and other **royalty** pass by.
3. Dave has enjoyed a successful career in **journalism.**
4. The **rivalry** between the two players was intense.
5. One of the biggest sources of income in Hawaii is **tourism.**
6. The soldiers pledged their **loyalty** to their country.
7. The entire **robbery** was video-taped by the hidden camera.
8. Her feelings of **uncertainty** showed on her face.
9. We showed our **patriotism** by singing the national anthem.
10. His **cruelty** drove his friends away.
11. The chef's **specialty** is eggs Benedict.

*(continued on next page)*

## Pretest
Administer the test on this page as a pretest. Say each word, use it in the sentence, and then repeat the word.   ACCESSING PRIOR KNOWLEDGE

**SELF-CHECK**   Have students check their own pretests against the list of Spelling Words. Remind students to write misspelled words in their Lesson Word Logs.   STUDENT SELF-ASSESSMENT

## Introducing the Lesson

### Option A (Open Sort)
Distribute the word cards (page 147) to individuals or small groups, and guide them in an open-sort activity. In open sort, students group the word cards according to a criterion they select themselves. Then guide students in comparing and discussing the criteria they selected.

### Option B (Modeling)
Read aloud with students the lesson title and the Spelling Words. Use this model sentence to introduce the lesson skill in a context.

*The group showed **unity** and **bravery** during the siege.*

## Teaching the Lesson

- Ask volunteers to name and spell the words that have the suffix *-ty.* List the words on the board. (*poverty, royalty, loyalty, uncertainty, cruelty, specialty, novelty*)
- Follow the same procedure for the suffixes *-ism* and *-ry/-ery.* List the words on the board. (*-ism: journalism, tourism, patriotism, realism, optimism, mechanism, criticism; -ry/-ery: rivalry, robbery*)
- Have students add other words with these suffixes to the columns. Then have volunteers read all the words aloud and underline the suffixes.

**IN SUMMARY**   Ask students to summarize the lesson in their own words. Elicit the fact that the suffix *-ty* forms nouns that mean "the state or quality of." The suffixes *-ism* and *-ry/-ery* form nouns that mean "the act, practice, theory, or occupation of."

**ASSIGNMENT**   Students can complete the first page of the lesson as a follow-up to the group activity, either in class or as homework.

# Lesson 22: Noun Endings *(continued)*

## Practicing the Lesson

### Spelling Clues: Identifying the Base Word

If necessary, point out that the base words students are looking for are *journal, mechanics, patriot, rob, special,* and *tour.* Remind them that sometimes the spelling of the base word changes a little when a suffix is added. If they have found the base word and are still not sure of the correct spelling, they should look the word up in a dictionary.   APPLYING SPELLING STRATEGIES

### Proofreading

You may wish to have students review Spelling Clues: Identifying the Base Word before proofreading the questions.

### Working with Meaning

Have students work together in small groups. They can help one another by sharing knowledge about word meanings. Then pairs of students can read the dialogue aloud.

## Posttest

Administer the test on page 48 as a posttest, or administer one of your own. Say each word, use it in a sentence, and then repeat the word.

## Reteaching the Lesson

Write the suffixes *-ty, -ism, -ry,* and *-ery,* as well as the root words appearing in the lesson, on index cards. Place the word cards in two boxes, labeled *Base Word* and *Suffix.* To begin, include only the base words to which suffixes can be added without spelling changes (for example, *special + ty*).

Have students select a card at random from each box, put the two cards together, and read the word. If the word does not exist, have them return one card to its box and choose another. When the cards form a real word, have students say the word, say it in segments, spell it aloud, and write it down.

For the Spelling Words that require spelling changes before a suffix is added, provide a sheet of paper with the base word and the suffix on it. Have students cross out the letter that is dropped or make any other spelling changes needed. Then, have them rewrite the base word and add the suffix. Have students say the word and spell it aloud.   VISUAL/AUDITORY MODALITIES

*(Pretest/Posttest, continued)*

12. Too much **realism** in a movie can make it boring.
13. Just for the **novelty** of it, Betty dyed her hair purple.
14. The rose-colored glasses added to Jean's feelings of **optimism.**
15. The clock's **mechanism** is very simple.
16. Vin seems to handle **criticism** well.

## PRACTICE ACTIVITY

The practice activity is on page 149.

### Answers: Spelling Clues

1. journalism
2. mechanism
3. patriotism
4. robbery
5. specialty
6. tourism

### Answers: Proofreading

7. optimism
8. novelty
9. uncertainty
10. realism

### Answers: Working with Meaning

11. rivalry
12. loyalty
13. poverty
14. cruelty
15. criticism
16. royalty

# Lesson 23: Prefix *ob-*

**OBJECTIVE**
To spell words that begin with the prefix *ob- (oc-, of-, op-)*

**HOME ACTIVITY**
The home activity is on page 151.

**SECOND-LANGUAGE SUPPORT**
Lead students to observe that only the *ob-* form of the prefix does not require a doubled consonant. Provide extra practice by distributing cards with *double* printed on one side and *do not double* printed on the other side. Pronounce aloud words that have the prefixes *ob-, oc-, of-,* and *op-*. For each word, have the students hold up the appropriate side of the card. Check student responses for accuracy before going on to the next word. LISTENING FOR SOUNDS

**PRETEST/POSTTEST**
1. Rosa kept her best necklace in an **oblong** box.
2. The **observation** about the group was correct.
3. Does anyone have an **objection** to postponing the test?
4. What was your **objective** in reading the book?
5. Lucy has chosen to make landscaping her **occupation.**
6. All children have **obtained** permission to go on the trip.
7. For lunch today, the cafeteria is **offering** turkey sandwiches and fruit.
8. The two girls try to look different, but they are **obviously** twins.
9. Because of his **offensive** behavior, everyone avoids him.
10. At the first **opportunity,** Lisa thanked Ms. Wilson for the gift.
11. What do you think of this **obscure** song from Dad's collection?

*(continued on next page)*

## Pretest
Administer the test on this page as a pretest. Say each word, use it in the sentence, and then repeat the word. ACCESSING PRIOR KNOWLEDGE

**SELF-CHECK** Have students check their own pretests against the list of Spelling Words. Remind students to write misspelled words in their Lesson Word Logs. STUDENT SELF-ASSESSMENT

## Introducing the Lesson

### Option A (Open Sort)
Distribute the word cards (page 150) to individuals or small groups, and guide them in an open-sort activity. In open sort, students group the word cards according to a criterion they select themselves. Then guide students in comparing and discussing the criteria they selected.

### Option B (Modeling)
Read aloud with students the lesson title and the Spelling Words. Use this model sentence to introduce the lesson skill in a context.

*The **official** strongly **objected** to her **opponent's** statement.*

## Teaching the Lesson

- Ask volunteers to name the Spelling Words that have a prefix spelled *ob-*. As students name words, list the words on the board. (*oblong, observation, objection, objective, obtained, obviously, obscure, obstacle, obsessions*)
- Continue this procedure with the prefixes spelled *oc-, of-,* and *op-*. As students name words, list the words on the board. (*oc-: occupation, occupant, occasionally; of-: offering, offensive; op-: opportunity, opposition*)
- Invite students to add to the columns words with these prefixes from their own writing. Then have volunteers read all the words aloud and underline the troublesome areas.

**IN SUMMARY** Have students summarize the lesson in their own words. Elicit the fact that *ob-* is an absorbed prefix that changes form, or spelling, to match the first letter of the word to which it is being added. Knowing this can help students spell words that have the prefix *ob-*.

**ASSIGNMENT** Students can complete the first page of the lesson as a follow-up to the group activity, either in class or as homework.

# Lesson 23: Prefix *ob-* (continued)

## Practicing the Lesson

### Spelling Clues: Prefixes

Suggest to students that when they consider how to spell words that have the prefix *oc-*, *of-*, or *op-*, they should check to make sure they have doubled the consonant before spelling the rest of the word. Then they should check the spelling of the rest of the word. If the word still doesn't look right, they should check a dictionary.    APPLYING SPELLING STRATEGIES

### Proofreading

You may wish to have students review Spelling Clues: Prefixes before proofreading the paragraph.

### Fun with Words

Students may complete this activity individually or with a partner. To extend the activity, you might have students write sentences of their own for each of the Spelling Words.

TRANSITIONAL SPELLERS    Have students complete this activity cooperatively with a partner or in a small group. Suggest that students use picture clues to help them figure out the missing words.

SECOND-LANGUAGE SUPPORT    Have students work together in small groups. They can help one another by sharing knowledge as they try to determine what context clues are given in the art.    USING PICTURE CLUES

## Posttest

Administer the test on page 50 as a posttest, or administer one of your own. Say each word, use it in a sentence, and then repeat the word.

## Reteaching the Lesson

Give students a strategy for dividing multisyllabic words into their component parts. Use an auditory and visual approach. Have students listen as you say the words. Then, have them divide a prewritten list of the words into their component parts by making slash marks between the syllables. Finally, have students write the words from dictation.

In preparing the prewritten list of words, group together words with the same form of the prefix.    VISUAL/AUDITORY MODALITIES

*(Pretest/Posttest, continued)*

12. The new **occupant** will move in on Friday.
13. No **obstacle** can stand in the way of our friendship.
14. There was no **opposition** to the helmet law in our city.
15. One of her **obsessions** is the need to keep her room spotless.
16. I try to avoid sweets, but **occasionally** I enjoy an ice-cream cone.

### PRACTICE ACTIVITY

The practice activity is on page 152.

### Answers: Spelling Clues

1. offensive
2. occupation
3. oblong
4. occupant
5. obsessions
6. opposition

### Answers: Proofreading

7. objective
8. obtained
9. occasionally
10. obscure
11. observation

### Answers: Fun with Words

12. offering
13. opportunity
14. obviously
15. obstacle
16. objection

# Unit 4 Review

## OBJECTIVES

- To review spelling patterns and strategies in Lessons 20–23

- To give students the opportunity to recognize and use these spelling patterns and Spelling Words in their writing

## UNIT 4 WORDS

The following words are reviewed in Practice Test, Parts A and B.

### Lesson 20: Prefixes—Size and Amount

| | |
|---|---|
| equivalent | microscopic |
| multiplication | magnificently |

### Lesson 21: Double Consonants

| | |
|---|---|
| exaggerated | satellite |
| parallel | terrific |
| vaccination | |

### Lesson 22: Noun Endings

| | |
|---|---|
| realism | rivalry |
| criticism | journalism |
| patriotism | |

### Lesson 23: Prefix *ob-*

| | |
|---|---|
| objection | objective |
| obstacle | occupant |
| opposition | opportunity |

## Review Strategies

Review with students the following spelling-clue strategies for Lessons 20–23.

### Lesson 20    Spelling Clues: Visualization

Pronounce the word *equivalent* aloud. Then ask students to visualize it as they have seen it written in other contexts—in math books, for example. Then write this on the board: ____*valent*. Ask students to spell the prefix that would complete the word. Do the same with *microscopic, multiplication,* and *magnificently.*

### Lesson 21    Spelling Clues: Double Consonants

Write these word pairs on the board: *terific—terrific, satelite—satellite, vaccination—vacination,* and *exaggerated—exagerated.* Suggest that students compare the two spellings of each word to see which one looks right. Remind them that writing a word two ways to see which one looks right is a good spelling strategy.

### Lesson 22    Spelling Clues: Identifying the Base Word

Write these words on the board: *rivalry, criticism, patriotism, journalism,* and *realism.* Ask a student to name the base word in each *(rival, critic, patriot, journal, and real).* Then, ask if the base word changes when a suffix is added. Remind students that identifying the base word is a good spelling strategy.

### Lesson 23    Spelling Clues: Prefixes

Write on the board: *occupation—ocupation, oportunity—opportunity,* and *offensive—ofensive.* Ask a volunteer to underline the words that are spelled correctly. Then, ask students why the prefix *ob-* is called an *absorbed prefix.* (It takes on the form of the root to which it is being added: spelled *oc-* with roots beginning with *c,* spelled *of-* with roots beginning with *f,* and spelled *op-* with roots beginning with *p.*)

# Unit 4 Review *(continued)*

## Practice Test

The Practice Test provides an opportunity to review Spelling Words and spelling generalizations in a standardized test format, complete with a sample answer card.

### Option 1

Use Practice Test: Part A as a pretest. Later, use Practice Test: Part B as a posttest.

### Option 2

Have students review their Lesson Word Log for this unit. If they need extra help, you may wish to review the spelling generalizations discussed in the individual lessons. Then administer both parts of the Practice Test to determine whether students have mastered the spelling generalizations.

### Practice Test: Part A

1. (D) equivalent
2. (C) exaggerated
3. (B) multiplication
4. (A) parallel
5. (A) microscopic
6. (D) vaccination
7. (C) objection
8. (D) realism
9. (D) magnificently
10. (C) satellite

### Practice Test: Part B

1. (B) critisism [criticism]
2. (A) patriatism [patriotism]
3. (B) terific [terrific]
4. (B) obstacal [obstacle]
5. (A) oposition [opposition]
6. (A) rivelry [rivalry]
7. (B) obgective [objective]
8. (A) ocupant [occupant]
9. (A) jurnalism [journalism]
10. (B) oportunity [opportunity]

## Options for Evaluation

- Have students check their own Practice Tests against their lists of Spelling Words. The list on the opposite page provides references to the lessons where they can find words they misspelled.
- You may prefer to assign partners and have students check each other's Practice Tests, using their own list of Spelling Words.

## REVIEW ACTIVITIES

### Activity 1

Provide an opportunity for students who draft and compose on a computer to review the uses of the spell-check function. Ask them how using the spell-check function has been helpful and what kinds of spelling problems they have been able to identify. Discuss how the spell-check function helps writers improve their spelling skills and in what ways, if any, it limits their development of spelling skills.

### Activity 2

Have a contest to write a sentence using the most words from this review lesson. Write the words on the board. Give students five (or ten) minutes to compose the longest sentence they can, using as many of the words from the list as possible. Have them read their sentence aloud as other students listen to make sure it makes sense.

### Activity 3

Write the words from this review lesson in random order, scattered on a piece of tagboard. Then, draw jigsaw-puzzle shapes on the tagboard—one piece per word. Cut out the puzzle along the lines. On the back of each piece, write a misspelling of the word. Mix up the pieces, spread them out on a desk, and have students put them together. The pieces won't match up if the misspelled version of the word is showing. When complete, the puzzle will show only correctly spelled words.

### Activity 4

Write each word from this review lesson on the board, along with a misspelled version of it. Have students who need a reteaching activity copy the correct spelling of each word on a sheet of paper.

## WHAT'S IN A WORD?

### *benefactor*

Have students write titles of stories, biographies, or autobiographies in which a person's life changes dramatically as the result of a benefactor's generosity. Then invite them to share these titles orally. They might enjoy explaining a few details of the plots of the stories, to show how a benefactor contributed to the outcome. A variation on this activity would be to have students make up a story about how a benefactor changed their own lives.

**WORKING TOGETHER** You may want to provide small groups of students with collections of books and stories (or book reports about them) in which benefactors play a role. Students can work together to list titles and discuss the literature.

### *dragon*

To extend this activity, invite volunteers to retell a story that involves dragons or other magical beasts. Most students will be familiar with folk tales, fairy tales, and modern stories that feature magical beasts that talk, fly, help humans, harm humans, or test humans.

## Unit Activity Options

### Question and Answer

A sample exchange between two students might be as follows: "Do you like to cook with a microwave oven?" "Yes, I do, but my aunt, who lives south of the equator, does not." Students might find it difficult to answer a question with a totally unrelated word, so remind them that the answers can be—and probably will be—very silly.

### Story Starter

Students might enjoy reading their stories aloud to the class after their partners have filled in the blanks.

### Proofreading Partners

Have students read the instructions for the activity. Then answer any questions they may have. Remind students to review the list carefully and to select the Spelling Words they find most troublesome. This approach will make the activity a useful tool for improving their spelling skills. Then, have students select their own partners and complete the activity.

### Practice in Pairs

As an additional requirement for keeping the cards, you might suggest that students use the words in sentences.

### What's the Sense?

After students finish writing several sentences, you may wish to have them choose one sentence to expand into a silly paragraph or story.

### What *IS* in a Word?

You might want to have a word-history sharing time occasionally, during which students read one or two of their selections to the class.

# Unit 4 Review *(continued)*

## Curriculum Options

### Health: Searching for Health

Have students identify any health-related Spelling Words in this unit. Then, have students brainstorm a longer list of health-related words. Record these words on the board.

Have students work independently or with partners to create their own word-search puzzles, using at least twelve different health words. Have students complete their puzzles by writing a brief clue for each hidden word.

You may want to have students exchange puzzles with a partner so they can solve each other's puzzles. You may also want to photocopy all the unsolved puzzles and make a collection of word-search puzzles for each student to solve.

### Language Arts: Collect Pairs

To prepare for this activity, make a deck of fifty cards (twenty-five pairs). Use Spelling Words from this unit. In this card game for two to five players, five cards are dealt to each player, and the rest of the deck is placed facedown in the center of the table. The object of the game is to get as many pairs as possible. Play begins when the person to the left of the dealer asks any other player if he or she holds any specific card by saying, for example, "Angela, do you have a *metallic?*" The player asking for the card must hold the mate to that card. If the other player has the card, he or she must hand it over. The first player places the matching pair on the table and takes another turn. Following a "no" answer, the player draws enough cards to make his or her hand equal five cards, and play passes to the left. The player with the most pairs at the end of the game wins.

### Social Studies: Trial Reenactment

Organize students into groups of four to eight members each. Have each group research a legal case, either one from history that might be described in their social studies textbook or one from a current newspaper. Challenge students to reenact the court case, with individuals portraying the defendant, the prosecuting attorney, the defense attorney, the judge, and the witnesses involved in the case. Students should prepare a script to follow during their reenactment. Ask them to use as many Spelling Words as possible in their script. After group members have rehearsed, they can present their trial reenactment for classmates.

## WHAT'S IN A WORD?

### *refuge/fugitive*

Some students might benefit from an oral discussion of the meaning of each word. You might also wish to have students use the words in sentences.

### *ponderous*

Ask students to use the dictionary to find other words related to the Latin roots *pondus* and *pendere* (for example, *suspense, ponder, preponderance,* and *depend*).

# Lesson 25: Prefixes—Position, III

## OBJECTIVE
To spell words with the prefixes *peri-*, *intra-/intro-*, *per-*, and *circu(m)-*

## HOME ACTIVITY
The home activity is on page 154.

## SECOND-LANGUAGE SUPPORT
After discussing the meanings of the prefixes, write the Spelling Words on the board, grouping them by prefix. Have students go to the board and underline the prefix in each group of words. Then have students write the words on index cards and work in pairs to practice spelling the words and using them in sentences. REINFORCEMENT/PRACTICE

## PRETEST/ POSTTESTS
1. The author wrote a brief **introduction** to the book.
2. Students from the same school compete in **intramural** sports.
3. The camera worked **perfectly** after I had it repaired.
4. The air **circulation** improved when we opened the windows.
5. We measured the **perimeter** of the yard before building a fence.
6. The pilot disappeared under mysterious **circumstances.**
7. After a visit to Hawaii, we decided to live there **permanently.**
8. The **circumference** of the earth is about 25,000 miles.
9. Discoveries in science can change our **perception** of the universe.
10. People in our state wanted an **intrastate** bus system.
11. Sam is quiet, but I wouldn't say he is an **introvert.**
12. My travels abroad changed my **perspective** on life here.
13. The **periodic** crashes of thunder startled us.

*(continued on next page)*

## Pretest
Administer the test on this page as a pretest. Say each word, use it in the sentence, and then repeat the word.   ACCESSING PRIOR KNOWLEDGE

**SELF-CHECK**   Have students check their own pretests against the list of Spelling Words. Remind students to write misspelled words in their Lesson Word Logs.   STUDENT SELF-ASSESSMENT

## Introducing the Lesson

### Option A (Open Sort)
Distribute the word cards (page 153) to individuals or small groups, and guide them in an open-sort activity. In open sort, students group the word cards according to a criterion they select themselves. Then guide students in comparing and discussing the criteria they selected.

### Option B (Modeling)
Read aloud with students the lesson title and the Spelling Words. Use this model sentence to introduce the lesson skill in a context.

*The coach **persuaded** me to try out for the **intramural** basketball team.*

## Teaching the Lesson

- Call on volunteers to name the Spelling Words that have the same prefix as *periscope*. As students name words, list the words on the board and discuss their meanings. (*perimeter, periodic, peripheral*)
- Follow the same procedure for words with the prefixes *intra-/intro-*, *per-*, and *circu(m)-*. (***intra-/intro-:** introduction, intramural, intrastate, introvert;* ***per-:** perfectly, permanently, perception, perspective, persuaded;* ***circu(m)-:** circulation, circumstances, circumference, circuit*)
- Have students add words from their own writing to the columns. Then, have volunteers read all the words aloud and discuss their meanings.

**IN SUMMARY**   Have students summarize the lesson in their own words, making sure they understand the meanings of the lesson prefixes. Elicit the observation that knowledge of prefixes can help students spell and understand words.

**ASSIGNMENT**   Students can complete the first page of the lesson as a follow-up to the group activity, either in class or as homework.

# Lesson 25: Prefixes—Position, III *(continued)*

## Practicing the Lesson

### Spelling Clues: Choosing Correct Spellings

Tell students that when they are unsure of the spelling of a word, they might be able to decide on the correct spelling by writing the word in several different ways. They should focus especially on the part of the word that does not look correct.

Summarize for students the variety of strategies that they can use to help them identify and correct the misspelled words in items 1–6. First, students should check the spelling of the lesson prefixes. Second, they should pronounce the words carefully to help them spot other spelling errors. Finally, they should use their knowledge of the spelling of related words to help them find other errors. APPLYING SPELLING STRATEGIES

**TRANSITIONAL SPELLERS** Transitional Spellers can work in pairs to complete items 1–6. Suggest that they look at the prefix of each word first and then at the rest of the word to help them pinpoint spelling errors.

### Proofreading

You may wish to have students review Spelling Clues: Choosing Correct Spellings before proofreading the letter.

### Fun with Words

Have students complete this activity individually or with a partner.

## Posttest

Administer the test on page 56 as a posttest, or administer one of your own. Say each word, use it in a sentence, and then repeat the word.

## Reteaching the Lesson

Students who need additional practice may use a tape recorder. With the recorder in the Record mode, have a student say a Spelling Word, spell it slowly, repeat the word, and then pause. Repeat the procedure with each Spelling Word. To provide practice in spelling the words, have a student play the tape, writing the word during the pause. Students can check their own spelling by referring to the list of Spelling Words. AUDITORY MODALITY

*(Pretest/Posttest, continued)*

**14.** The glasses improved my **peripheral** vision.

**15.** The candidate **persuaded** most of us to vote for him.

**16.** A simple electrical **circuit** consists of two wires.

### PRACTICE ACTIVITY

The practice activity is on page 155.

### Answers: Spelling Clues

| | |
|---|---|
| **1.** circulation | **4.** permanently |
| **2.** persuaded | **5.** circumstances |
| **3.** perfectly | **6.** periodic |

### Answers: Proofreading

| | |
|---|---|
| **7.** intrastate | **10.** circuit |
| **8.** perspective | **11.** perimeter |
| **9.** perception | **12.** introduction |

### Answers: Fun with Words

| | |
|---|---|
| **13.** intramural | **15.** introvert |
| **14.** peripheral | **16.** circumference |

# Lesson 26: More Greek Word Parts

## OBJECTIVE
To recognize and spell words formed from Greek word parts

## HOME ACTIVITY
The home activity is on page 157.

## SECOND-LANGUAGE SUPPORT
Many Greek word parts are found in Spanish words as well as in English words, with occasional spelling differences. In Spanish, the word part *archae-* may be written as *archi-* or *arqui-*, and *-soph-* as *-sof-*. Ask students who speak Spanish to compare the Spelling Words with their Spanish equivalents.   COMPARING AND CONTRASTING

## PRETEST/POSTTEST
1. The freeways were crowded with **automobiles** and trucks.
2. Most restaurants have a no-smoking **policy.**
3. We searched the **archives** to find documents from the Civil War era.
4. Pat received an award for her **scholastic** achievement.
5. After a long career in **politics,** the senator retired.
6. Most modern hospitals use **sophisticated** medical equipment.
7. The small town became a large **metropolitan** area.
8. The **optic** nerve carries visual information to the brain.
9. The student's **scholarship** paid for her entire college education.
10. The **philosopher** spoke about the nature of reality.
11. The mirrored walls created an **optical** illusion of more space.
12. The **optometrist** fitted the lenses into the eyeglass frames.
13. Word processors are making typewriters seem **archaic.**

*(continued on next page)*

## Pretest
Administer the test on this page as a pretest. Say each word, use it in the sentence, and then repeat the word.   ACCESSING PRIOR KNOWLEDGE

**SELF-CHECK**   Have students check their own pretests against the list of Spelling Words. Remind students to write misspelled words in their Lesson Word Logs.   STUDENT SELF-ASSESSMENT

## Introducing the Lesson
### Option A (Open Sort)
Distribute the word cards (page 156) to individuals or small groups, and guide them in an open-sort activity. In open sort, students group the word cards according to a criterion they select themselves. Then guide students in comparing and discussing the criteria they selected.

### Option B (Modeling)
Read aloud with students the lesson title and the Spelling Words. Use this model sentence to introduce the lesson skill in a context.

*The politician **explained** his **philosophy** of government.*

## Teaching the Lesson
- Ask volunteers to name the Spelling Words that include the Greek word part *auto-*. List the words on the board. *(automobiles, automatically)*
- Follow the same procedure for the other Greek word parts. Discuss the meaning of each part. (*-soph-* means "wise"; *opt-* means "eye"; *schol-* means "schooling"; *archae-* means "old"; *arch-* means *"rank"*; *-poli-* means "city.") Explain that *archaeologist* is sometimes spelled *archeologist*. (**-soph-:** *sophisticated, philosopher, sophomore;* **opt-:** *optic, optical, optometrist;* **schol-:** *scholastic, scholarship;* **archae-/arch-:** *archives, archaic, archaeologist;* **-poli-:** *policy, politics, metropolitan*)
- After students have added words from their own writing to the columns, have volunteers read all the words aloud and discuss their meanings.

**IN SUMMARY**   Ask students to summarize the lesson in their own words. Elicit the observation that familiarity with Greek word parts will help them spell many words.

**ASSIGNMENT**   Students can complete the first page of the lesson as a follow-up to the group activity, either in class or as homework.

# Lesson 26: More Greek Word Parts (continued)

## Practicing the Lesson

### Spelling Clues: Say It Aloud

Explain to students that the spelling of most Latin- and Greek-derived words is closely related to the way they sound. If students are unsure of the spelling of a word, they should begin by pronouncing the word carefully, listening for familiar word parts.

As they proofread the words in items 1–6, students should check the spelling of the prefixes first. If they cannot use pronunciation as a guide to determining the spelling, they should try to think of related words.    APPLYING SPELLING STRATEGIES

### Proofreading

You may wish to have students review Spelling Clues: Say It Aloud before proofreading the report.

**TRANSITIONAL SPELLERS**    Have students work in pairs to proofread the school newspaper report.

### Fun with Words

Before asking students to complete this activity, you might give them some background information about Pompeii. This Italian city was destroyed by the eruption of Mount Vesuvius in A.D. 79. It lay buried under ashes for about 1,700 years before archaeologists began excavating its public buildings and houses.

## Posttest

Administer the test on page 58 as a posttest, or administer one of your own. Say each word, use it in a sentence, and then repeat the word.

## Reteaching the Lesson

Use this activity to help students with learning difficulties see that the word parts derived from Greek have both a consistent meaning and a consistent spelling, making words with these word parts easy to learn to spell.

Have students write each Spelling Word with a plus sign between the Greek word part and the other parts. Then have them rewrite the word, joining the parts. All words that contain the same word part should be written as a group. Discuss the meaning of the Greek word part and then the meaning of the whole word.    VISUAL MODALITY

*(Pretest/Posttest, continued)*

14. The tape **automatically** rewinds itself.
15. Dave has just begun his **sophomore** year in college.
16. The **archaeologist** explained how fossils are preserved.

### PRACTICE ACTIVITY

The practice activity is on page 158.

**Answers: Spelling Clues**

1. automobiles
2. metropolitan
3. politics
4. optic
5. sophisticated
6. philosopher

**Answers: Proofreading**

7. sophomore
8. scholarship
9. optometrist
10. automatically
11. archaic
12. scholastic

**Answers: Fun with Words**

13. optical
14. archaeologist
15. archives
16. policy

# Lesson 27: Words from Other Languages, I

## OBJECTIVE
To spell some common words that come from other languages

## HOME ACTIVITY
The home activity is on page 160.

## SECOND-LANGUAGE SUPPORT
You may wish to ask speakers of other languages to identify words from their native languages that are commonly used in English. Discuss whether the words have undergone any changes in spelling or meaning. You may also wish to ask students to name English words that are commonly used in their native languages. COMPARING AND CONTRASTING

## PRETEST/POSTTEST
1. The artist's **landscape** showed fields of flowers.
2. We watched the dock workers unload the ship's **cargo.**
3. I learned to play my favorite song on the **piano.**
4. I had not seen the **opera,** but I was familiar with the story.
5. The **carnival** included a magic show and amusement rides.
6. The **chipmunk** gathered nuts and seeds for winter.
7. Our **parakeet** has bright green feathers and an orange beak.
8. The summer **monsoon** brought rain to the dry region.
9. The **hickory** tree produces wood that is extremely strong and hard.
10. Sara's **heroic** rescue of her brother proved her great courage.
11. The museum displayed a model of a dinosaur's **skeleton.**
12. My cousin made a delicious sauce for the **spaghetti.**
13. A **walrus** uses its tusks to defend itself from polar bears.
14. The **yacht** with the yellow sail won the race.

*(continued on next page)*

## Pretest
Administer the test on this page as a pretest. Say each word, use it in the sentence, and then repeat the word.   ACCESSING PRIOR KNOWLEDGE

**SELF-CHECK**   Have students check their own pretests against the list of Spelling Words. Remind students to write misspelled words in their Lesson Word Logs.   STUDENT SELF-ASSESSMENT

## Introducing the Lesson
### Option A (Open Sort)
Distribute the word cards (page 159) to individuals or small groups, and guide them in an open-sort activity. In open sort, students group the word cards according to a criterion they select themselves. Then guide students in comparing and discussing the criteria they selected.

### Option B (Modeling)
Read aloud with students the lesson title and the Spelling Words. Use this model sentence to introduce the lesson skill in a context.

*Which do you prefer—spaghetti or macaroni?*

## Teaching the Lesson
- Before students consult a dictionary to check word origins, encourage them to use their general knowledge to guess the origin of a word. You might provide some hints, such as the suggestion that many words pertaining to music come from Italian, or that the European settlers in North America often used Native American words for plants and animals of the region. (**French and Spanish:** *carnival, parakeet, cargo, barbecue;* **Greek:** *heroic, skeleton;* **Italian:** *piano, opera, spaghetti, macaroni;* **Dutch:** *landscape, walrus, yacht;* **Arabic:** *monsoon;* **Algonquian:** *chipmunk, hickory*)
- After students have added words from their own writing to the columns, have volunteers read all the words aloud and discuss their origins.

**IN SUMMARY**   Have students summarize the lesson in their own words. Elicit the fact that the more students learn about a word, the more familiar the word becomes and the easier it is to recall its spelling.

**ASSIGNMENT**   Students can complete the first page of the lesson as a follow-up to the group activity, either in class or as homework.

# Lesson 27: Words from Other Languages, I (continued)

## Practicing the Lesson

### Spelling Clues: Word Shapes

Have students look over the list of Spelling Words to find the word that matches each shape. After students have completed the activity, point out that associating a particular shape with a word can be helpful in remembering the spelling of words that cannot be spelled phonetically, such as *yacht*.   APPLYING SPELLING STRATEGIES

### Proofreading

You may wish to have students review Spelling Clues: Word Shapes before proofreading the paragraph.

**TRANSITIONAL SPELLERS**   Suggest to students that they look at the part of each word that may have been misspelled, such as the two *c*'s in *maccaroni* or the schwa sound in *hickery,* and either visualize the shape of the word or experiment with other ways of spelling it until they think they can spell the word correctly.

### Fun with Words

You may wish to extend this activity by asking students to make up two-line rhymes for other Spelling Words and challenge the rest of the class to provide the missing word.

## Posttest

Administer the test on page 60 as a posttest, or administer one of your own. Say each word, use it in a sentence, and then repeat the word.

## Reteaching the Lesson

Since most of the words in this lesson must be learned by rote, the more students are exposed to the words, the greater the likelihood that they will learn to spell them.

Dictate the Spelling Words to the students. Encourage them to write the letters they are unsure about. Then, have them check their spelling and underline the parts of the word that they misspelled. Analyze the misspellings to determine whether there are any consistent patterns to the errors.

Quiz students on four of the Spelling Words at least once a day so that they will have frequent exposure to the words. Follow the strategy of having students check their quizzes immediately and correct any misspellings.   VISUAL MODALITY

*(Pretest/Posttest, continued)*

**15.** We had **macaroni** and cheese for lunch.

**16.** Tonight we'll cook outdoors on the **barbecue.**

### PRACTICE ACTIVITY

The practice activity is on page 161.

### Answers: Spelling Clues

| | | | |
|---|---|---|---|
| **1.** | yacht | **4.** | opera |
| **2.** | monsoon | **5.** | heroic |
| **3.** | cargo | **6.** | landscape |

### Answers: Proofreading

| | | | |
|---|---|---|---|
| **7.** | carnival | **10.** | macaroni |
| **8.** | piano | **11.** | barbecue |
| **9.** | spaghetti | **12.** | hickory |

### Answers: Fun with Words

| | | | |
|---|---|---|---|
| **13.** | chipmunk | **15.** | skeleton |
| **14.** | parakeet | **16.** | walrus |

# Lesson 28: More Related Words

## OBJECTIVE
To spell and understand relationships among word parts

## HOME ACTIVITY
The home activity is on page 163.

## SECOND-LANGUAGE SUPPORT
Dividing the words into syllables may help students acquiring English learn the multisyllabic words of the lesson. Give students a list of the Spelling Words, grouping words with the same root together. Read each word aloud, and ask students to divide the word into syllables.   AUDITORY ANALYSIS

## PRETEST/POSTTEST
1. The **supermarket** sold a huge variety of frozen foods.
2. The United States is considered a **superpower.**
3. I was one of the **alto** singers in the chorus.
4. The airplane reached an **altitude** of 20,000 feet.
5. The map showed **geographic** features of the region.
6. The **astronauts** brought back samples of the moon's rocks.
7. Mark studied **geology** to learn about earthquakes and volcanoes.
8. We learned about circles and triangles in **geometry.**
9. The patient remained under the doctor's close **supervision.**
10. The ship's captain recounted his most exciting **nautical** adventures.
11. The **navigation** of large ships is best done by trained personnel.
12. The **odometer** showed that we had driven 400 miles.
13. I put an **asterisk** next to all the words I knew.

*(continued on next page)*

## Pretest
Administer the test on this page as a pretest. Say each word, use it in the sentence, and then repeat the word.   ACCESSING PRIOR KNOWLEDGE

**SELF-CHECK**   Have students check their own pretests against the list of Spelling Words. Remind students to write misspelled words in their Lesson Word Logs.   STUDENT SELF-ASSESSMENT

## Introducing the Lesson

### Option A (Open Sort)
Distribute the word cards (page 162) to individuals or small groups, and guide them in an open-sort activity. In open sort, students group the word cards according to a criterion they select themselves. Then guide students in comparing and discussing the criteria they selected.

### Option B (Modeling)
Read aloud with students the lesson title and the Spelling Words. Use this model sentence to introduce the lesson skill in a context.

*The astronauts checked the altitude of the spacecraft.*

## Teaching the Lesson

- As students name words that belong in each group, list the words on the board. Call on volunteers to give the meanings of the words. (*alt-: alto, altitude; -meter-: odometer, altimeter, seismometer; nav-/-naut-: navigation, astronauts, nautical, cosmonaut; ast(e)r-/-astro-: asterisk; geo-: geographic, geology, geometry; super-: supermarket, superpower, supervision*)
- After each list is complete, ask students to consider the root each group of words has in common. Then discuss the meanings of the roots. (*alt-*, high; *-meter-*, measure; *nav-/-naut-*, having to do with sailors or ships; *ast(e)r-/astro-*, star; *geo-*, earth; *super-*, upper or higher)
- After students have added words from their own writing to the columns, have volunteers read all the words aloud and discuss their meanings.

**IN SUMMARY**   Review the meanings of the Greek and Latin word parts. Elicit the fact that many English words, especially scientific and technical words, contain these word parts.

**ASSIGNMENT**   Students can complete the first page of the lesson as a follow-up to the group activity, either in class or as homework.

# Lesson 28: More Related Words *(continued)*

## Practicing the Lesson

### Spelling Clues: Word Parts

Explain to students that recognizing common word parts can help them spell many words. If students are unsure how to spell a word, they should try to think of words with the same or similar word parts. If, for example, they are not sure of the spelling of the last syllable of *cosmonaut,* recognizing that *cosmonaut* is related to *astronaut* can help them determine the correct spelling.    APPLYING SPELLING STRATEGIES

### Proofreading

You may wish to have students review Spelling Clues: Word Parts before proofreading the note.

**TRANSITIONAL SPELLERS**    Have Transitional Spellers work in pairs as they proofread the note. Suggest to students that they name related words as they correct errors in the misspelled words.

### Working with Meaning

You may wish to extend this activity by having students make up similar sentences for other Spelling Words and challenge a partner to complete them.

**SECOND-LANGUAGE SUPPORT**    Have students work in pairs or small groups to complete the sentences in Working with Meaning. Ask students to underline or circle the key word or word in each sentence that function as clues. In item 13, for example, *captain* and *ship* provide the context for *navigation.* USING CONTEXT CLUES

## Posttest

Administer the test on page 62 as a posttest, or administer one of your own. Say each word, use it in a sentence, and then repeat the word.

## Reteaching the Lesson

Many students with memory deficits have difficulty recalling the correct spelling of multisyllabic words. To help students learn multisyllabic words, teach one word part at a time until you are sure that the student has learned it. For example, ask students to make an index card for each Spelling Word that contains the word part *geo-.* Have them underline the word part with a marker or crayon. Each day of the week, have students make a set of cards for one of the other word parts in the lesson. At the end of the week, ask students to spell words selected at random from their sets of word cards.    VISUAL MODALITY

*(Pretest/Posttest, continued)*

**14.** According to their **altimeter,** the climbers were halfway to the top.

**15.** The Russian **cosmonauts** set up a space station.

**16.** The **seismometer** recorded small ground movements.

## PRACTICE ACTIVITY
The practice activity is on page 164.

### Answers: Spelling Clues
**1.** altimeter     **5.** alto

**2.** supervision     **6.** odometer

**3.** superpower     **7.** asterisk

**4.** seismometer

### Answers: Proofreading
**8.** altitude     **11.** geometry

**9.** cosmonauts     **12.** geology

**10.** astronauts     **13.** supermarket

### Answers: Working with Meaning
**14.** navigation     **16.** geographic

**15.** nautical

# Unit 5 Review

## OBJECTIVES

- To review spelling patterns and strategies in Lessons 25–28
- To give students the opportunity to recognize and use these spelling patterns and Spelling Words in their writing

## UNIT 5 WORDS

The following words are reviewed in Practice Test, Parts A and B.

### Lesson 25: Prefixes—Position, III

| | |
|---|---|
| introvert | permanently |
| perception | perspective |
| perimeter | |

### Lesson 26: More Greek Word Parts

| | |
|---|---|
| archaic | automatically |
| archives | sophomore |

### Lesson 27: Words from Other Languages, I

| | |
|---|---|
| heroic | parakeet |
| hickory | spaghetti |
| landscape | |

### Lesson 28: More Related Words

| | |
|---|---|
| asterisk | nautical |
| cosmonauts | navigation |
| geographic | supermarket |

## Review Strategies

Review with students the following spelling-clue strategies for Lessons 25–28.

### Lesson 25    Spelling Clues: Choosing Correct Spellings

Write on the board: *We need a teacher's permisson to leave school.* Ask students to find the misspelled word *(permisson)* and to tell you how to spell it correctly. Write all their responses on the board, and ask which spelling is correct. Remind them that when they are not sure how to spell a word, they can try different spellings and choose the one that looks correct.

### Lesson 26    Spelling Clues: Say It Aloud

Say the word *predicament*. Ask a student to suggest two ways in which the /k/ sound in the word could be spelled (for example, *ck* or *c*). Write the responses on the board. Ask students to think of other words with a /k/ sound in the middle, and have them spell the words (for example, *political, comical,* and *indicate*). Then have students identify the correct spelling of the /k/ sound in *predicament*. Remind students that saying a word aloud, listening for sounds, and thinking of ways to spell the sound can help them spell the word.

### Lesson 27    Spelling Clues: Word Shapes

Say aloud the word *allotment*. Ask students to guess how the word might be spelled (*alottment* and *allotmint,* for example). Then ask students to visualize the shape of the word represented by each spelling. Draw word shapes for each of the spellings given. Have students choose the correct spelling of the word. Discuss how visualizing the shape of a word can help them spell the word correctly.

### Lesson 28    Spelling Clues: Word Parts

Write on the board: *tellegraph/telegraph*. Ask students to choose the correct spelling *(telegraph)*. Call on students to suggest other words that have the word part *tele-* (for example, *telephone* and *television*). Remind students that noticing common word parts and thinking about their spellings can help them spell unfamiliar or challenging words.

# Unit 5 Review *(continued)*

## Practice Test

The Practice Test provides an opportunity to review Spelling Words and spelling generalizations in a standardized test format, complete with a sample answer card.

### Option 1

Use Practice Test: Part A as a pretest. Later, use Practice Test: Part B as a posttest.

### Option 2

Have students review their Lesson Word Log for this unit. If they need extra help, you may wish to review the spelling generalizations discussed in the individual lessons. Then, administer both parts of the Practice Test to determine whether students have mastered the spelling generalizations.

### Practice Test: Part A

1. (C) perseption [perception]
2. (B) intravert [introvert]
3. (A) permanantly [permanently]
4. (A) sphageti [spaghetti]
5. (C) sophmore [sophomore]
6. (C) optomatrist [optometrist]
7. (D) astonauts [astronauts]
8. (C) supermarkit [supermarket]
9. (C) automaticaly [automatically]
10. (A) hickery [hickory]

### Practice Test: Part B

1. (C) cosmanauts [cosmonauts]
2. (A) pirspective [perspective]
3. (B) lanscape [landscape]
4. (C) nauticul [nautical]
5. (D) navagation [navigation]
6. (B) geografic [geographic]
7. (A) heroick [heroic]
8. (D) pirimeter [perimeter]
9. (C) astrick [asterisk]
10. (C) arckives [archives]

## Options for Evaluation

- Have students check their own Practice Tests against their lists of Spelling Words. The list on the opposite page provides references to the lessons where they can find words they misspelled.

- You may prefer to assign partners and have students check each other's Practice Tests, using their own list of Spelling Words.

## REVIEW ACTIVITIES

### Activity 1

Make a list on the board or on chart paper of the prefixes and roots used in the words of this review lesson. Choose one of the listed words and ask students to identify and write the word that you are thinking of. Give students hints or ask questions that will lead them to choose one of the words, such as "This goes all around and ends in *meter*." *(perimeter)* Students can look at the chart to help them recall and spell the answers.

### Activity 2

Have students work in pairs for this activity. Give each pair of students a list of the words from this review lesson, and ask them to prepare a short dialogue using at least four of them. Suggest that students look at the words to find a context in which several might be used. Some possibilities are dialogues between explorers on a sea voyage, astronauts on a space mission, or friends planning a party. Call on pairs of students to present their dialogues. Classmates should identify list words that were used.

### Activity 3

Students might like to make up analogies that must be completed with one of the Spelling Words from Unit 5. Give them this example:

key : _____ :: string : guitar. *(piano)*

Pairs of students can exchange and solve each other's analogies.

### Activity 4

Students can discover other words with the prefixes and roots in the Unit 5 Spelling Words by browsing through a dictionary. Encourage them to enter interesting words in their Lesson Word Logs.

# Unit 5 Review *(continued)*

## WHAT'S IN A WORD?

### ◆ *archaic*

Ask students to use the dictionary to find other archaic words (for example, *thou, thee*). Then, invite them to write sentences using these words.

### ◆ *astronaut*

Discuss the literal meaning of *astronaut*—"star sailor"—and how the word captures the adventure and mystery of space travel. Explain to students that the Russian word *cosmonaut* is formed by combining *cosmos*, Greek for "universe," with the word part *-naut-*.

Call on volunteers to share other words with the word parts *aster-* and *-naut-*. Discuss how the meaning of each word is related to the word part.

### ◆ *automobile*

Discuss the meanings of words with *auto-*, such as *autobiography, autobus, automatic,* and *autopilot*. You may wish to have students consult a dictionary to find other words that use the Greek word part *auto-*.

## Unit Activity Options

### Round Robin

After students have completed their round-robin stories, you may wish to have groups exchange and read each other's stories.

**WORKING TOGETHER** You may wish to alter the round-robin activity by having groups of students work together to write stories about a wilderness adventure.

### Word Race

You might want to vary the game by having students who are not playing write sentences for the words and leave blanks where the words should go. Players can complete the sentences with Spelling Words instead of matching words with their definitions.

### Proofreading Partners

Have students read the instructions for the activity, and answer any questions they may have. Remind students to review the list carefully and to select the Spelling Words they find most troublesome; this approach will make the activity a useful tool for improving their spelling skills. Then, have students select their own partners and complete the activity.

### Finding Synonyms

After students have completed the activity, you may wish to discuss which Spelling Words are so specific that they do not have synonyms.

### Prefixes That Describe Where

Write the prefixes *de-* and *ex-* on the board. After students have read the introductory paragraph, lead them in a discussion of the meanings of the prefixes. After they have completed the activity, have volunteers read their responses aloud.

**WORKING TOGETHER** You may want to have students complete this activity in pairs. Provide a dictionary for each pair of students to use in checking the spelling of their responses.

◆ This indicates a Unit Spelling Word.

# Unit 5 Review *(continued)*

## Curriculum Options

### Language Arts: Pick a Pair

Have pairs of students make a set of cards for the Spelling Words in this unit, with each card showing one word. Have students place the cards face down. One student in each pair chooses two cards and thinks of a sentence using both Spelling Words. Since many pairs of words would not ordinarily appear in the same sentence, the sentences may be as humorous or imaginative as students wish to make them, but they should also provide a context for the words. A possible example is *Every time I played the piano, my pet walrus bared its tusks.* The student then writes the sentence on a piece of paper, substituting blanks for the Spelling Words, and challenges his or her partner to fill in the blanks with the correct words.

### Science: Words of Science

Have students work in groups of three or four for this activity. Ask students to take turns making up sentences using one of the Spelling Words in this unit or another word with one of the same word parts. The sentence should be about a scientific process, activity, or invention. Have the rest of the students listen for and spell the Spelling Word or the related word. An example of a sentence might be *The cosmonauts succeeded in putting the space station into orbit.*

### Social Studies: Headline News

Write down on cards or slips of paper a variety of career or academic areas, such as government, history, transportation, medicine, law enforcement, philosophy, and archaeology. Distribute one card to each pair of students. Have students work together to make up a newspaper headline pertaining to the subject area on their card, using at least one of the Spelling Words from this unit. An example for the subject area *transportation* might be *Car Manufacturers Display First Self-Navigating Automobiles.* As students read their headlines to the class, have the rest of the students listen for and spell the word or words.

## WHAT'S IN A WORD?

### ◆ carnival

You may wish to ask students to discuss the meanings of other words with the Latin word part *carn-*, such as *carnivorous* (meat-eating) and *carnage* (massacre).

### ◆ introvert

Discuss with students the main characters of some books or stories they have read. Ask them whether they would describe the characters as introverts or extroverts. Discuss with students whether most people are dominated by one type of personality or whether they have a mixture of the personality traits associated with introverts and those associated with extroverts.

◆ This indicates a Unit Spelling Word.

# Lesson 30: Words from Names

## OBJECTIVE
To spell words that come from names

## HOME ACTIVITY
The home activity is on page 166.

## SECOND-LANGUAGE SUPPORT
The concept of forming words from the names of people, places, and fictional characters should be familiar to most of your students acquiring English. Ask students to translate some of the Spelling Words into their first language, write the Spelling Word and the translation on the board, and compare the two spellings.    COMPARING WORDS FROM DIFFERENT LANGUAGES

## PRETEST/ POSTTEST
1. Kim ordered a grilled cheese **sandwich** for lunch.
2. John always orders extra pickles on his **hamburger.**
3. The **mercury** in the thermometer rose steadily all morning.
4. The **tuxedo** that Jake rented looked terrific on him.
5. In an obvious **spoonerism,** Lois said she put a son of toil on her lawn.
6. When Carol said she was wearing neon stockings, she wasn't using a **malapropism.**
7. This **sequoia** has been growing for a very long time.
8. We decided to **boycott** the movie theater because the prices were too high.
9. My friend from England calls his raincoat a **mackintosh.**
10. Would you like mustard on this **frankfurter**?
11. If we didn't **pasteurize** our milk, we might get sick.
12. This book has been printed in **Braille** so that it can be read by people who are blind.

*(continued on next page)*

## Pretest
Administer the test on this page as a pretest. Say each word, use it in the sentence, and then repeat the word.    ACCESSING PRIOR KNOWLEDGE

**SELF-CHECK**    Have students check their own pretests against the list of Spelling Words. Remind students to write misspelled words in their Lesson Word Logs.    STUDENT SELF-ASSESSMENT

## Introducing the Lesson

### Option A (Open Sort)
Distribute the word cards (page 165) to individuals or small groups, and guide them in an open-sort activity. In open sort, students group the word cards according to a criterion they select themselves. Then guide students in comparing and discussing the criteria they selected.

### Option B (Modeling)
Read aloud with students the lesson title and the Spelling Words. Use this model sentence to introduce the lesson skill in a context.

*Jack ate* **tangerines** *and* **graham** *crackers for a snack.*

## Teaching the Lesson

- Write the headings *people, fictional characters,* and *places* on the board.
- Ask volunteers to name the Spelling Words that come from the names of real people. List the words on the board. (*sandwich, spoonerism, sequoia, boycott, mackintosh, pasteurize, Braille, Celsius, Fahrenheit, zeppelin*)
- Ask volunteers to name words that come from the names of literary and mythological characters. List the words on the board. (*mercury, malapropism, odyssey*)
- Follow the same procedure for words that come from names of places. (*hamburger, tuxedo, frankfurter*)

**IN SUMMARY**    Ask students to summarize the lesson in their own words. Elicit the information that even though the Spelling Words come from proper names, most of them are not capitalized.

**ASSIGNMENT**    Students can complete the first page of the lesson as a follow-up to the group activity, either in class or as homework.

# Lesson 30: Words from Names *(continued)*

## Practicing the Lesson

### Spelling Clues: Listening to Sounds

Suggest to students that when they encounter a word whose spelling they are unsure of, they say the word aloud and think about the letters that usually spell the sounds they hear. You may wish to pronounce the words in items 1–5 for students as they work individually to make their choices.   APPLYING SPELLING STRATEGIES

**TRANSITIONAL SPELLERS**   Have students complete this activity cooperatively with a partner or in a small group.

### Proofreading

You may wish to have students review Spelling Clues: Listening to Sounds before proofreading the letter.

### Fun with Words

Students may complete this activity individually or with a partner. Tell students to look for clues in the art and to choose the correct Spelling Words based on those clues.

**WORKING TOGETHER**   Students might enjoy doing this activity in small groups. They can take turns reading each sentence in the cartoon and providing the Spelling Word to fit in the blank.

## Posttest

Administer the test on page 68 as a posttest, or administer one of your own. Say each word, use it in a sentence, and then repeat the word.

## Reteaching the Lesson

Students with learning difficulties often have trouble modifying their behavior to meet the demands of the task and situation. Give students a strategy for analyzing multisyllabic words. Use a combination of auditory and visual approaches. Prepare a written list of the Spelling Words. Say a word for students and have them repeat it. Have students divide the word into its component parts by drawing slash marks between the syllables (for example: ham/bur/ger). Encourage students to whisper the word to themselves several times so they can analyze it. Finally, have students write the word from dictation. Repeat the procedure for each Spelling Word. VISUAL/AUDITORY MODALITIES

*(Pretest/Posttest, continued)*

13. At a temperature of 100° **Celsius,** water boils.
14. At a temperature of 212° **Fahrenheit,** water boils.
15. Dan had many adventures during his **odyssey** around the world.
16. A **zeppelin** is an airship shaped like a cylinder.

### PRACTICE ACTIVITY

The practice activity is on page 167.

### Answers: Spelling Clues

1. pasteurize
2. malapropism
3. zeppelin
4. sequoia
5. Braille

### Answers: Proofreading

6. boycott
7. Fahrenheit
8. mackintosh
9. spoonerisms
10. odyssey

### Answers: Fun with Words

11. tuxedo
12. sandwich
13. hamburger (frankfurter)
14. frankfurter (hamburger)
15. mercury
16. Celsius

# Lesson 31: Latin Roots, II

## OBJECTIVE
To spell words that have Latin roots

## HOME ACTIVITY
The home activity is on page 169.

## SECOND-LANGUAGE SUPPORT
Write on the board the Latin roots used in this lesson. Below the headings, list several words containing each root. Have a volunteer say each word aloud and underline the Latin root. Point out to students the different ways the roots can be spelled. You might ask students to list words from their first language that contain these roots and discuss any differences in the way the roots are spelled. RECOGNIZING SPELLING CHANGES

## PRETEST/POSTTEST
1. The orchestra leader **conducted** the symphony with great skill.
2. A teacher's job is to **educate** students.
3. Please put the leftover stew in this large **container.**
4. The car will not be safe until you **adjust** the brakes.
5. Billy is being **detained** for an hour after school today.
6. The locket I lost had great **sentimental** value.
7. Sandra is the company's most **productive** employee.
8. When Jim found out that he had been **deceived,** he was quite angry.
9. Several thousand people **attended** the performance last night.
10. Pat paid the bill after the **adjustments** had been made.
11. When the thief was sent to jail, we felt that **justice** had been done.

*(continued on next page)*

## Pretest
Administer the test on this page as a pretest. Say each word, use it in the sentence, and then repeat the word.   ACCESSING PRIOR KNOWLEDGE

**SELF-CHECK**   Have students check their own pretests against the list of Spelling Words. Remind students to write misspelled words in their Lesson Word Logs.   STUDENT SELF-ASSESSMENT

## Introducing the Lesson
### Option A (Open Sort)
Distribute the word cards (page 168) to individuals or small groups, and guide them in an open-sort activity. In open sort, students group the word cards according to a criterion they select themselves. Then guide students in comparing and discussing the criteria they selected.

### Option B (Modeling)
Read aloud with students the lesson title and the Spelling Words. Use this model sentence to introduce the lesson skill in a context.

*At the **reception** Jan said, "It's not **sensible** to be so **tense**."*

## Teaching the Lesson
- Ask volunteers to name and spell the Spelling Words that come from the Latin root *-sens* or *-sent*. Write the heading on the board, and list the words below it. (*sensation, sensory, sentimental*)
- Follow the same procedure for the Latin roots *-duc-/-duct-*, *-jus-*, *-ceive-/-cept-*, *-ten-/-tain-*, and *-ten(d)-*. Help students understand that *attended* comes from the root *-ten(d)-* rather than *-ten-*. (**-duc-/-duct-:** *educate, conducted, productive;* **-jus-:** *adjust, adjustments, justice;* **-ceive-/-cept-:** *deceived, perceived, acceptable, acceptance;* **-ten-/-tain-:** *container, detained;* **-ten(d)-:** *attended*)
- Then have students name and spell other words that have these roots. List the words on the board.

**IN SUMMARY**   Ask students to summarize the lesson in their own words. Elicit the information that when a Latin root is used to form an English word, the spelling of the root sometimes changes, depending on the other word parts.

**ASSIGNMENT**   Students can complete the first page of the lesson as a follow-up to the group activity, either in class or as homework.

# Lesson 31: Latin Roots, II *(continued)*

## Practicing the Lesson

### Spelling Clues: Looking at Words

Suggest that when students are unsure of the spelling of a word, they try writing it several ways and then choose the spelling that looks correct.   APPLYING SPELLING STRATEGIES

### Proofreading

You may wish to have students review Spelling Clues: Looking at Words before proofreading the poster.

### Fun with Words

Students may complete this activity individually or with a partner. You may wish to expand the activity by having students write their own sentences using the words. As an additional challenge, suggest that they write sentences that tell a story.

**SECOND-LANGUAGE SUPPORT**   To help your second-language students complete this activity, suggest that they look for clues in the art. Such clues will help them figure out the intended meaning.   USING PICTURE CLUES

## Posttest

Administer the test on page 70 as a posttest, or administer one of your own. Say each word, use it in a sentence, and then repeat the word.

## Reteaching the Lesson

Have students work in pairs to make a set of flashcards for the Spelling Words. Instruct students to print one word on each card, using a colored marker to print the letters that make up the Latin root. Have students write the meaning of the root on the back of each card. You may wish to have students check their cards for accuracy as you spell the root in each word aloud.

Then have the partners practice spelling the words. One student can dictate the words from the cards for the other to spell, either orally or in writing; then they can reverse roles. After a word is dictated and spelled, the speller should be shown the flashcard immediately to check his or her spelling. VISUAL MODALITY

*(Pretest/Posttest, continued)*

12. It is not **acceptable** behavior to argue at the table.
13. Please sign the form to indicate your **acceptance** of the terms.
14. Dotty's pet snake caused quite a **sensation** at the party.
15. I experienced a **sensory** overload in the perfume shop.
16. Even in the darkness, we **perceived** another presence in the cave.

### PRACTICE ACTIVITY

The practice activity is on page 170.

### Answers: Spelling Clues
1. educate
2. perceived
3. acceptance
4. detained
5. deceived
6. justice

### Answers: Proofreading
7. sentimental
8. conducted
9. attended
10. adjust
11. acceptable
12. sensation

### Answers: Fun with Words
13. adjustment
14. container
15. productive
16. sensory

# Lesson 32: Noun Endings—Diminutives

## OBJECTIVE
To spell words that have diminutive suffixes

## HOME ACTIVITY
The home activity is on page 172.

## SECOND-LANGUAGE SUPPORT
To provide practice with words having diminutive suffixes, prepare a set of flashcards for the Spelling Words. Have volunteers pick a card, read the word aloud, and use it in a sentence. Discuss with students the meanings of the words and, when appropriate, discuss how the suffix changes the meaning of a word to reflect a similar size. Invite students to give examples of diminutive suffixes used in their first languages.   COMPARING MEANINGS

## PRETEST/POSTTEST
1.  This **booklet** will tell you how to take care of your bicycle.
2.  The young art student filled an entire **tablet** with pictures of trees.
3.  At the meeting, they gave me a **leaflet** that explains the contest rules.
4.  Please take this **packet** of old letters and save them for me.
5.  A calf becomes a **yearling** on its first birthday.
6.  You will find the information you need on this **diskette.**
7.  At the **luncheonette,** Wendy ordered juice and a sandwich.
8.  There was not a **particle** of dust to be found in the room.
9.  If that **icicle** falls from the eaves, it could hurt somebody.
10. The **sapling** will someday be as tall as the elm tree we cut down.
11. We all enjoyed the food at the **banquet.**

*(continued on next page)*

## Pretest
Administer the test on this page as a pretest. Say each word, use it in the sentence, and then repeat the word.   ACCESSING PRIOR KNOWLEDGE

**SELF-CHECK**   Have students check their own pretests against the list of Spelling Words. Remind students to write misspelled words in their Lesson Word Logs.  STUDENT SELF-ASSESSMENT

## Introducing the Lesson
### Option A (Open Sort)
Distribute the word cards (page 171) to individuals or small groups, and guide them in an open-sort activity. In open sort, students group the word cards according to a criterion they select themselves. Then guide students in comparing and discussing the criteria they selected.

### Option B (Modeling)
Read aloud with students the lesson title and the Spelling Words. Use this model sentence to introduce the lesson skill in a context.

*This **article** gives the rules of **etiquette** for a formal dinner.*

## Teaching the Lesson
- Ask volunteers to name and spell the Spelling Words that have the diminutive suffixes *-let* and *-et*. Write the suffixes on the board and list the words below them. (*-let: booklet, tablet, leaflet, bracelet, pamphlet; -et: banquet, cabinet, packet*)
- Follow the same procedure for the suffixes *-cle, -ette,* and *-ling.* (*-cle: particle, icicle; -ette: diskette, luncheonette, cassette, statuette; -ling: yearling, sapling*)
- Have students find words with these suffixes in their own writing and add them to the columns. Then have volunteers read all the words aloud and underline the suffixes.

**IN SUMMARY**   Ask students to summarize the lesson in their own words. Elicit the fact that the suffixes *-let, -et, -cle, -ette,* and *-ling* are called diminutive suffixes because they usually indicate a diminished size.

**ASSIGNMENT**   Students can complete the first page of the lesson as a follow-up to the group activity, either in class or as homework.

# Lesson 32: Noun Endings—Diminutives (continued)

## Practicing the Lesson

### Spelling Clues: Word Shapes
Point out to students that remembering the shape of a word can help them remember the spelling of the word. Some words have very unusual shapes. Students might enjoy drawing the shapes of other words on the list.   APPLYING SPELLING STRATEGIES

### Proofreading
You may wish to have students review Spelling Clues: Word Shapes before proofreading the letter.

### Working with Meaning
Suggest to students that a good method for finding the missing word in an analogy is to figure out the relationship of the two words that are given. Are they synonyms or antonyms? Does one word tell a quality of the other? Is one word a type of the other? Is one word a tool that is used by the other? The relationship of the words in the second pair must match the relationship of the words in the first pair.

SECOND-LANGUAGE SUPPORT   Have students work together in small groups. They can help one another by sharing knowledge about word definitions. They can discuss how each analogy suggests a Spelling Word.

## Posttest
Administer the test on page 72 as a posttest, or administer one of your own. Say each word, use it in a sentence, and then repeat the word.

## Reteaching the Lesson
Students with visual memory deficits may need additional practice with word endings. Review the meaning of *suffix* (a word part that is added to the end of a word). For most words in this lesson, each suffix changes the meaning of the base word by making it a diminutive.

   For individual students who need tactile-kinesthetic reinforcement for spelling the Spelling Words, have them write the word plus the suffix (for example: *book + let = booklet*), trace the word using a colored marker or felt-tip pen, copy the word underneath the model, saying the name of each letter as it is written, and cover the model and write the word from memory.   KINESTHETIC MODALITY

*(Pretest/Posttest, continued)*

12. The ointment Johnny needs is in the medicine **cabinet.**
13. Laura lost her **bracelet** because the clasp on it came undone.
14. The **cassette** was lost when it fell out of the case.
15. This **pamphlet** explains how you can help stop pollution.
16. Vic put a **statuette** of a baseball player on top of his television.

## PRACTICE ACTIVITY
The practice activity is on page 173.

### Answers: Spelling Clues
1. booklet
2. diskette
3. packet
4. pamphlet
5. particle
6. tablet

### Answers: Proofreading
7. banquet
8. luncheonette
9. leaflet
10. cabinet
11. statuette
12. yearling

### Answers: Working with Meaning
13. icicle
14. sapling
15. bracelet
16. cassette

# Lesson 33: Latin Roots, III

## OBJECTIVE
To spell words that contain Latin roots

## HOME ACTIVITY
The home activity is on page 175.

## SECOND-LANGUAGE SUPPORT
Students acquiring English may experience difficulty in spelling words with these Latin roots. Provide extra practice by distributing cards with the roots printed on them. As you pronounce each word on the list, have students hold up the corresponding card. Check student responses for accuracy before going on to the next word. For those roots that have two spellings, ask students which spelling applies to the given word.   LISTENING FOR ROOTS

## PRETEST/POSTTEST
1. The dog felt **confined** when it was inside.
2. Hawaii and Alaska used to be **territories** of the United States.
3. Melinda, the jeweler, spent many years **refining** her skills.
4. Kurt was trying to grow tomatoes in a big pot on his **terrace.**
5. Sharon made a **duplicate** key to the door of her apartment.
6. Eric's interest in **financial** matters will someday make him rich.
7. The directions for putting the bicycle together were **complicated.**
8. We strained our **vocal** cords by yelling during the baseball game.
9. The two groups worked in **conjunction** to solve the problem.
10. The mother of that demanding child seems to have **infinite** patience.
11. In Spanish class today, we added ten new words to our **vocabulary.**

*(continued on next page)*

## Pretest
Administer the test on this page as a pretest. Say each word, use it in the sentence, and then repeat the word.   ACCESSING PRIOR KNOWLEDGE

**SELF-CHECK**   Have students check their own pretests against the list of Spelling Words. Remind students to write misspelled words in their Lesson Word Logs.   STUDENT SELF-ASSESSMENT

## Introducing the Lesson

### Option A (Open Sort)
Distribute the word cards (page 174) to individuals or small groups, and guide them in an open-sort activity. In open sort, students group the word cards according to a criterion they select themselves. Then guide students in comparing and discussing the criteria they selected.

### Option B (Modeling)
Read aloud with students the lesson title and the Spelling Words. Use this model sentence to introduce the lesson skill in a context.

*Albert finally completed the application.*

## Teaching the Lesson

- Ask volunteers to name the Spelling Words that are based on the Latin root *-plic-* or *-plex,* meaning "fold." List the words on the board. *(duplicate, applicable, complicated)*
- Follow the same procedure for the remaining Latin roots. Explain that *-fin-* means "end," *-junct-* means "join," *-voc-* or *-vok-* means "voice," and *-terr-* means "earth." (**-fin-:** *confined, refining, financial, infinite, definitely;* **-voc-** or **-vok-:** *vocal, vocabulary, vocational;* **-junct-:** *conjunction, juncture;* **-terr-:** *territories, terrace, territorial)*
- Have students add other words with these roots to the columns. After they do so, have volunteers read all the words aloud and underline the Latin roots.

**IN SUMMARY**   Have students summarize the lesson in their own words. Elicit the fact that some Latin roots have a consistent spelling.

**ASSIGNMENT**   Students can complete the first page of the lesson as a follow-up to the group activity, either in class or as homework.

# Lesson 33: Latin Roots, III *(continued)*

## Practicing the Lesson

### Spelling Clues: Find the Root

Suggest that students look for both Latin roots and base words as they complete items 1–6. First they should check the spelling of the Latin root (*-terr-*, for example). Then they should identify the base word (such as *territory*) and determine whether any spelling changes are needed before a prefix or suffix is added (as in *territorial* and *territories*).   APPLYING SPELLING STRATEGIES

### Proofreading

You may wish to have students review Spelling Clues: Find the Root before proofreading the sentences.

### Fun with Words

Students may complete this activity individually or with a partner. To extend this activity, you might have students write sentences of their own with each of the Spelling Words used in the cartoon.

TRANSITIONAL SPELLERS   Have students complete this activity cooperatively with a partner or in a small group. To help students with this activity, suggest that they use the picture clues in the cartoon to help them figure out the missing words.

## Posttest

Administer the test on page 74 as a posttest, or administer one of your own. Say each word, use it in a sentence, and then repeat the word.

## Reteaching the Lesson

Students with learning difficulties sometimes have trouble analyzing a task and completing it. Point out that the roots in this lesson have both a meaning and a consistent spelling.

Help students identify the Latin roots so they will know how to spell at least a portion of a word. Have students study the roots until they are visually identifiable. Then have the students look through various written materials to see if they can identify words with the Latin roots from this lesson. Have students practice spelling each word by copying the word, tracing over it, covering the model, and writing the word from memory.

All words that contain the same root should be written together. Discussing the meaning of the root and then the meaning of the whole word will also give the student something to remember.   KINESTHETIC MODALITY

*(Pretest/Posttest, continued)*

12. The **vocational** training will help you get a good job.
13. We are **definitely** going to Alaska in the summer.
14. We are not allowed to fish in the **territorial** waters of that country.
15. At this **juncture,** we must seriously consider our options.
16. When you fill out this form, check all the **applicable** boxes.

### PRACTICE ACTIVITY

The practice activity is on page 176.

### Answers: Spelling Clues

1. territorial
2. terrace
3. vocal
4. applicable
5. infinite
6. territories

### Answers: Proofreading

7. complicated
8. vocabulary
9. refining
10. duplicate
11. definitely
12. confined

### Answers: Fun with Words

13. juncture
14. conjunction
15. vocational
16. financial

# Lesson 34: Words from Other Languages, II

## OBJECTIVE
To spell words from other languages

## HOME ACTIVITY
The home activity is on page 178.

## SECOND-LANGUAGE SUPPORT
To provide extra practice, make illustrated flashcards. Write a word or phrase on one side, and provide an illustration representing the word on the other side. Have students choose a card at random, read and define the word, and use the illustration to check their answers.   USING PICTURE CLUES

## PRETEST/POSTTEST
1. Because it was so cold, Annie used the hood on her **parka.**
2. The artist was famous for creating **mammoth** statues.
3. Mustard is very good on a fresh, hot **pretzel.**
4. The **waffle** is served with strawberries and whipped cream.
5. You could be surprised at how warm it is inside an **igloo.**
6. For self-defense and physical fitness, Henry is taking a **karate** class.
7. A **harpoon** was used by the hunters.
8. While I was in Japan, I bought a beautiful **kimono** to wear.
9. Andrew started **kindergarten** before his fifth birthday.
10. At the **caucus,** the election committee nominated Bob for president.
11. We coasted down the snow-covered hill on our new **toboggan.**
12. Judy used her **kayak** to travel down the river.

*(continued on next page)*

## Pretest
Administer the test on this page as a pretest. Say each word, use it in the sentence, and then repeat the word.   ACCESSING PRIOR KNOWLEDGE

**SELF-CHECK**   Have students check their own pretests against the list of Spelling Words. Remind students to write misspelled words in their Lesson Word Logs.   STUDENT SELF-ASSESSMENT

## Introducing the Lesson

### Option A (Open Sort)
Distribute the word cards (page 177) to individuals or small groups, and guide them in an open-sort activity. In open sort, students group the word cards according to a criterion they select themselves. Then guide students in comparing and discussing the criteria they selected.

### Option B (Modeling)
Read aloud with students the lesson title and the Spelling Words. Use this model sentence to introduce the lesson skill in a context.

*Betty bought dill* **pickles** *at the* **delicatessen.**

## Teaching the Lesson

- Ask volunteers to name the Spelling Words that come from Russian. Write *Russian* on the board and list the words below the heading. *(parka, mammoth, tundra)*
- Follow the same procedure for the remaining languages. Encourage students to refer to dictionaries as needed. (***Inuit:*** *igloo, kayak;* ***German:*** *pretzel, kindergarten;* ***Algonquian:*** *caucus, toboggan, persimmon;* ***Dutch:*** *waffle, harpoon;* ***Japanese:*** *karate, kimono, hibachi, haiku)*
- Invite students to find words from different languages in their own writing and add the words to the columns. Then have volunteers read all the words aloud and briefly define them.

**IN SUMMARY**   Ask students to summarize the lesson in their own words. Elicit the information that many English words come from other languages.

**ASSIGNMENT**   Students can complete the first page of the lesson as a follow-up to the group activity, either in class or as homework.

# Lesson 34: Words from Other Languages, II *(continued)*

## Practicing the Lesson

### Spelling Clues: Checking Syllables

Suggest that when students encounter a word whose spelling they are unsure of, they say the word aloud, listening for each syllable. They should be certain to include letters to represent all the syllables and avoid adding extra syllables. If they are still unsure of the correct spelling, they should look up the word in a dictionary.   APPLYING SPELLING STRATEGIES

### Proofreading

You may wish to have students review Spelling Clues: Checking Syllables before proofreading the letter.

### Fun with Words

Students may complete this activity individually or with a partner. After students have completed the activity, you might wish to provide more practice by suggesting to students that they write their own paragraphs, using as many of the words as they can.

## Posttest

Administer the test on page 76 as a posttest, or administer one of your own. Say each word, use it in a sentence, and then repeat the word.

## Reteaching the Lesson

Most of the words in this lesson must be learned by rote. This presents problems for students with visual-memory deficiencies and specific language difficulties. Frequent exposure to the words will increase the likelihood that they will learn how to spell them.

   Have students write the Spelling Words from dictation. Encourage students to write the letters that they know and to leave spaces for the letters of which they are unsure. Immediately, have students check their own spelling against a model, and have them underline the parts of the words that were incorrectly spelled. Analyze the misspellings to determine whether there are any consistent errors.

   Quiz students at least once a day on four of the Spelling Words so they will have high exposure. Follow the strategy of having the students correct their quizzes immediately and correct any misspellings.   VISUAL MODALITY

*(Pretest/Posttest, continued)*

13. The **tundra** had no trees or other landmarks to help show us our way.
14. The **persimmon** was sour because it was not ripe yet.
15. Our **hibachi** is big enough to hold four hamburgers at a time.
16. William's **haiku** about the bird won the poetry contest at our school.

### PRACTICE ACTIVITY

The practice activity is on page 179.

### Answers: Spelling Clues

| 1. tundra | 4. mammoth |
|---|---|
| 2. caucus | 5. kindergarten |
| 3. persimmon | |

### Answers: Proofreading

| 6. parka | 9. waffle |
|---|---|
| 7. kimono | 10. haiku |
| 8. hibachi | 11. karate |

### Answers: Fun with Words

| 12. igloo | 15. harpoon |
|---|---|
| 13. toboggan | 16. kayak |
| 14. pretzel | |

# Lesson 35: Suffixes in Combination

## OBJECTIVE
To spell words that have suffixes in combination

## HOME ACTIVITY
The home activity is on page 181.

## SECOND-LANGUAGE SUPPORT
To provide practice with words that have suffixes in combination, prepare a set of flashcards. On one side of each card, write a Spelling Word. On the other side write a sentence, leaving a blank for the Spelling Word and using the base word as a clue. For example: *Do me a* **favor** *and comment* _____ *on my nephew's artwork.* Have students choose a flashcard, read the sentence, provide the Spelling Word that fits in the blank, and check their answer by looking at the other side of the card. USING CONTEXT CLUES

## PRETEST/POSTTEST
1. The puppy was wandering **aimlessly** through the neighborhood.
2. Dorothy threw her coat **carelessly** across the couch.
3. The sound of the rain gave me a feeling of **peacefulness.**
4. Gary suffered terrible feelings of **loneliness** when he first moved.
5. Many **historically** important buildings are being preserved now.
6. The sun shone **favorably** on the day of our trip.
7. If you treat the cat nicely, **eventually** she will trust you.
8. Many people in this city work for **governmental** agencies.
9. Traffic was heavy, but **fortunately** there were no accidents.
10. To prosper **economically,** most people must work hard.

*(continued on next page)*

## Pretest
Administer the test on this page as a pretest. Say each word, use it in the sentence, and then repeat the word.   ACCESSING PRIOR KNOWLEDGE

**SELF-CHECK**   Have students check their own pretests against the list of Spelling Words. Remind students to write misspelled words in their Lesson Word Logs.   STUDENT SELF-ASSESSMENT

## Introducing the Lesson

### Option A (Open Sort)
Distribute the word cards (page 180) to individuals or small groups, and guide them in an open-sort activity. In open sort, students group the word cards according to a criterion they select themselves. Then guide students in comparing and discussing the criteria they selected.

### Option B (Modeling)
Read aloud with students the lesson title and the Spelling Words. Use this model sentence to introduce the lesson skill in a context.

*Tim arranged the* **illustrators'** *names* **alphabetically** *on the list.*

## Teaching the Lesson

- Ask volunteers to name and spell the Spelling Words that have two suffixes. List the words on the board. *(aimlessly, carelessly, peacefulness, loneliness, favorably, eventually, governmental, fortunately, architectural, significantly, mysteriously)*
- Ask volunteers to name and spell the words that have three suffixes. List the words on the board. *(historically, economically, sensationally, naturalization, rhythmically)*
- Then have students name and spell other words that have these patterns. List the words on the board.
- Invite volunteers to read all the words aloud and briefly define them.

**IN SUMMARY**   Have students summarize the lesson in their own words. Elicit the information that some words are formed by the addition of two or more suffixes to a base word.

**ASSIGNMENT**   Students can complete the first page of the lesson as a follow-up to the group activity, either in class or as homework.

# Lesson 35: Suffixes in Combination *(continued)*

## Practicing the Lesson

### Spelling Clues: Checking Base Words and Suffixes

Suggest that when students encounter a word that has suffixes in combination, they check each part of the word separately. First, students should consider whether the base word needs any spelling changes when the first suffix is added. Then they should consider the spelling of each suffix. If they are still unsure of the spelling, they should look up the word in a dictionary.    APPLYING SPELLING STRATEGIES

### Proofreading

You may wish to have students review Spelling Clues: Checking Base Words and Suffixes before proofreading the paragraph.

### Fun with Words

Students may complete this activity individually or with a partner. You may wish to extend the activity by having students write their own sentences using the words. As an additional challenge, suggest that they write sentences that tell a story.

## Posttest

Administer the test on page 78 as a posttest, or administer one of your own. Say each word, use it in a sentence, and then repeat the word.

## Reteaching the Lesson

Attention deficits often accompany learning difficulties. A strategy of guided reduction of cues is used in this activity.

Have students make a series of flip cards with decreasing cues for spelling the Spelling Words. Have them make four to five cards for each word. Write the series as follows: for_ _ _ ately, for_ _ _ _ _ _ly, for_ _ _ _ _ _ _ _,
_ _ _ _ _ _ _ _ _ _ _.

On the first card or two, omit medial sounds. On the next card, omit the final suffix. Then omit the initial sounds. The lines on the cards indicate the number of letters and provide additional cues for the student who is uncertain about how many letters are in the word. Staple the cards together on one side so that after the student has completed one card, it can be folded back and the word on the new card can be spelled.

Say the word for students, and have them repeat it softly so they can determine the letters of the missing syllable. Have them complete the series independently.    VISUAL MODALITY

*(Pretest/Posttest, continued)*

11. The **architectural** plan for this building was drawn by Carl.
12. They drove **sensationally** and won the race.
13. The process of **naturalization** can be a lengthy one.
14. The crime rate has dropped **significantly** in our city.
15. Amy **mysteriously** disappeared for a week.
16. Clara tapped her shoes **rhythmically** on the sidewalk.

### PRACTICE ACTIVITY

The practice activity is on page 182.

### Answers: Spelling Clues

1. historically
2. governmental
3. economically
4. naturalization
5. significantly
6. architectural
7. sensationally

### Answers: Proofreading

8. aimlessly
9. peacefulness
10. loneliness
11. favorably

### Answers: Fun with Words

12. mysteriously
13. rhythmically
14. carelessly
15. fortunately
16. eventually

## OBJECTIVES
- To review spelling patterns and strategies in Lessons 30–35
- To give students the opportunity to recognize and use these spelling patterns and Spelling Words in their writing

## UNIT 6 WORDS
The following words are reviewed in Practice Test, Parts A and B.

**Lesson 30: Words from Names**

sandwich      hamburger

tuxedo

**Lesson 31: Latin Roots, II**

container      deceived

adjustments      educate

acceptable

**Lesson 32: Noun Endings— Diminutives**

cassette      icicle

bracelet

**Lesson 33: Latin Roots, III**

financial      refining

terrace

**Lesson 34: Words from Other Languages, II**

persimmon      karate

pretzel      haiku

**Lesson 35: Suffixes in Combination**

fortunately      carelessly

## Review Strategies
Review with students the following spelling-clue strategies for Lessons 30–35.

### Lesson 30   Spelling Clues: Listening to Sounds
Write the word *sandwich* on the board. Then have a student say it aloud, pronouncing all the sounds clearly. Ask students to listen carefully to the pronunciation and think about other words they know that have the same sounds. Have them consider how those sounds are spelled in other words. Do the same with *tuxedo* and *hamburger*.

### Lesson 31   Spelling Clues: Looking at Words
Suggest that students try several different spellings for words they find problematic. When they see the word written down, they might find it easier to choose the correct spelling.

### Lesson 32   Spelling Clues: Word Shapes
Draw the word shapes for *cassette, bracelet*, and *icicle* on the board. Ask volunteers to suggest words that would fit into each shape. Remind them to consider whether the word has any tall letters or any letters that go below the line. Remembering the distinctive shape of a problematic word is an effective spelling strategy.

### Lesson 33   Spelling Clues: Find the Root
Call on a student to identify the base words in *financial* and *refining (finance* and *refine)*. Ask the student to explain how the spelling of the base word changes when a suffix is added. Then have students identify the Latin root in each word *(-fin-)*.

### Lesson 34   Spelling Clues: Checking Syllables
Ask a volunteer to say aloud the words *persimmon, pretzel, karate*, and *haiku*, taking care to pronounce each syllable. Remind students that pronouncing each syllable of a word can often help them determine the correct spelling.

### Lesson 35   Spelling Clues: Checking Base Words and Suffixes
Write the words *fortunately* and *carelessly* on the board. For each word, have students identify the base word and two suffixes. Remind students to consider whether the base word needs any spelling changes before the first suffix is added and to check each suffix separately.

# Unit 6 Review *(continued)*

## Practice Test

The Practice Test provides an opportunity to review Spelling Words and spelling generalizations in a standardized test format, complete with a sample answer card.

### Option 1

Use Practice Test: Part A as a pretest. Later, use Practice Test: Part B as a posttest.

### Option 2

Have students review their Lesson Word Log for this unit. If they need extra help, you may wish to review the spelling generalizations discussed in the individual lessons. Then administer both parts of the Practice Test to determine whether students have mastered the spelling generalizations.

| Practice Test: Part A | Practice Test: Part B |
|---|---|
| 1. (C) sandwich | 1. (D) bracelet |
| 2. (B) persimmon | 2. (A) icicle |
| 3. (A) tuxedo | 3. (C) carelessly |
| 4. (D) financial | 4. (B) terrace |
| 5. (A) container | 5. (D) refining |
| 6. (C) adjustments | 6. (B) pretzel |
| 7. (B) acceptable | 7. (A) karate |
| 8. (C) deceived | 8. (C) haiku |
| 9. (D) cassette | 9. (D) hamburger |
| 10. (A) fortunately | 10. (C) Educate |

## Options for Evaluation

- Have students check their own Practice Tests against their lists of Spelling Words. The list on the opposite page provides references to the lessons where they can find words they misspelled.
- You may prefer to assign partners and have students check each other's Practice Tests, using their own list of Spelling Words.

## REVIEW ACTIVITIES

### Activity 1

Have students list the Unit 6 Spelling Words that they would like to review and then sort the words according to their own criteria. For example, they might sort the words according to part of speech, word structure, or lesson category.

### Activity 2

Have students work with partners. Taking turns, each person chooses a Spelling Word and draws one blank for each letter. The partner must try to figure out the word by guessing one letter at a time. Each time he or she guesses a letter correctly, the other partner writes it in the blank or blanks where it belongs. Students can try to arrive at the answer more quickly by asking whether the word has a certain prefix, suffix, or root. If it does, the student's partner must then write those letters in the blanks.

### Activity 3

Write each word from this review lesson on a separate index card and place the cards face down on a desk. Have a student pick a card, make up a sentence using the word on the card, and place the card face up in another pile. Then have another student pick the next card and do the same thing. Suggest that the students try to have each pair of sentences relate to each other in some way. Continue this activity until all the cards have been used.

## WHAT'S IN A WORD?

**♦ Braille**

Ask students to research the life of Louis Braille and to report their findings to the class.

**♦ complicated**

You may wish to have students write pairs of words in which one word has a simple meaning *(addition)* and the other has a complicated meaning *(algebra)*.

**♦ diskette and disk**

Have students research the origin of the words and write a sentence for each one.

## Unit Activity Options

### Label a Mural

Before students begin this activity, discuss the meaning of the word *mural*. Remind them that a mural can be as big as they want it, so they will have opportunities to use all the Spelling Words.

### A Secret Tablet

Students might enjoy hearing one another's secret messages. Invite volunteers to read their messages aloud.

### Picture Clues

Ask students to select three Spelling Words for this activity and to work independently to draw their clues. Then have students exchange clues with partners. Invite volunteers to share drawings with other students.

### Synonym/Antonym Spelling

You may want to have students write the Spelling Words in one column and the synonym or antonym for each word in another column.

**WORKING TOGETHER** For the Synonym/Antonym Spelling activity, allow time for pairs of students to play the game. Remind them to tell their partners whether the word being used is a synonym or antonym of the Spelling Word.

### Locating Unfamiliar Words

To extend the activity, have students write pronunciations for several other Spelling Words and use a dictionary to check their work. Encourage them to discuss any differences between their written pronunciations and those given in the dictionary.

### Puzzle Maker

You may wish to supply grid paper for this activity.

### Proofreading Partners

Have students read the instructions for the activity, and answer any questions they may have. Remind students to review the list carefully and to select the Spelling Words they find most troublesome; this approach will make the activity a useful tool for improving their spelling skills. Then have students select their own partners and complete the activity.

♦ This indicates a Unit Spelling Word.

# Unit 6 Review *(continued)*

## Curriculum Options

### Language Arts: Play a Board Game

To prepare for this activity, trace a path on poster board. Mark off one-inch spaces. Write a Spelling Word in each space. Students advance from Start by tossing dice or using a spinner. As they land on a space, they must pronounce the word and use it in a sentence that shows they know the meaning. If they do this, they can remain on the space. If not, they must go back to where they were before the turn began. The first player to reach the finish line wins.

### Science: Word Search

Remind students that many words with an unusual plural form are words related to science, such as *bacteria, larvae, fungi, stimuli,* and *nuclei.* Organize students in small groups, and give each group a science textbook or another science reference. Give group members time to peruse the contents of their reference book to locate examples of plural words with unusual spellings. Assign a Recorder to each group to write down examples that each group finds. Later, have group members list the unusual plurals on the board. As an additional activity, students can determine the singular form of each plural found and make a separate list of these spellings as well.

### Social Studies: In the News

Students will need to prepare for this game by creating questions that can be answered by a Spelling Word. Questions can be based on local or national events. The game is played in two teams of three or four persons per team. Team A begins by asking Team B a question. If a member of Team B answers it correctly and spells the Spelling Word correctly, Team B gets two points. If the answer is wrong, but the word is spelled correctly, the team gets one point. (You may want to make up a rule about players taking turns answering questions so that one student doesn't answer them all for his or her team.) Teams should take turns asking questions. The team with more points wins.

## WHAT'S IN A WORD?

### ♦ *Fahrenheit*

Ask students to find out in which countries the two temperature systems are used. (The United States uses *Fahrenheit;* most other countries use *Celsius.*)

### ♦ *fortunately*

Ask students to think about a time that a decision, an event, or a meeting could have gone any one of several ways. What do they think might have influenced the outcome to make it favorable? Was it all just luck, or were there other factors? Invite volunteers to share their responses.

### ♦ *hamburgers* and *frankfurters*

Have students locate, on a map, the two German cities for which these foods are named.

♦ This indicates a Unit Spelling Word.

# Management Charts

This section of the Teacher's Guide contains the following reproducible management charts.

**Percent Conversion Chart**
The Percent Conversion Chart indicates percentage scores on tests that have from 4 to 24 test items. To find the percentage score a particular student has earned, find the box where the appropriate horizontal and vertical rows meet. The percent score appears in that box.

**Spelling Progress Chart**
The Spelling Progress Chart may be used to track individual students' scores for the Pretest, Posttest, and Practice Test over the course of six units. Make one photocopy of the Spelling Progress Chart for each student. Keep a copy of the Spelling Progress Chart for each student. Keep a copy of this chart in each student's portfolio and refer to it during student-and-teacher conferences. If you prefer, you may want to allow the students themselves to record and to keep a copy of the record to monitor their own progress as a form of self-assessment.

The Practice Test at the end of each unit is designed to give students practice with the standardized test format and help them become comfortable with test-taking procedures. The number of correctly spelled words should be recorded in the appropriate column of the chart.

**Class Record-Keeping Chart**
Use the Class Record-Keeping Chart to keep track of the progress of your class. This chart can hold all students' scores for the Pretest, the Posttest, and the Practice Test. Make six copies of this page. Use one copy with each unit.

**Error Analysis Chart for Writing Activities**
The Error Analysis Chart for Writing Activities is designed to help you analyze the nature of students' spelling errors and thereby customize instruction to meet individual needs.

# Percent Conversion Chart

Use the matrix below to convert the raw score for each test to a percentage.

| Number of Test Items | \ Number Correct 2 | 3 | 4 | 5 | 6 | 7 | 8 | 9 | 10 | 11 | 12 | 13 | 14 | 15 | 16 | 17 | 18 | 19 | 20 | 21 | 22 | 23 | 24 |
|---|---|---|---|---|---|---|---|---|---|---|---|---|---|---|---|---|---|---|---|---|---|---|---|
| For 4-item test | 50 | 75 | 100 | | | | | | | | | | | | | | | | | | | | |
| For 5-item test | 40 | 60 | 80 | 100 | | | | | | | | | | | | | | | | | | | |
| For 6-item test | | 50 | 67 | 83 | 100 | | | | | | | | | | | | | | | | | | |
| For 7-item test | | 43 | 57 | 71 | 86 | 100 | | | | | | | | | | | | | | | | | |
| For 8-item test | | | 50 | 63 | 75 | 88 | 100 | | | | | | | | | | | | | | | | |
| For 9-item test | | | 44 | 56 | 67 | 78 | 89 | 100 | | | | | | | | | | | | | | | |
| For 10-item test | | | | 50 | 60 | 70 | 80 | 90 | 100 | | | | | | | | | | | | | | |
| For 11-item test | | | | 45 | 55 | 64 | 73 | 82 | 91 | 100 | | | | | | | | | | | | | |
| For 12-item test | | | | | 50 | 58 | 67 | 75 | 83 | 92 | 100 | | | | | | | | | | | | |
| For 13-item test | | | | | 46 | 54 | 62 | 69 | 77 | 85 | 92 | 100 | | | | | | | | | | | |
| For 14-item test | | | | | | 50 | 57 | 64 | 71 | 79 | 86 | 93 | 100 | | | | | | | | | | |
| For 15-item test | | | | | | 47 | 53 | 60 | 67 | 73 | 80 | 87 | 93 | 100 | | | | | | | | | |
| For 16-item test | | | | | | | 50 | 56 | 63 | 69 | 75 | 81 | 88 | 94 | 100 | | | | | | | | |
| For 17-item test | | | | | | | 47 | 53 | 59 | 65 | 71 | 76 | 82 | 88 | 94 | 100 | | | | | | | |
| For 18-item test | | | | | | | | 50 | 56 | 61 | 67 | 72 | 78 | 83 | 89 | 94 | 100 | | | | | | |
| For 19-item test | | | | | | | | 47 | 53 | 58 | 63 | 68 | 74 | 79 | 84 | 89 | 95 | 100 | | | | | |
| For 20-item test | | | | | | | | | 50 | 55 | 60 | 65 | 70 | 75 | 80 | 85 | 90 | 95 | 100 | | | | |
| For 21-item test | | | | | | | | | 48 | 52 | 57 | 62 | 67 | 71 | 76 | 81 | 86 | 90 | 95 | 100 | | | |
| For 22-item test | | | | | | | | | | 50 | 55 | 59 | 64 | 68 | 73 | 77 | 82 | 86 | 91 | 95 | 100 | | |
| For 23-item test | | | | | | | | | | 48 | 52 | 57 | 61 | 65 | 70 | 74 | 78 | 83 | 87 | 91 | 96 | 100 | |
| For 24-item test | | | | | | | | | | | 50 | 54 | 58 | 63 | 67 | 71 | 75 | 79 | 83 | 88 | 92 | 96 | 100 |

**Management Charts**

# Spelling Progress Chart

**Directions** Write in Pretest, Posttest, and Practice Test scores. If a student shows improvement but has missed one or more items, fill in dot under Showed Improvement. For perfect scores, fill in dot under Mastered Words.

| LESSON | NUMBER OF WORDS CORRECTLY SPELLED | | PROGRESS | |
|---|---|---|---|---|
| | Pretest | Posttest | Showed Improvement | Mastered Words |
| **Unit 1** Lesson 1 | | | ○ | ○ |
| Lesson 2 | | | ○ | ○ |
| Lesson 3 | | | ○ | ○ |
| Lesson 4 | | | ○ | ○ |
| Lesson 5 | | | ○ | ○ |
| Lesson 6 | | | ○ | ○ |
| Unit 1 Review    Practice Test | | | ○ | ○ |
| **Unit 2** Lesson 8 | | | ○ | ○ |
| Lesson 9 | | | ○ | ○ |
| Lesson 10 | | | ○ | ○ |
| Lesson 11 | | | ○ | ○ |
| Lesson 12 | | | ○ | ○ |
| Unit 2 Review    Practice Test | | | ○ | ○ |
| **Unit 3** Lesson 14 | | | ○ | ○ |
| Lesson 15 | | | ○ | ○ |
| Lesson 16 | | | ○ | ○ |
| Lesson 17 | | | ○ | ○ |
| Lesson 18 | | | ○ | ○ |
| Unit 3 Review    Practice Test | | | ○ | ○ |
| **Unit 4** Lesson 20 | | | ○ | ○ |
| Lesson 21 | | | ○ | ○ |
| Lesson 22 | | | ○ | ○ |
| Lesson 23 | | | ○ | ○ |
| Unit 4 Review    Practice Test | | | ○ | ○ |
| **Unit 5** Lesson 25 | | | ○ | ○ |
| Lesson 26 | | | ○ | ○ |
| Lesson 27 | | | ○ | ○ |
| Lesson 28 | | | ○ | ○ |
| Unit 5 Review    Practice Test | | | ○ | ○ |
| **Unit 6** Lesson 30 | | | ○ | ○ |
| Lesson 31 | | | ○ | ○ |
| Lesson 32 | | | ○ | ○ |
| Lesson 33 | | | ○ | ○ |
| Lesson 34 | | | ○ | ○ |
| Lesson 35 | | | ○ | ○ |
| Unit 6 Review    Practice Test | | | ○ | ○ |

# Class Record-Keeping Chart

**Directions** Make six copies of this page, and use one copy with each unit.

| ▶NAME | ▶LESSON Pretest/ Posttest | ▶LESSON Pretest/ Posttest | ▶LESSON Pretest/ Posttest | ▶LESSON Pretest/ Posttest | ▶LESSON Pretest/ Posttest | ▶LESSON Pretest/ Posttest | ▶UNIT REVIEW Practice Test |
|---|---|---|---|---|---|---|---|
| | | | | | | | |
| | | | | | | | |
| | | | | | | | |
| | | | | | | | |
| | | | | | | | |
| | | | | | | | |
| | | | | | | | |
| | | | | | | | |
| | | | | | | | |
| | | | | | | | |
| | | | | | | | |
| | | | | | | | |
| | | | | | | | |
| | | | | | | | |
| | | | | | | | |
| | | | | | | | |
| | | | | | | | |
| | | | | | | | |
| | | | | | | | |
| | | | | | | | |
| | | | | | | | |
| | | | | | | | |
| | | | | | | | |
| | | | | | | | |
| | | | | | | | |
| | | | | | | | |
| | | | | | | | |
| | | | | | | | |
| | | | | | | | |
| | | | | | | | |
| | | | | | | | |

# Error Analysis Chart for Writing Activities

**Directions** Make as many copies of this chart as necessary.

| | | Misspelling | Correct Spelling | | | | | | | | |
|---|---|---|---|---|---|---|---|---|---|---|---|
| **Where the Error Appears in the Word** | Beginning | | | | | | | | | | |
| | Middle | | | | | | | | | | |
| | End | | | | | | | | | | |
| **Substitutions, Omissions, Insertions, Reversals** | Vowel | | | | | | | | | | |
| | Consonant | | | | | | | | | | |
| | Silent Letters | | | | | | | | | | |
| | Double Letters | | | | | | | | | | |
| **Other** | Compounds, Homophones, Contractions | | | | | | | | | | |
| | Irregular Words | | | | | | | | | | |
| | Inflectional Endings and Suffixes | | | | | | | | | | |

# Student Worksheets and Answer Key

This section of the Teacher's Guide contains the following reproducible worksheets and answers.

## Word Cards

The Word Cards are designed to be used in open-sort activities. In open sort, students group the word cards according to a criterion they select themselves. They might group words that share the same beginning or middle sound, words that are related by topic, or words that have a similar shape.

## Home Activities

The Home Activity is designed to involve family members in the spelling instruction of your students. It includes a brief introductory letter about the lesson being developed in class as well as an activity designed to help family members become an integral part of the learning process.

## Practice Activities

The Practice Activity is designed to provide students with additional practice on the spelling concepts developed in class.

## Answer Key for Practice Activities

The Answer Key for Practice Activities provides answers for all Practice Activities.

# Lesson 1: Compound Words

| | | | |
|---|---|---|---|
| homesick | evergreen | well-wisher | picnic basket |
| homemade | long-term | underground | handkerchief |
| large-scale | gingerbread | furthermore | heart attack |
| stagecoach | good-natured | headquarters | loudspeaker |

# Lesson 1: Compound Words

Dear Parent or Guardian,

Your child _____ has just begun this spelling lesson. This week's test of words will be held on

_____ .

Please contact me if you have any questions. Use the Comment Box to make any comments on your child's progress, noting any words that he or she still needs to review.

Sincerely,

_____

## Spelling Words

1. homesick
2. evergreen
3. well-wisher
4. picnic basket
5. homemade
6. long-term
7. underground
8. handkerchief
9. large-scale
10. gingerbread
11. furthermore
12. heart attack
13. stagecoach
14. good-natured
15. headquarters
16. loudspeaker

## Home Activity

Prepare a flashcard for each Spelling Word. Show your child each card for a few seconds, and then place it facedown on the table. Ask your child to spell the word.

### COMMENT BOX

# Lesson 1: Compound Words

**A.** Write the Spelling Word that matches each clue.

1. You can carry lunch for a group in this.

_____

2. This kind of tree doesn't lose its leaves in winter.

_____

3. If you want everyone to hear what you say, you might use this. _____

4. Many people like this for dessert.

_____

5. You might feel this way when you're away from the family. _____

6. You might use this for blowing your nose.

_____

7. If you smile most of the time, people will assume you're this. _____

8. If you have this kind of project, you work on it over an extended period of time. _____

9. This is a person who wants good things to happen to you.

_____

10. This is another word for *moreover*.

_____

11. This is where you'd expect to find the people in charge.

_____

12. This is the kind of gift you create yourself.

_____

13. If you know CPR, you can help a person who has this.

_____

14. Something that isn't above the surface of the earth must be this. _____

15. A map of this kind includes many details.

_____

16. In the old West, this carried both mail and passengers.

_____

**B.** Write a paragraph on a topic of your choice. Use at least five Spelling Words.

_____

_____

_____

_____

## Spelling Words

1. *homesick*
2. *evergreen*
3. *well-wisher*
4. *picnic basket*
5. *homemade*
6. *long-term*
7. *underground*
8. *handkerchief*
9. *large-scale*
10. *gingerbread*
11. *furthermore*
12. *heart attack*
13. *stagecoach*
14. *good-natured*
15. *headquarters*
16. *loudspeaker*

# Lesson 2: Homophones

| | | | |
|---|---|---|---|
| border | capital | fowl | principal |
| boarder | bard | stationary | principle |
| palette | stationery | burro | pallet |
| Capitol | burrow | foul | barred |

Dear Parent or Guardian,
    Your child _____ has just begun this spelling lesson. This week's test of words will be held on

_____ .

    Please contact me if you have any questions. Use the Comment Box to make any comments on your child's progress, noting any words that he or she still needs to review.
    Sincerely,

_____

## Spelling Words

1. border
2. capital
3. fowl
4. principal
5. boarder
6. bard
7. stationary
8. principle
9. palette
10. stationery
11. burro
12. pallet
13. Capitol
14. burrow
15. foul
16. barred

**Home Activity**

Write a sentence using each Spelling Word. Read each sentence, leaving out the Spelling Word. Ask your child to write the Spelling Word that best completes each sentence.

COMMENT BOX

# Lesson 2: Homophones

**A.** The sentences below can be completed with pairs of homophones. Write two Spelling Words to finish each sentence.

1. Many visitors to Washington, D.C., the _____ of the country, visit the _____, the official building of the United States Congress.

2. The artist mixed a few colors on her _____ and began painting a picture of the children as they slept on a _____.

3. The only other _____ in the rooming house plans to drive to the _____ in the morning.

4. Wild _____ no longer live near the lake because the water has become _____.

5. The _____ explained that everyone in the school was expected to uphold the _____ of honesty.

6. The train was expected to remain _____ for almost an hour, so I took out a piece of _____ and began writing to my parents.

7. Many other poets are invited to read their work here, but that _____ has been _____ from the premises.

8. The _____ stood and gazed curiously into the rabbit's _____.

**B.** Write a paragraph on a topic of your choice. Use at least five Spelling Words.

_____

_____

_____

_____

_____

## Spelling Words

1. border
2. capital
3. fowl
4. principal
5. boarder
6. bard
7. stationary
8. principle
9. palette
10. stationery
11. burro
12. pallet
13. Capitol
14. burrow
15. foul
16. barred

# Lesson 3: Adding Endings to Words

| | | | |
|---|---|---|---|
| potatoes | separating | harvesting | contained |
| programming | refused | omitted | produced |
| acquired | abilities | submitted | justified |
| forbidding | petrified | nutrients | resources |

# Lesson 3: Adding Endings to Words

Dear Parent or Guardian,
    Your child _____ has just begun this spelling lesson. This week's test of words will be held on
_____ .
    Please contact me if you have any questions. Use the Comment Box to make any comments on your child's progress, noting any words that he or she still needs to review.
    Sincerely,

_____

## Spelling Words

1. potatoes
2. separating
3. harvesting
4. contained
5. programming
6. refused
7. omitted
8. produced
9. acquired
10. abilities
11. submitted
12. justified
13. forbidding
14. petrified
15. nutrients
16. resources

## Home Activity

Copy the list of Spelling Words, scrambling the letters in each word. Give the list to your child, and ask him or her to unscramble the letters in each word so that each spells a Spelling Word.

COMMENT BOX

# Lesson 3: Adding Endings to Words

**PRACTICE ACTIVITY**

**A.** Add the given ending to each base word, making any necessary spelling changes. Write the Spelling Word on the line.

1. refuse + ed _____

2. separate + ing _____

3. ability + es _____

4. submit + ed _____

5. potato + es _____

6. produce + ed _____

7. program + ing _____

8. resource + s _____

9. omit + ed _____

10. petrify + ed _____

11. harvest + ing _____

12. justify + ed _____

13. contain + ed _____

14. nutrient + s _____

15. forbid + ing _____

16. acquire + ed _____

## Spelling Words

1. *potatoes*
2. *separating*
3. *harvesting*
4. *contained*
5. *programming*
6. *refused*
7. *omitted*
8. *produced*
9. *acquired*
10. *abilities*
11. *submitted*
12. *justified*
13. *forbidding*
14. *petrified*
15. *nutrients*
16. *resources*

**B.** Write a paragraph on a topic of your choice. Use at least five Spelling Words.

_____

_____

_____

_____

_____

_____

_____

_____

_____

# Lesson 4: Related Words

| | | | |
|---|---|---|---|
| awful | drama | strain | awfully |
| continue | profession | dramatic | despair |
| awe | professionally | continuous | strenuous |
| continuously | dramatically | desperately | strenuously |

# Lesson 4: Related Words

Dear Parent or Guardian,
    Your child _____ has just begun this
spelling lesson. This week's test of words will be held on
_____ .
    Please contact me if you have any questions. Use the
Comment Box to make any comments on your child's progress,
noting any words that he or she still needs to review.
    Sincerely,

_____

## Spelling Words

1. awful
2. drama
3. strain
4. awfully
5. continue
6. profession
7. dramatic
8. despair
9. awe
10. professionally
11. continuous
12. strenuous
13. continuously
14. dramatically
15. desperately
16. strenuously

## Home Activity
Think of a synonym or antonym for each Spelling Word. Say the synonym or antonym, and ask your child to write the corresponding Spelling Word.

COMMENT BOX

# Lesson 4: Related Words

**A.** Write the Spelling Word that fits each clue. Then write the other Spelling Word or Spelling Words that are related to the first word you wrote.

**1.** a play performed by actors

_____

**2.** to make a great effort

_____

**3.** to go on

_____

**4.** a feeling of fear and wonder

_____

**5.** to give up all hope

_____

**6.** an occupation that requires a good education and involves mental rather than physical labor

_____

**B.** Write a paragraph on a topic of your choice. Use at least five Spelling Words.

_____

_____

_____

_____

_____

_____

_____

_____

_____

_____

_____

_____

## Spelling Words

1. awful
2. drama
3. strain
4. awfully
5. continue
6. profession
7. dramatic
8. despair
9. awe
10. professionally
11. continuous
12. strenuous
13. continuously
14. dramatically
15. desperately
16. strenuously

# Lesson 5: Easily Confused Words

| | | | |
|---|---|---|---|
| breath | finally | bazaar | antidote |
| conscious | excess | bizarre | finely |
| breadth | persecuted | conscience | prosecuted |
| futile | access | anecdote | feudal |

# Lesson 5: Easily Confused Words

Dear Parent or Guardian,
    Your child _____ has just begun this
spelling lesson. This week's test of words will be held on

_____ .

    Please contact me if you have any questions. Use the
Comment Box to make any comments on your child's progress,
noting any words that he or she still needs to review.
    Sincerely,

_____

## Spelling Words

1. breath
2. finally
3. bazaar
4. antidote
5. conscious
6. excess
7. bizarre
8. finely
9. breadth
10. persecuted
11. conscience
12. prosecuted
13. futile
14. access
15. anecdote
16. feudal

## Home Activity

For each Spelling Word, write a word or phrase that describes or suggests the Spelling Word but does not include it. Have your child write and pronounce the Spelling Word that goes with each word or phrase.

COMMENT BOX

# Lesson 5: Easily Confused Words

**A.** Write each pair of similar Spelling Words. Match each word with the correct clue.

1. br ___ th: air _____

   br ___ th: width _____

2. fi ___ ly: at last _____

   fi ___ ly: in small pieces _____

3. b ___: odd _____

   b ___: marketplace _____

4. an ___ te: story _____

   an ___ te: medicine _____

5. p ___ ted: put on trial _____

   p ___ ted: mistreated _____

6. f ___: Middle Ages _____

   f ___: useless _____

7. con ___: aware _____

   con ___: right and wrong _____

8. ___ss: entrance _____

   ___ss: too much _____

**B.** Write a paragraph on a topic of your choice. Use at least five Spelling Words.

_____

_____

_____

_____

_____

_____

_____

_____

_____

_____

_____

## Spelling Words

1. breath
2. finally
3. bazaar
4. antidote
5. conscious
6. excess
7. bizarre
8. finely
9. breadth
10. persecuted
11. conscience
12. prosecuted
13. futile
14. access
15. anecdote
16. feudal

# Lesson 6: Prefixes *ad-*, *in-*

| | | | |
|---|---|---|---|
| arrested | improved | included | irrigated |
| inspection | insisted | illustrated | advice |
| approved | agreeable | investigated | announcement |
| impressed | accomplished | affectionate | irresponsible |

Dear Parent or Guardian,
    Your child _____ has just begun this
spelling lesson. This week's test of words will be held on
_____ .
    Please contact me if you have any questions. Use the
Comment Box to make any comments on your child's progress,
noting any words that he or she still needs to review.
    Sincerely,
    _____

## Spelling Words

1. arrested
2. improved
3. included
4. irrigated
5. inspection
6. insisted
7. illustrated
8. advice
9. approved
10. agreeable
11. investigated
12. announcement
13. impressed
14. accomplished
15. affectionate
16. irresponsible

**Home Activity**

Find an example of a crossword puzzle in a newspaper or magazine, and ask your child to create a crossword puzzle using the Spelling Words. Clues can be definitions or synonyms of the Spelling Words. You or another family member can solve the puzzle.

**COMMENT BOX**

# Lesson 6: Prefixes *ad-*, *in-*

**A.** Find the Spelling Words in the word-search puzzle. A word may be written down, up, across, or diagonally. Circle the word, and then write it on the line.

```
a j v w i l l u s t r a t e d p i s e q u n a
x n i z h i u e q c a p p r o v e d g n o r f
w k n l i u i r e y n g h t o p b e v c b d f
d j s o t t e r c o h b q u a x i t m n b t e
e d p d u b b r i s s i j e g l m s e d e e c
t y e i n n m t o o c k s h r u x i v e l l t
s x c g a c c o m p l i s h e d s s r s t t i
e g t y i n v e s t i g a t e d c n m s x m o
r p i b c d a r m n t i n g a d v i c e p r n
r e o i n c l u d e d w r e b s t e d r l o a
a z n q u c i n g r n p n e l b e w o p s e t
y s t r o i r r i g a t e d e c u v x m n g e
i r r e s p o n s i b l e g g r e g h i u y m
g h e t l o e w h f k c v b d d i l l o u r t
```

_____    _____

_____    _____

_____    _____

_____    _____

_____    _____

_____    _____

_____    _____

_____    _____

**B.** Write a paragraph on a topic of your choice. Use at least five Spelling Words.

_____

_____

_____

_____

_____

_____

_____

_____

## Spelling Words

1. arrested
2. improved
3. included
4. irrigated
5. inspection
6. insisted
7. illustrated
8. advice
9. approved
10. agreeable
11. investigated
12. announcement
13. impressed
14. accomplished
15. affectionate
16. irresponsible

# Lesson 8: Words from French

| | | | |
|---|---|---|---|
| pigeon | perfume | depot | elite |
| suite | matinee | blouse | debris |
| surgeon | embarrassed | chauffeur | croquet |
| amateur | crochet | plateau | coup |

# Lesson 8: Words from French

Dear Parent or Guardian,
    Your child _____ has just begun this spelling lesson. This week's test of words will be held on

_____ .

    Please contact me if you have any questions. Use the Comment Box to make any comments on your child's progress, noting any words that he or she still needs to review.
    Sincerely,

_____

## Spelling Words

1. pigeon
2. perfume
3. depot
4. elite
5. suite
6. matinee
7. blouse
8. debris
9. surgeon
10. embarrassed
11. chauffeur
12. croquet
13. amateur
14. crochet
15. plateau
16. coup

### Home Activity
Ask your child to write an acrostic. Write each Spelling Word vertically down the left-hand side of the paper. For each letter in the Spelling Word, have your child write a phrase that starts with that letter. Encourage your child to do several acrostics each day.

COMMENT BOX

Copyright © by Holt, Rinehart and Winston. All rights reserved.

ELEMENTS OF LANGUAGE | Second Course | *Spelling Teacher's Guide*

# Lesson 8: Words from French

**A.** Write the Spelling Word that fits each word shape.

1.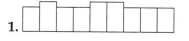

2.

3.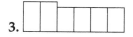

4.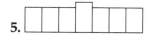

5.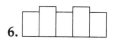

6.

7.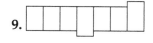

8.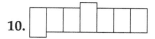

9.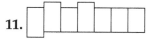

10.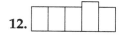

11.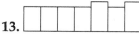

12.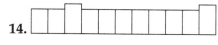

13.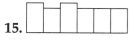

14.

15.

16.

**B.** Write a paragraph on a topic of your choice. Use at least five Spelling Words.

## Spelling Words

1. pigeon
2. perfume
3. depot
4. elite
5. suite
6. matinee
7. blouse
8. debris
9. surgeon
10. embarrassed
11. chauffeur
12. croquet
13. amateur
14. crochet
15. plateau
16. coup

# Lesson 9: Adjective Endings

| | | | |
|---|---|---|---|
| horrid | stupid | crooked | electronic |
| historic | ragged | magnetic | barefooted |
| democratic | passionate | rigid | contented |
| poetic | undersized | metallic | confederate |

# Lesson 9: Adjective Endings

Dear Parent or Guardian,
    Your child _____ has just begun this spelling lesson. This week's test of words will be held on

_____ .

    Please contact me if you have any questions. Use the Comment Box to make any comments on your child's progress, noting any words that he or she still needs to review.
    Sincerely,

_____

## Spelling Words

1. horrid
2. stupid
3. crooked
4. electronic
5. historic
6. ragged
7. magnetic
8. barefooted
9. democratic
10. passionate
11. rigid
12. contented
13. poetic
14. undersized
15. metallic
16. confederate

**Home Activity**

Prepare a simple definition for each Spelling Word. Read the definition aloud, and ask your child to write the Spelling Word that corresponds to the definition.

COMMENT BOX

# Lesson 9: Adjective Endings

**A.** Write a Spelling Word to replace the underlined word or words. Do not change the meaning of the sentence.

1. Watching the sun set, they felt peaceful and <u>satisfied</u>.

   _____

2. The <u>shoeless</u> children scurried down the dusty path.

   _____

3. Unfortunately, we made a <u>senseless</u> mistake.

   _____

4. Members must agree to abide by <u>strict</u> regulations.

   _____

5. It was a <u>frightful</u> situation. _____

6. He landed only one <u>smaller-than-normal</u> fish.

   _____

7. Why do you insist on wearing that <u>tattered</u> jacket?

   _____

8. The actor gave a <u>very emotional</u> performance.

   _____

9. She had found only one large, <u>twisted</u> stick. _____

10. They established a more <u>representative</u> government.

    _____

11. People often quote from that old and <u>famous</u> speech.

    _____

12. The smell of flowers is <u>attractive</u>. _____

13. He is my <u>associate</u>. _____

14. They installed a new <u>electron-based</u> system. _____

15. She often uses <u>imaginatively</u> <u>beautiful</u> language.

    _____

16. They were surprised by the sharp, <u>clanging</u> sounds.

    _____

**B.** Write a paragraph on a topic of your choice. Use at least five Spelling Words.

_____

_____

_____

_____

## Spelling Words

1. horrid
2. stupid
3. crooked
4. electronic
5. historic
6. ragged
7. magnetic
8. barefooted
9. democratic
10. passionate
11. rigid
12. contented
13. poetic
14. undersized
15. metallic
16. confederate

# Lesson 10: Greek Word Parts

| | | | |
|---|---|---|---|
| telephones | cycle | recycle | phonograph |
| symbolic | microphone | generation | cyclone |
| symptoms | genius | synonyms | generator |
| synthetic | genes | sympathetic | symphony |

# Lesson 10: Greek Word Parts

Dear Parent or Guardian,

Your child _____ has just begun this spelling lesson. This week's test of words will be held on

_____ .

Please contact me if you have any questions. Use the Comment Box to make any comments on your child's progress, noting any words that he or she still needs to review.

Sincerely,

_____

## Spelling Words

1. telephones
2. cycle
3. recycle
4. phonograph
5. symbolic
6. microphone
7. generation
8. cyclone
9. symptoms
10. genius
11. synonyms
12. generator
13. synthetic
14. genes
15. sympathetic
16. symphony

**Home Activity**

Make a list of the Spelling Words. Beginning with the second letter of each word, substitute a blank for every other letter. Ask your child to complete the words by filling in the blanks.

<u>COMMENT BOX</u>

# Lesson 10: Greek Word Parts

**A.** Write the Spelling Word that best fits each definition.

1. words with the same meaning _____

2. to use again _____

3. a storm with whirling winds _____

4. a piece of music composed to be played by an orchestra

   _____

5. a special talent or knack _____

6. segments of chromosomal DNA _____

7. serving as a representation for something else

   _____

8. a device that amplifies sounds _____

9. showing shared feelings _____

10. a device that produces sound from the grooves in a record

    _____

11. devices for sending and receiving the sounds of speech

    _____

12. signs of a disease _____

13. a machine that changes mechanical energy into electric

    energy _____

14. a series of events that always occur in the same order

    _____

15. not true or real _____

16. a group of people born at about the same time

    _____

**B.** Write a paragraph on a topic of your choice. Use at least
five Spelling Words.

_____

_____

_____

_____

## Spelling Words

1. telephones
2. cycle
3. recycle
4. phonograph
5. symbolic
6. microphone
7. generation
8. cyclone
9. symptoms
10. genius
11. synonyms
12. generator
13. synthetic
14. genes
15. sympathetic
16. symphony

# Lesson 11: Words from Greek

| | | | |
|---|---|---|---|
| alphabet | arithmetic | heroes | stadium |
| physical | aroma | episode | marathon |
| chorus | pneumonia | rhythm | labyrinth |
| melancholy | philosophy | phenomenon | architecture |

# Lesson 11: Words from Greek

Dear Parent or Guardian,
    Your child _____ has just begun this spelling lesson. This week's test of words will be held on
_____ .
    Please contact me if you have any questions. Use the Comment Box to make any comments on your child's progress, noting any words that he or she still needs to review.
    Sincerely,
_____

## Spelling Words

1. alphabet
2. arithmetic
3. heroes
4. stadium
5. physical
6. aroma
7. episode
8. marathon
9. chorus
10. pneumonia
11. rhythm
12. labyrinth
13. melancholy
14. philosophy
15. phenomenon
16. architecture

## Home Activity

Have your child make a word-search puzzle by writing the Spelling Words horizontally or vertically in a grid of cells. One letter should be written in each cell. The remaining cells should be filled with letters chosen at random. A family member can work the puzzle.

### COMMENT BOX

# Lesson 11: Words from Greek

**PRACTICE ACTIVITY**

**A.** Write the Spelling Word that would most likely follow each word in a dictionary.

1. phylum _____
2. labor-saving _____
3. alpaca _____
4. epilogue _____
5. rhyme _____
6. pheasant _____
7. megastructure _____
8. maracas _____
9. archipelago _____
10. chortle _____
11. aristocrat _____
12. philology _____
13. pneumatic _____
14. hermit _____
15. army _____
16. stack _____

**B.** Write a paragraph on a topic of your choice. Use at least five Spelling Words.

_____
_____
_____
_____
_____
_____
_____
_____
_____
_____
_____

## Spelling Words

1. alphabet
2. arithmetic
3. heroes
4. stadium
5. physical
6. aroma
7. episode
8. marathon
9. chorus
10. pneumonia
11. rhythm
12. labyrinth
13. melancholy
14. philosophy
15. phenomenon
16. architecture

ELEMENTS OF LANGUAGE | Second Course | *Spelling Teacher's Guide*

# Lesson 12: Science/Technology Words

| | | | |
|---|---|---|---|
| radar | electrical | scuba | universe |
| chemical | scientists | sonar | instruments |
| atmosphere | experiments | hemisphere | environment |
| laser | probability | technological | molecules |

# Lesson 12: Science/Technology Words

Dear Parent or Guardian,
Your child _____ has just begun this
spelling lesson. This week's test of words will be held on

_____ .

Please contact me if you have any questions. Use the
Comment Box to make any comments on your child's progress,
noting any words that he or she still needs to review.
Sincerely,

_____

## Spelling Words

1. radar
2. electrical
3. scuba
4. universe
5. chemical
6. scientists
7. sonar
8. instruments
9. atmosphere
10. experiments
11. hemisphere
12. environment
13. laser
14. probability
15. technological
16. molecules

**Home Activity**
Write a sentence using each Spelling Word. Read each sentence, leaving out the Spelling Word. Ask your child to write the Spelling Word that best completes each sentence.

COMMENT BOX

**124**

# Lesson 12: Science/Technology Words

**PRACTICE ACTIVITY**

**A.** Write the Spelling Word that fits each set of letter spaces.

s

c

1. _ _ _ _ i _ _ _

2. _ _ e _ _ _ _ _ _

3. _ n _ _ _ _ _ _ _ _

4. _ _ _ c _ _ _ _

5. _ _ _ e _

6. _ _ _ a _

7. _ _ _ _ n _ _ _ _ _ _

8. _ _ d _ _

9. _ _ _ _ t _ _ _ _

10. _ _ _ e _ _ _ _ _ _

11. _ c _ _ _

12. _ _ _ _ _ _ h _ _ _

13. _ n _ _ _ _ _ _

14. _ _ _ _ _ o _ _ _ _ _

15. _ _ _ _ _ _ _ l _ _ _

16. _ _ _ o _ _ _ _ _

g

y

## Spelling Words

1. radar
2. electrical
3. scuba
4. universe
5. chemical
6. scientists
7. sonar
8. instruments
9. atmosphere
10. experiments
11. hemisphere
12. environment
13. laser
14. probability
15. technological
16. molecules

**B.** Write a paragraph on a topic of your choice. Use at least five Spelling Words.

_____

_____

_____

_____

_____

_____

# Lesson 14: Latin Roots, I

| | | | |
|---|---|---|---|
| exported | imported | migrate | portable |
| predicting | dictator | supported | verdict |
| dictionaries | reservation | preservation | conservation |
| observatory | indictment | emigrate | immigration |

# Lesson 14: Latin Roots, I

Dear Parent or Guardian,
Your child _____ has just begun this spelling lesson. This week's test of words will be held on
_____ .
Please contact me if you have any questions. Use the Comment Box to make any comments on your child's progress, noting any words that he or she still needs to review.
Sincerely,
_____

## Spelling Words

1. exported
2. imported
3. migrate
4. portable
5. predicting
6. dictator
7. supported
8. verdict
9. dictionaries
10. reservation
11. preservation
12. conservation
13. observatory
14. indictment
15. emigrate
16. immigration

## Home Activity

Make a list of the Spelling Words. Beginning with the second letter of each word, substitute a blank for every other letter. Ask your child to complete the words by filling in the blanks.

COMMENT BOX

# Lesson 14: Latin Roots, I

**A.** Write the first ten Spelling Words in alphabetical order.

1. _ O _ _ _ _ _ _ _
2. _ _ _ _ _ _ O _ _ _ _ _ _
3. _ _ _ _ O _ _ _ _ _
4. _ _ _ _ _ _ O _ _
5. O _ _ _ _ _ _ _
6. _ _ O _ _ _ _ _
7. _ _ _ O _ _ _ _ _
8. _ _ _ _ _ _ _ O _ _
9. _ _ _ _ _ _ O _ _
10. _ _ _ O _ _

---

Now write all the circled letters. _____

Unscramble them to find another Spelling Word.

11. _____

---

Write the Spelling Word that matches each clue.

12. increases a country's population _____

13. opposite of "wasteful use" _____

14. opposite of "stay put" _____

15. place for stargazers _____

16. policy that will protect historic landmarks _____

**B.** Write a paragraph on a topic of your choice. Use at least five Spelling Words.

_____

_____

_____

_____

_____

_____

## Spelling Words

1. exported
2. imported
3. migrate
4. portable
5. predicting
6. dictator
7. supported
8. verdict
9. dictionaries
10. reservation
11. preservation
12. conservation
13. observatory
14. indictment
15. emigrate
16. immigration

# Lesson 15: More Related Words

| | | | |
|---|---|---|---|
| propose | proposition | disposed | disposition |
| combine | combination | patriots | patriotic |
| distribute | distribution | repeated | repetition |
| oblige | obligation | medicine | medicinal |

# Lesson 15: More Related Words

Dear Parent or Guardian,
   Your child _____ has just begun this
spelling lesson. This week's test of words will be held on
_____ .

   Please contact me if you have any questions. Use the
Comment Box to make any comments on your child's progress,
noting any words that he or she still needs to review.
   Sincerely,
   _____

## Spelling Words

1. propose
2. proposition
3. disposed
4. disposition
5. combine
6. combination
7. patriots
8. patriotic
9. distribute
10. distribution
11. repeated
12. repetition
13. oblige
14. obligation
15. medicine
16. medicinal

## Home Activity

With your child, write a pair of sentences for each pair of Spelling Words. For example, while your child writes a sentence using *propose*, you could write one using *proposition*. Read your sentences aloud, and continue with the next pair of Spelling Words.

**COMMENT BOX**

# Lesson 15: More Related Words

**A.** Say the Spelling Words to yourself in pairs. Then use the clues in parentheses to help you find the pair of related words that completes each sentence.

1. The schwa sound in _____ becomes a long *i* sound

   in _____.
   (It's all mixed up.)

2. The schwa sound in _____ becomes a short *o*

   sound in _____.
   (Nathan Hale)

3. The schwa sound in _____ becomes a long *e*

   sound in _____.
   (Could you say that again?)

4. The schwa sound in _____ becomes a long *i*

   sound in _____.
   (You must!)

5. The schwa sound in _____ becomes a long *o*

   sound in _____.
   (Are you asking me to marry you?)

6. The schwa sound in _____ becomes a short *i*

   sound in _____.
   (It's not supposed to taste good.)

7. The schwa sound in _____ becomes a short *i*

   sound in _____.
   (Give one to each.)

8. The schwa sound in _____ becomes a long *o*

   sound in _____.
   (Get rid of it!)

**B.** Write a paragraph on a topic of your choice. Use at least five Spelling Words.

_____

_____

_____

_____

_____

## Spelling Words

1. propose
2. proposition
3. disposed
4. disposition
5. combine
6. combination
7. patriots
8. patriotic
9. distribute
10. distribution
11. repeated
12. repetition
13. oblige
14. obligation
15. medicine
16. medicinal

# Lesson 16: Prefixes—Position, I

| protested | undertake | telegram | telegraph |
|-----------|-----------|----------|-----------|
| provisions | international | interview | telescopes |
| underlying | underneath | profitable | proceeds |
| intermediate | prosperity | interrupted | intercept |

# Lesson 16: Prefixes—Position, I

Dear Parent or Guardian,
    Your child _____ has just begun this spelling lesson. This week's test of words will be held on
_____ .
    Please contact me if you have any questions. Use the Comment Box to make any comments on your child's progress, noting any words that he or she still needs to review.
    Sincerely,
_____

## Spelling Words

1. protested
2. undertake
3. telegram
4. telegraph
5. provisions
6. international
7. interview
8. telescopes
9. underlying
10. underneath
11. profitable
12. proceeds
13. intermediate
14. prosperity
15. interrupted
16. intercept

## Home Activity

Prepare a flashcard for each Spelling Word. Show your child each card for a few seconds, and then place it facedown on the table. Ask your child to spell the word.

COMMENT BOX

# Lesson 16: Prefixes—Position, I

**A.** The answer to each clue in the puzzle is a Spelling Word.

## Spelling Words

1. *protested*
2. *undertake*
3. *telegram*
4. *telegraph*
5. *provisions*
6. *international*
7. *interview*
8. *telescopes*
9. *underlying*
10. *underneath*
11. *profitable*
12. *proceeds*
13. *intermediate*
14. *prosperity*
15. *interrupted*
16. *intercept*

**Across**

2. football word
6. instruments of astronomers
8. between extremes
9. supplies for a trip
10. opposite of over
11. often describes issues or reasons
12. invented by Samuel Morse

**Down**

1. goes forward
3. what most people want
4. reversed, this means "take below"
5. do well on this to get the job
7. bringing financial success

What's another way of saying "The chairperson complained when someone broke into the meeting of leaders from all over the world to read an urgent message"? Use four Spelling Words.

_____

_____

_____

**B.** Write a paragraph on a topic of your choice. Use at least five Spelling Words.

_____

_____

_____

_____

# Lesson 17: Prefixes—Position, II

| | | | |
|---|---|---|---|
| subway | subjected | subtracting | transportation |
| abstract | transaction | absolute | extravagant |
| subdued | abolished | translation | submerged |
| transferred | transient | extraordinary | extraterrestrial |

Dear Parent or Guardian,
    Your child _____ has just begun this spelling lesson. This week's test of words will be held on

_____ .

    Please contact me if you have any questions. Use the Comment Box to make any comments on your child's progress, noting any words that he or she still needs to review.
        Sincerely,

    _____

## Spelling Words

1. subway
2. subjected
3. subtracting
4. transportation
5. abstract
6. transaction
7. absolute
8. extravagant
9. subdued
10. abolished
11. translation
12. submerged
13. transferred
14. transient
15. extraordinary
16. extraterrestrial

**Home Activity**

Copy the list of Spelling Words, scrambling the letters in each word. Give the list to your child, and ask him or her to unscramble the letters in each word so that each spells a Spelling Word.

COMMENT BOX

# Lesson 17: Prefixes—Position, II

**A.** Replace each underlined word or phrase with a Spelling Word.

The (1) <u>underground means of traveling</u> is a fast method of (2) <u>transit</u>, (3) <u>taking away</u> the time you spend changing from one route to another. One day, after I had (4) <u>switched</u> from one route to another three times, my confusion was (5) <u>complete</u>. I said to myself, "Why have I (6) <u>exposed</u> myself to this!" Then I noticed a (7) <u>calm</u> passenger reading what looked like a French (8) <u>version</u> of a Sherlock Holmes mystery. "Are you French?" I asked. "Yes," he replied, smiling. "And a detective, too. Like Sherlock Holmes, I've been a (9) <u>temporary</u> guest in many places." As we talked, my spirits rose, and I heartily thanked the man. "Sir, you're (10) <u>overly generous</u> with your praise," he said. "I'm just a man who enjoys talking."

_____  _____

_____  _____

_____  _____

_____

Each clue below contains a prefix, a definition or synonym, and sometimes an extra hint. Write the Spelling Word that is formed by solving each word problem. An example is given.

*trans* + harbor + *ation* = <u>transportation</u>

*trans* + deed = _____

*extra* + common = _____

*extra* + *ter* + take a break − *t* + a legal action =

_____

*ab* + made smooth − *p* = _____

*abs* + plot of land = _____

*sub* + join + *d* = _____

**B.** Write a paragraph on a topic of your choice. Use at least five Spelling Words.

_____

_____

## Spelling Words

1. subway
2. subjected
3. subtracting
4. transportation
5. abstract
6. transaction
7. absolute
8. extravagant
9. subdued
10. abolished
11. translation
12. submerged
13. transferred
14. transient
15. extraordinary
16. extraterrestrial

# Lesson 18: Noun and Verb Endings

| | | | |
|---|---|---|---|
| debate | regulate | decorate | estimate |
| hesitate | demonstrate | investigate | delegate |
| concentrate | mandate | eliminate | advocate |
| simulate | participate | negotiate | phosphate |

# Lesson 18: Noun and Verb Endings

Dear Parent or Guardian,
    Your child _____ has just begun this spelling lesson. This week's test of words will be held on
_____ .
    Please contact me if you have any questions. Use the Comment Box to make any comments on your child's progress, noting any words that he or she still needs to review.
    Sincerely,
_____

## Spelling Words

1. debate
2. regulate
3. decorate
4. estimate
5. hesitate
6. demonstrate
7. investigate
8. delegate
9. concentrate
10. mandate
11. eliminate
12. advocate
13. simulate
14. participate
15. negotiate
16. phosphate

### Home Activity
Have your child write a phrase that describes or suggests each Spelling Word but does not include it. Then you can identify the Spelling Word that goes with each phrase. As an alternative, you may write the phrases and have your child identify the Spelling Words.

COMMENT BOX

# Lesson 18: Noun and Verb Endings

**A.** Write the Spelling Word that is a synonym of each word below.

remove _____    govern _____

show _____    support _____

adorn _____    falter _____

command _____    argue _____

If you use four of the letters from the word *fabricate*, you can spell the word *crab*. For each of the words below, find the Spelling Word that has the letters needed to make the word listed.

trap _____

slim _____

shop _____

mitt _____

once _____

deal _____

ingot _____

vine _____

**B.** Write a paragraph on a topic of your choice. Use at least five Spelling Words.

_____

_____

_____

_____

_____

_____

_____

_____

_____

_____

_____

_____

## Spelling Words

1. debate
2. regulate
3. decorate
4. estimate
5. hesitate
6. demonstrate
7. investigate
8. delegate
9. concentrate
10. mandate
11. eliminate
12. advocate
13. simulate
14. participate
15. negotiate
16. phosphate

# Lesson 20: Prefixes—Size and Amount

| | | | |
|---|---|---|---|
| microwave | microcomputer | multiplication | magnify |
| multicolored | magnitude | equality | multitude |
| microscopic | equation | multimedia | equator |
| microorganism | multicultural | magnificently | equivalent |

Dear Parent or Guardian,

Your child _____ has just begun this spelling lesson. This week's test of words will be held on

_____ .

Please contact me if you have any questions. Use the Comment Box to make any comments on your child's progress, noting any words that he or she still needs to review.

Sincerely,

_____

## Spelling Words

1. microwave
2. microcomputer
3. multiplication
4. magnify
5. multicolored
6. magnitude
7. equality
8. multitude
9. microscopic
10. equation
11. multimedia
12. equator
13. microorganism
14. multicultural
15. magnificently
16. equivalent

**Home Activity**
Prepare a simple definition for each Spelling Word. Read the definition, and ask your child to write the Spelling Word that corresponds to the definition.

COMMENT BOX

# Lesson 20: Prefixes—Size and Amount PRACTICE ACTIVITY

**A.** Write the Spelling Word that fits each clue.

**1.** It's a math operation that's the opposite of division.

_____

**2.** It's an imaginary line around the earth. _____

**3.** It's a plant or animal so small you can't see it without a special instrument. _____

**4.** This word describes anything too small to be seen without a special instrument. _____

**5.** Something that has many different hues is _____.

**6.** This describes doing things in a grand fashion. _____

**7.** It can be used to heat or cook food quickly. _____

**8.** Instruments that make things look larger than they really are do this. _____

**9.** It's a mathematical statement of quantities that are equal.

_____

**10.** This kind of show might include slides, recorded music, and live performers. _____

**11.** It's the size or extent of something. _____

**12.** It's a PC. _____

**13.** You can use this word to describe two things that are the same. _____

**14.** It's a crowd. _____

**15.** This represents members from many different cultures.

_____

**16.** It's the condition of being the same. _____

**B.** Write a paragraph on a topic of your choice. Use at least five Spelling Words.

_____

_____

_____

_____

_____

_____

## Spelling Words

1. microwave
2. microcomputer
3. multiplication
4. magnify
5. multicolored
6. magnitude
7. equality
8. multitude
9. microscopic
10. equation
11. multimedia
12. equator
13. microorganism
14. multicultural
15. magnificently
16. equivalent

# Lesson 21: Double Consonants

| | | | |
|---|---|---|---|
| chattering | uttered | triggered | terrific |
| scattering | polluted | summoned | satellite |
| vaccination | intellectual | narrative | penniless |
| parallel | embassy | exaggerated | torrential |

# Lesson 21: Double Consonants

Dear Parent or Guardian,
    Your child _____ has just begun this spelling lesson. This week's test of words will be held on

_____ .

    Please contact me if you have any questions. Use the Comment Box to make any comments on your child's progress, noting any words that he or she still needs to review.
    Sincerely,

_____

## Spelling Words

1. chattering
2. uttered
3. triggered
4. terrific
5. scattering
6. polluted
7. summoned
8. satellite
9. vaccination
10. intellectual
11. narrative
12. penniless
13. parallel
14. embassy
15. exaggerated
16. torrential

## Home Activity

Scramble the letters in each word from the list of Spelling Words. Give the list to your child, and ask him or her to unscramble the words so that each spells a Spelling Word.

COMMENT BOX

# Lesson 21: Double Consonants

**A.** The middle letters in these Spelling Words are represented by *s. Write each word, adding the correct letters.

1. t r * * * * * e d _____
2. p a * * * * e l _____
3. p e * * * * * s s _____
4. e m * * * * y _____
5. s c * * * * * * n g _____
6. n a * * * * * v e _____
7. t o * * * * * * a l _____
8. u t * * * e d _____
9. s a * * * * * t e _____
10. c h * * * * *i n g _____
11. e x * * * * * * * * e d _____
12. s u * * * * e d _____
13. i n * * * * * * * * * a l _____
14. v a * * * * * * * * o n _____
15. p o * * * * e d _____
16. t e * * * * i c _____

**B.** Write a paragraph on a topic of your choice. Use at least five Spelling Words.

_____
_____
_____
_____
_____
_____
_____
_____
_____
_____
_____
_____
_____
_____

## Spelling Words

1. chattering
2. uttered
3. triggered
4. terrific
5. scattering
6. polluted
7. summoned
8. satellite
9. vaccination
10. intellectual
11. narrative
12. penniless
13. parallel
14. embassy
15. exaggerated
16. torrential

# Lesson 22: Noun Endings

| | | | |
|---|---|---|---|
| poverty | royalty | journalism | rivalry |
| tourism | loyalty | robbery | uncertainty |
| patriotism | cruelty | specialty | realism |
| novelty | optimism | mechanism | criticism |

# Lesson 22: Noun Endings

Dear Parent or Guardian,
    Your child _____ has just begun this
spelling lesson. This week's test of words will be held on
_____ .
    Please contact me if you have any questions. Use the
Comment Box to make any comments on your child's progress,
noting any words that he or she still needs to review.
    Sincerely,

_____

## Spelling Words

1. poverty
2. royalty
3. journalism
4. rivalry
5. tourism
6. loyalty
7. robbery
8. uncertainty
9. patriotism
10. cruelty
11. specialty
12. realism
13. novelty
14. optimism
15. mechanism
16. criticism

## Home Activity

For each Spelling Word that begins with a consonant, have
your child write a sentence using alliteration. Several words in
the sentence should have the same initial sound as the
Spelling Word—for example, *Jane Jordan just joined a journalism
club.*

COMMENT BOX

# Lesson 22: Noun Endings

**A.** Fill in the crossword puzzle with Spelling Words that fit the clues.

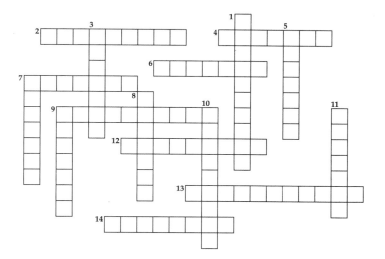

## Spelling Words

1. poverty
2. royalty
3. journalism
4. rivalry
5. tourism
6. loyalty
7. robbery
8. uncertainty
9. patriotism
10. cruelty
11. specialty
12. realism
13. novelty
14. optimism
15. mechanism
16. criticism

**Across**

2. an outstanding talent
4. people of noble rank
6. competition
7. unlawful taking of property
9. love of one's country
12. unfavorable comment
13. doubt
14. a tendency to see the bright side of everything

**Down**

1. the occupation of writing or editing a newspaper
3. pitiless behavior
5. the condition of remaining faithful to family and friends
7. a tendency to face facts
8. traveling for pleasure
9. the condition of being very poor
10. a working part of a machine
11. something new or different

**B.** Write a paragraph on a topic of your choice. Use at least five Spelling Words.

_____

_____

_____

_____

_____

_____

_____

_____

_____

# Lesson 23: Prefix *ob-*

| | | | |
|---|---|---|---|
| oblong | observation | objection | objective |
| occupation | obtained | offering | obviously |
| offensive | opportunity | obscure | occupant |
| obstacle | opposition | obsessions | occasionally |

Dear Parent or Guardian,
    Your child _____ has just begun this spelling lesson. This week's test of words will be held on

_____ .

    Please contact me if you have any questions. Use the Comment Box to make any comments on your child's progress, noting any words that he or she still needs to review.
    Sincerely,

_____

## Spelling Words

1. oblong
2. observation
3. objection
4. objective
5. occupation
6. obtained
7. offering
8. obviously
9. offensive
10. opportunity
11. obscure
12. occupant
13. obstacle
14. opposition
15. obsessions
16. occasionally

### Home Activity
Have your child make a word-search puzzle by writing the Spelling Words horizontally or vertically in a grid of cells. One letter should be written in each cell. The remaining cells should be filled with letters chosen at random. A family member can work the puzzle.

**COMMENT BOX**

# Lesson 23: Prefix *ob-*

**A.** The vowels have been left out of these Spelling Words. Write each word by adding the missing vowels.

1. ccptn _____
2. ffrng _____
3. pprtnt _____
4. ccpnt _____
5. blng _____
6. bjctv _____
7. bsssns _____
8. ffnsv _____
9. bjctn _____
10. bvsl _____
11. bscr _____
12. bsrvtn _____
13. bstcl _____
14. ccsnll _____
15. btnd _____
16. ppstn _____

## Spelling Words

1. oblong
2. observation
3. objection
4. objective
5. occupation
6. obtained
7. offering
8. obviously
9. offensive
10. opportunity
11. obscure
12. occupant
13. obstacle
14. opposition
15. obsessions
16. occasionally

**B.** Write a paragraph on a topic of your choice. Use at least five Spelling Words.

_____
_____
_____
_____
_____
_____
_____
_____
_____
_____
_____
_____

# Lesson 25: Prefixes—Position, III

| | | | |
|---|---|---|---|
| introduction | intramural | perfectly | circulation |
| perimeter | circumstances | permanently | circumference |
| perception | intrastate | introvert | perspective |
| periodic | peripheral | persuaded | circuit |

# Lesson 25: Prefixes—Position, III

Dear Parent or Guardian,
    Your child _____ has just begun this spelling lesson. This week's test of words will be held on
_____ .
    Please contact me if you have any questions. Use the Comment Box to make any comments on your child's progress, noting any words that he or she still needs to review.
    Sincerely,
_____

## Spelling Words

1. introduction
2. intramural
3. perfectly
4. circulation
5. perimeter
6. circumstances
7. permanently
8. circumference
9. perception
10. intrastate
11. introvert
12. perspective
13. periodic
14. peripheral
15. persuaded
16. circuit

## Home Activity

For each Spelling Word, write two words that can be formed from the letters. For example, *permanently* includes the letters of the words *man* and *rent*. Have your child identify and write the Spelling Word from which each pair of words is formed.

COMMENT BOX

ELEMENTS OF LANGUAGE | Second Course | *Spelling Teacher's Guide*

# Lesson 25: Prefixes—Position, III

**A.** Complete each analogy with a Spelling Word.

1. _____ : end :: preface : conclusion

2. _____ : temporarily :: often : seldom

3. _____ : central :: outside : inside

4. area : inside :: _____ : outside

5. praise : compliment :: _____ : convinced

6. intermittent : _____ :: calm : peaceful

7. faultlessly : _____ :: quickly : rapidly

8. _____ : electricity :: pipe : water

9. braggart : _____ :: boastful : withdrawn

10. lungs : respiration :: heart : _____

Unscramble these words.

11. mralnutair _____

12. teerpecivps _____

13. asnatirtet _____

14. eitperonpc _____

15. unrasccseitmc _____

16. ucrcemnifecer _____

**B.** Write a paragraph on a topic of your choice. Use at least five Spelling Words.

_____

_____

_____

_____

_____

_____

_____

_____

_____

_____

_____

## Spelling Words

1. introduction
2. intramural
3. perfectly
4. circulation
5. perimeter
6. circumstances
7. permanently
8. circumference
9. perception
10. intrastate
11. introvert
12. perspective
13. periodic
14. peripheral
15. persuaded
16. circuit

# Lesson 26: More Greek Word Parts

| | | | |
|---|---|---|---|
| automobiles | policy | archives | scholastic |
| politics | sophisticated | metropolitan | optic |
| scholarship | philosopher | optical | optometrist |
| archaic | automatically | sophomore | archaeologist |

# Lesson 26: More Greek Word Parts

HOME ACTIVITY

Dear Parent or Guardian,
Your child _____ has just begun this
spelling lesson. This week's test of words will be held on

_____ .

Please contact me if you have any questions. Use the
Comment Box to make any comments on your child's progress,
noting any words that he or she still needs to review.
Sincerely,

_____

## Spelling Words

1. automobiles
2. policy
3. archives
4. scholastic
5. politics
6. sophisticated
7. metropolitan
8. optic
9. scholarship
10. philosopher
11. optical
12. optometrist
13. archaic
14. automatically
15. sophomore
16. archaeologist

**Home Activity**
Make a list of the Spelling Words. Beginning with the second
letter of each word, substitute a blank for every other letter.
Ask your child to complete the words by filling in the blanks.

COMMENT BOX

Copyright © by Holt, Rinehart and Winston. All rights reserved.

LESSON 26 | More Greek Word Parts | Home Activity

**157**

# Lesson 26: More Greek Word Parts

**A.** • Which words are derived from the Greek word for "sight"?

_____

• Which words include a Greek root that means "first in time" or "first in rank"?

_____

• Which words are derived from the Greek word for "city"?

_____

• Which words are derived from a Greek word meaning "wise"?

_____

• Which words are derived from a Greek word meaning "school"?

_____

• Which words include the Greek word for "self"?

_____

**B.** Write a paragraph on a topic of your choice. Use at least five Spelling Words.

_____

_____

_____

_____

_____

_____

_____

_____

_____

_____

_____

## Spelling Words

1. automobiles
2. policy
3. archives
4. scholastic
5. politics
6. sophisticated
7. metropolitan
8. optic
9. scholarship
10. philosopher
11. optical
12. optometrist
13. archaic
14. automatically
15. sophomore
16. archaeologist

# Lesson 27: Words from Other Languages, I  WORD CARDS

| | | | |
|---|---|---|---|
| landscape | cargo | piano | opera |
| carnival | chipmunk | parakeet | monsoon |
| hickory | heroic | skeleton | spaghetti |
| walrus | yacht | macaroni | barbecue |

Dear Parent or Guardian,
    Your child _____ has just begun this spelling lesson. This week's test of words will be held on

_____ .

    Please contact me if you have any questions. Use the Comment Box to make any comments on your child's progress, noting any words that he or she still needs to review.
    Sincerely,

    _____

## Spelling Words

1. landscape
2. cargo
3. piano
4. opera
5. carnival
6. chipmunk
7. parakeet
8. monsoon
9. hickory
10. heroic
11. skeleton
12. spaghetti
13. walrus
14. yacht
15. macaroni
16. barbecue

**Home Activity**

Write riddles for four Spelling Words. Have your child write the Spelling Word that solves each riddle. Then switch roles. Continue with the remaining Spelling Words. An example riddle is *I hold the keys to music. (piano)*

### COMMENT BOX

# Lesson 27: Words from Other Languages, I PRACTICE ACTIVITY

**A.** Use one or more Spelling Words to complete each series.

chestnut, oak, _____

noodles, _____ _____

squirrel, woodchuck, _____

concert, play, _____

parrot, canary, _____

hurricane, tornado, _____

seal, dolphin, _____

trumpet, violin, _____

canoe, schooner, _____

Find the Spelling Word that has the letters needed to make each of the words below.

note _____          cog _____

chore _____        larva _____

sled _____          race _____

**B.** Write a paragraph on a topic of your choice. Use at least five Spelling Words.

_____

_____

_____

_____

_____

_____

_____

_____

_____

_____

_____

_____

_____

_____

_____

## Spelling Words

1. landscape
2. cargo
3. piano
4. opera
5. carnival
6. chipmunk
7. parakeet
8. monsoon
9. hickory
10. heroic
11. skeleton
12. spaghetti
13. walrus
14. yacht
15. macaroni
16. barbecue

# Lesson 28: More Related Words

| | | | |
|---|---|---|---|
| supermarket | superpower | alto | altitude |
| geographic | astronauts | geology | geometry |
| supervision | nautical | navigation | odometer |
| asterisk | altimeter | cosmonauts | seismometer |

# Lesson 28: More Related Words

Dear Parent or Guardian,
    Your child _____ has just begun this
spelling lesson. This week's test of words will be held on
_____ .
    Please contact me if you have any questions. Use the
Comment Box to make any comments on your child's progress,
noting any words that he or she still needs to review.
    Sincerely,
    _____

## Spelling Words

1. supermarket
2. superpower
3. alto
4. altitude
5. geographic
6. astronauts
7. geology
8. geometry
9. supervision
10. nautical
11. navigation
12. odometer
13. asterisk
14. altimeter
15. cosmonauts
16. seismometer

### Home Activity

Make up a question using each Spelling Word. (For example, "From which supermarket did you buy that food?") Ask the questions orally, and have your child answer each in writing, using the same Spelling Word in the answer.

COMMENT BOX

PRACTICE ACTIVITY

# Lesson 28: More Related Words

**A.** Write the Spelling Word that answers each question.

What instrument is used to predict and study earthquakes?

_____

What instrument is used to measure height?

_____

What instrument is used to measure distance traveled?

_____

What is another word for the "star" symbol on a keyboard?

_____

What is the study of the earth's features and history called?

_____

What are two words for people who travel in space?

_____

_____

What is the science of getting ships from place to place called?

_____

What branch of mathematics deals with the measurement of lines, angles, and shapes? _____

What is another word for *height*? _____

You can write in code by leaving out all the vowels in a word, and then substituting the next letter in the alphabet for each letter that remains in the word. For example, WORD becomes XSE if you drop the O and replace W with X, R with S, and D with E. Write the Spelling Word for each coded word below.

HHSQUID _____  TQSNSLU _____
TQSQXS _____  MU _____
OUDM _____  TQSWTO _____

**B.** Write a paragraph on a topic of your choice. Use at least five Spelling Words.

_____

_____

_____

_____

_____

_____

_____

## Spelling Words

1. supermarket
2. superpower
3. alto
4. altitude
5. geographic
6. astronauts
7. geology
8. geometry
9. supervision
10. nautical
11. navigation
12. odometer
13. asterisk
14. altimeter
15. cosmonauts
16. seismometer

# Lesson 30: Words from Names

| | | | |
|---|---|---|---|
| sandwich | hamburger | mercury | tuxedo |
| spoonerism | malapropism | sequoia | boycott |
| mackintosh | frankfurter | pasteurize | Braille |
| Celsius | Fahrenheit | odyssey | zeppelin |

# Lesson 30: Words from Names

Dear Parent or Guardian,
Your child _____ has just begun this spelling lesson. This week's test of words will be held on
_____ .

Please contact me if you have any questions. Use the Comment Box to make any comments on your child's progress, noting any words that he or she still needs to review.
Sincerely,

_____

## Spelling Words

1. sandwich
2. hamburger
3. mercury
4. tuxedo
5. spoonerism
6. malapropism
7. sequoia
8. boycott
9. mackintosh
10. frankfurter
11. pasteurize
12. Braille
13. Celsius
14. Fahrenheit
15. odyssey
16. zeppelin

## Home Activity

Ask your child to create a crossword puzzle using the Spelling Words. Your child may use either the definition or a synonym of each Spelling Word to write the clues. You or another family member can solve the puzzle.

COMMENT BOX

# Lesson 30: Words from Names

**A.** Write the Spelling Word that fits each clue.

1. A man might wear this to a party. _____

2. It's made from ground beef. _____

3. You read this writing with your fingers. _____

4. You make this kind of mistake when you mix up the sounds of words. _____

5. You and your friends might do this to the products of a company you think is unfair. _____

6. It's a long journey, filled with adventures.

_____

7. It's a kind of evergreen. _____

8. In this temperature scale, 32 degrees marks the freezing point of water. _____

9. In this temperature scale, 0 degrees marks the freezing point of water. _____

10. It's a kind of coat. _____

11. It's similar to a blimp. _____

12. You make this kind of mistake when you unintentionally use the wrong word. _____

13. It's the metallic element used in thermometers.

_____

14. Dairies do this to destroy bacteria in milk.

_____

15. It's a kind of sausage. _____

16. It's two slices of bread enclosing almost any kind of filling.

_____

**B.** Write a paragraph on a topic of your choice. Use at least five Spelling Words.

_____

_____

## Spelling Words

1. sandwich
2. hamburger
3. mercury
4. tuxedo
5. spoonerism
6. malapropism
7. sequoia
8. boycott
9. mackintosh
10. frankfurter
11. pasteurize
12. Braille
13. Celsius
14. Fahrenheit
15. odyssey
16. zeppelin

# Lesson 31: Latin Roots, II

| | | | |
|---|---|---|---|
| conducted | educate | container | adjust |
| detained | sentimental | productive | deceived |
| attended | adjustments | justice | acceptable |
| acceptance | sensation | sensory | perceived |

ELEMENTS OF LANGUAGE | Second Course | *Spelling Teacher's Guide*

# Lesson 31: Latin Roots, II

Dear Parent or Guardian,
    Your child _____ has just begun this spelling lesson. This week's test of words will be held on

_____ .

    Please contact me if you have any questions. Use the Comment Box to make any comments on your child's progress, noting any words that he or she still needs to review.
        Sincerely,

    _____

## Spelling Words

1. conducted
2. educate
3. container
4. adjust
5. detained
6. sentimental
7. productive
8. deceived
9. attended
10. adjustments
11. justice
12. acceptable
13. acceptance
14. sensation
15. sensory
16. perceived

## Home Activity

For each Spelling Word, think of a synonym or antonym. Say the synonym or antonym, and ask your child to write the corresponding Spelling Word.

COMMENT BOX

# Lesson 31: Latin Roots, II

**A.** Fill in the missing vowels to reveal the Spelling Word.

1. *tt*nd*d _____

2. *cc*pt*nc* _____

3. s*ns*t**n _____

4. c*nd*ct*d _____

5. p*rc**v*d _____

6. *dj*st _____

7. j*st*c* _____

8. s*ns*r* _____

9. *d*c*t _____

10. *cc*pt*bl* _____

11. c*nt**n*r _____

12. *dj*stm*nts _____

13. pr*d*ct*v* _____

14. d*t**n*d _____

15. d*c**v*d _____

16. s*nt*m*nt*l _____

**B.** Write a paragraph on a topic of your choice. Use at least five Spelling Words.

_____
_____
_____
_____
_____
_____
_____
_____
_____
_____
_____
_____

## Spelling Words

1. conducted
2. educate
3. container
4. adjust
5. detained
6. sentimental
7. productive
8. deceived
9. attended
10. adjustments
11. justice
12. acceptable
13. acceptance
14. sensation
15. sensory
16. perceived

# Lesson 32: Noun Endings—Diminutives

| | | | |
|---|---|---|---|
| booklet | tablet | leaflet | packet |
| yearling | diskette | luncheonette | particle |
| icicle | sapling | banquet | cabinet |
| bracelet | cassette | pamphlet | statuette |

# Lesson 32: Noun Endings—Diminutives HOME ACTIVITY

Dear Parent or Guardian,
    Your child _____ has just begun this spelling lesson. This week's test of words will be held on

_____ .

    Please contact me if you have any questions. Use the Comment Box to make any comments on your child's progress, noting any words that he or she still needs to review.
    Sincerely,

_____

## Spelling Words

1. booklet
2. tablet
3. leaflet
4. packet
5. yearling
6. diskette
7. luncheonette
8. particle
9. icicle
10. sapling
11. banquet
12. cabinet
13. bracelet
14. cassette
15. pamphlet
16. statuette

**Home Activity**
Ask your child to use the Spelling Words to create a word-search puzzle. You may also create one. Then solve each other's word-search puzzles.

COMMENT BOX

Copyright © by Holt, Rinehart and Winston. All rights reserved.

**172**   ELEMENTS OF LANGUAGE | Second Course | Spelling Teacher's Guide

# Lesson 32: Noun Endings–Diminutives

**A.** Fill in this crossword puzzle with the Spelling Words that fit the clues.

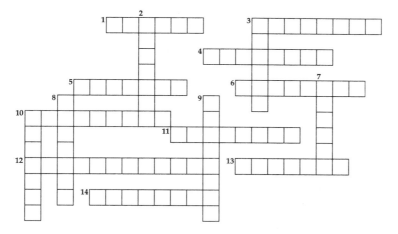

## Spelling Words

1. booklet
2. tablet
3. leaflet
4. packet
5. yearling
6. diskette
7. luncheonette
8. particle
9. icicle
10. sapling
11. banquet
12. cabinet
13. bracelet
14. cassette
15. pamphlet
16. statuette

**Across**

1. a pad of paper
3. a very small piece
4. jewelry to be worn on the wrist
5. a small, printed sheet of paper, usually folded
6. an animal between one and two years old
10. a small statue
11. a case holding a spool of tape for insertion into a tape recorder
12. a small restaurant
13. a formal dinner
14. a booklet with a paper cover

**Down**

2. a small book
3. a small package
7. a hanging rod of ice
8. a piece of furniture fitted with shelves
9. a floppy disk
10. a young tree

**B.** Write a paragraph on a topic of your choice. Use at least five Spelling Words.

_____

_____

_____

_____

_____

_____

_____

# Lesson 33: Latin Roots, III

| | | | |
|---|---|---|---|
| confined | territories | refining | terrace |
| duplicate | financial | complicated | vocal |
| conjunction | infinite | vocabulary | vocational |
| definitely | territorial | juncture | applicable |

Dear Parent or Guardian,
    Your child _____ has just begun this
spelling lesson. This week's test of words will be held on
_____ .
    Please contact me if you have any questions. Use the
Comment Box to make any comments on your child's progress,
noting any words that he or she still needs to review.
    Sincerely,
    _____

## Spelling Words

1. confined
2. territories
3. refining
4. terrace
5. duplicate
6. financial
7. complicated
8. vocal
9. conjunction
10. infinite
11. vocabulary
12. vocational
13. definitely
14. territorial
15. juncture
16. applicable

### Home Activity

Write a sentence for each Spelling Word. Read each sentence, leaving out the Spelling Word. Ask your child to write the Spelling Word that best completes each sentence.

COMMENT BOX

# Lesson 33: Latin Roots, III

**A.** Write the Spelling Word that best fits each definition.

1. made difficult to understand _____
2. a small porch or balcony _____
3. suitable _____
4. the fact of joining together _____
5. having to do with an occupation or trade

   _____
6. kept shut in _____
7. limited to a particular region _____
8. having to do with money _____
9. having no limits _____
10. making more pure _____
11. the total number of words a person knows and can use

    _____
12. without question _____
13. a joint or union _____
14. geographical areas _____
15. having to do with the voice _____
16. an exact copy _____

**B.** Write a paragraph on a topic of your choice. Use at least five Spelling Words.

_____
_____
_____
_____
_____
_____
_____
_____
_____
_____

## Spelling Words

1. confined
2. territories
3. refining
4. terrace
5. duplicate
6. financial
7. complicated
8. vocal
9. conjunction
10. infinite
11. vocabulary
12. vocational
13. definitely
14. territorial
15. juncture
16. applicable

# Lesson 34: Words from Other Languages, II WORD CARDS

| | | | |
|---|---|---|---|
| parka | mammoth | pretzel | waffle |
| igloo | karate | harpoon | kimono |
| kindergarten | caucus | toboggan | kayak |
| tundra | persimmon | hibachi | haiku |

# Lesson 34: Words from Other Languages, II HOME ACTIVITY

Dear Parent or Guardian,
    Your child _____ has just begun this spelling lesson. This week's test of words will be held on
_____ .
    Please contact me if you have any questions. Use the Comment Box to make any comments on your child's progress, noting any words that he or she still needs to review.
    Sincerely,

_____

## Spelling Words

1. parka
2. mammoth
3. pretzel
4. waffle
5. igloo
6. karate
7. harpoon
8. kimono
9. kindergarten
10. caucus
11. toboggan
12. kayak
13. tundra
14. persimmon
15. hibachi
16. haiku

**Home Activity**
Ask your child to write sentence-acrostics for several Spelling Words: After choosing a Spelling Word, your child should write a word that starts with each letter. The words should form a sentence. For example, _Karen and Ron ate the eggs._ (karate)

COMMENT BOX

# Lesson 34: Words from Other Languages, II PRACTICE ACTIVITY

**A.** Write the Spelling Word that fits each word shape.

1.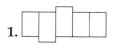
2.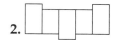
3.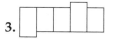
4.
5.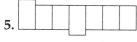
6.
7.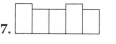
8.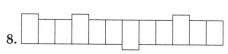
9.
10.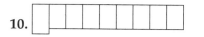
11.
12.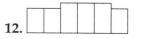
13.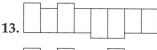
14.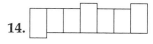
15.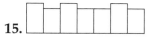
16.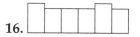

**B.** Write a paragraph on a topic of your choice. Use at least five Spelling Words.

## Spelling Words

1. parka
2. mammoth
3. pretzel
4. waffle
5. igloo
6. karate
7. harpoon
8. kimono
9. kindergarten
10. caucus
11. toboggan
12. kayak
13. tundra
14. persimmon
15. hibachi
16. haiku

# Lesson 35: Suffixes in Combination

| | | | |
|---|---|---|---|
| aimlessly | carelessly | peacefulness | loneliness |
| historically | favorably | eventually | governmental |
| fortunately | economically | architectural | sensationally |
| naturalization | significantly | mysteriously | rhythmically |

# Lesson 35: Suffixes in Combination

Dear Parent or Guardian,
    Your child _____ has just begun this spelling lesson. This week's test of words will be held on
_____ .
    Please contact me if you have any questions. Use the Comment Box to make any comments on your child's progress, noting any words that he or she still needs to review.
    Sincerely,
_____

## Spelling Words

1. aimlessly
2. carelessly
3. peacefulness
4. loneliness
5. historically
6. favorably
7. eventually
8. governmental
9. fortunately
10. economically
11. architectural
12. sensationally
13. naturalization
14. significantly
15. mysteriously
16. rhythmically

## Home Activity

Prepare a flashcard for each Spelling Word. Show your child each card for a few seconds, and then place it facedown on the table. Ask your child to spell the word.

COMMENT BOX

# Lesson 35: Suffixes in Combination

**A.** Find the Spelling Words in this word-search puzzle. The word may be written down, up, across, or diagonally. Circle the word, and then write it on the line.

```
c f k u n a t u r a l i z a t i o n s
s i g n i f i c a n t l y e r d g m y
i r l v w e a i m l e s s l y d h l l
y x a g v p n v g m s r e t u o i p s
l z r o u s t l o n e l i n e s s b u
e b u v s t r m o r g u i p c s t l o
t y t e j m r u c h a g h i e n o d i
a v c r x o o w l i n b d n b n r i r
n s e n s a t i o n a l l y d y i s e
u r t m t y q u i b e u n y v r c h t
t j i e n y p w i u f a a c d n a s s
r e h n a v a l x e v e n t u a l l y
o r c t p d s t c n o i s m r i l l m
f a r a x u c a r e l e s s l y y z o
y i a l n q e c o n o m i c a l l y t
s y o u n p r h y t h m i c a l l y o
```

## Spelling Words

1. aimlessly _____
2. carelessly _____
3. peacefulness _____
4. loneliness _____
5. historically _____
6. favorably _____
7. eventually _____
8. governmental _____
9. fortunately _____
10. economically _____
11. architectural _____
12. sensationally _____
13. naturalization _____
14. significantly _____
15. mysteriously _____
16. rhythmically _____

1. _____
2. _____
3. _____
4. _____
5. _____
6. _____
7. _____
8. _____

9. _____
10. _____
11. _____
12. _____
13. _____
14. _____
15. _____
16. _____

**B.** Write a paragraph on a topic of your choice. Use at least five Spelling Words.

_____

_____

_____

_____

ELEMENTS OF LANGUAGE | Second Course | *Spelling Teacher's Guide*

# Answer Key for Practice Activities

**p. 95 | Lesson 1: Compound Words**

**A.**
1. picnic basket
2. evergreen
3. loudspeaker
4. gingerbread
5. homesick
6. handkerchief
7. good-natured
8. long-term
9. well-wisher
10. furthermore
11. headquarters
12. homemade
13. heart attack
14. underground
15. large-scale
16. stagecoach

**B.** *(Answers will vary.)*

**p. 98 | Lesson 2: Homophones**

**A.**
1. capital, Capitol
2. palette, pallet
3. boarder, border
4. fowl, foul
5. principal, principle
6. stationary, stationery
7. bard, barred
8. burro, burrow

**B.** *(Answers will vary.)*

**p. 101 | Lesson 3: Adding Endings to Words**

**A.**
1. refused
2. separating
3. abilities
4. submitted
5. potatoes
6. produced
7. programming
8. resources
9. omitted
10. petrified
11. harvesting
12. justified
13. contained
14. nutrients
15. forbidding
16. acquired

**B.** *(Answers will vary.)*

**p. 104 | Lesson 4: Related Words**

**A.**
1. drama, dramatic, dramatically
2. strain, strenuous, strenuously
3. continue, continuous, continuously
4. awe, awful, awfully
5. despair, desperately
6. profession, professionally

**B.** *(Answers will vary.)*

**p. 107 | Lesson 5: Easily Confused Words**

**A.**
1. breath, breadth
2. finally, finely
3. bizarre, bazaar
4. anecdote, antidote
5. prosecuted, persecuted
6. feudal, futile
7. conscious, conscience
8. access, excess

**B.** *(Answers will vary.)*

**p. 110 | Lesson 6: Prefixes *ad-, in-***

**A.** *Across, top to bottom:* illustrated, approved, accomplished, investigated, advice, included, irrigated, irresponsible; *Down, left to right:* inspection, agreeable, affectionate; *Up, left to right:* arrested, insisted, impressed; *Diagonal:* announcement, improved

**B.** *(Answers will vary.)*

**p. 113 | Lesson 8: Words from French**

**A.**
1. chauffeur
2. depot
3. blouse
4. coup
5. amateur
6. elite
7. pigeon
8. surgeon
9. croquet
10. perfume
11. plateau
12. suite
13. crochet
14. embarrassed
15. debris
16. matinee

**B.** *(Answers will vary.)*

**p. 116 | Lesson 9: Adjective Endings**

**A.**
1. contented
2. barefooted
3. stupid
4. rigid
5. horrid
6. undersized
7. ragged
8. passionate
9. crooked
10. democratic
11. historic
12. magnetic
13. confederate
14. electronic
15. poetic
16. metallic

**B.** *(Answers will vary.)*

**p. 119 | Lesson 10: Greek Word Parts**

**A.**
1. synonyms
2. recycle
3. cyclone
4. symphony
5. genius
6. genes
7. symbolic
8. microphone
9. sympathetic
10. phonograph
11. telephones
12. symptoms
13. generator
14. cycle
15. synthetic
16. generation

**B.** *(Answers will vary.)*

**p. 122 | Lesson 11: Words from Greek**

**A.**
1. physical
2. labyrinth
3. alphabet
4. episode
5. rhythm
6. phenomenon
7. melancholy
8. marathon
9. architecture
10. chorus
11. arithmetic
12. philosophy
13. pneumonia
14. heroes
15. aroma
16. stadium

**B.** *(Answers will vary.)*

# Answer Key for Practice Activities *(continued)*

**p. 125 | Lesson 12: Science/Technology Words**

**A.**
1. chemical
2. electrical
3. instruments
4. molecules
5. laser
6. sonar
7. technological
8. radar
9. scientists
10. experiments
11. scuba
12. hemisphere
13. universe
14. environment
15. probability
16. atmosphere

**B.** *(Answers will vary.)*

**p. 128 | Lesson 14: Latin Roots, I**

**A.**
1. dictator
2. dictionaries
3. exported
4. imported
5. migrate
6. portable
7. predicting
8. reservation
9. supported
10. verdict

Circled letters: intdmtcnei

11. indictment
12. immigration
13. conservation
14. emigrate
15. observatory
16. preservation

**B.** *(Answers will vary.)*

**p. 131 | Lesson 15: More Related Words**

**A.**
1. combination, combine
2. patriots, patriotic
3. repetition, repeated
4. obligation, oblige
5. proposition, propose
6. medicine, medicinal
7. distribution, distribute
8. disposition, disposed

**B.** *(Answers will vary.)*

**p. 134 | Lesson 16: Prefixes—Position, I**

**A.** ACROSS: **2.** intercept **6.** telescopes **8.** intermediate **9.** provisions **10.** underneath **11.** underlying **12.** telegraph
DOWN: **1.** proceeds **3.** prosperity **4.** undertake **5.** interview **7.** profitable

The chairperson *protested* when someone *interrupted* the meeting of *international* leaders to read an urgent *telegram*.

**B.** *(Answers will vary.)*

**p. 137 | Lesson 17: Prefixes—Position, II**

**A.**
1. subway
2. transportation
3. subtracting
4. transferred
5. absolute
6. subjected
7. subdued
8. translation
9. transient
10. extravagant

transaction, extraordinary, extraterrestrial, abolished, abstract, submerged

**B.** *(Answers will vary.)*

**p. 140 | Lesson 18: Noun and Verb Endings**

**A.** *(column 1)* eliminate, demonstrate, decorate, mandate
*(column 2)* regulate, advocate, hesitate, debate
participate, simulate, phosphate, estimate, concentrate, delegate, negotiate, investigate

**B.** *(Answers will vary.)*

**p. 143 | Lesson 20: Prefixes—Size and Amount**

**A.**
1. multiplication
2. equator
3. microorganism
4. microscopic
5. multicolored
6. magnificently
7. microwave
8. magnify
9. equation
10. multimedia
11. magnitude
12. microcomputer
13. equivalent
14. multitude
15. multicultural
16. equality

**B.** *(Answers will vary.)*

**p. 146 | Lesson 21: Double Consonants**

**A.**
1. triggered
2. parallel
3. penniless
4. embassy
5. scattering
6. narrative
7. torrential
8. uttered
9. satellite
10. chattering
11. exaggerated
12. summoned
13. intellectual
14. vaccination
15. polluted
16. terrific

**B.** *(Answers will vary.)*

**p. 149 | Lesson 22: Noun Endings**

**A.** ACROSS: **2.** specialty **4.** royalty **6.** rivalry **7.** robbery **9.** patriotism **12.** criticism **13.** uncertainty **14.** optimism
DOWN: **1.** journalism **3.** cruelty **5.** loyalty **7.** realism **8.** tourism **9.** poverty **10.** mechanism **11.** novelty

**B.** *(Answers will vary.)*

**p. 152 | Lesson 23: Prefix *ob-***

**A.**
1. occupation
2. offering
3. opportunity

# Answer Key for Practice Activities *(continued)*

4. occupant
5. oblong
6. objective
7. obsessions
8. offensive
9. objection
10. obviously
11. obscure
12. observation
13. obstacle
14. occasionally
15. obtained
16. opposition

**B.** *(Answers will vary.)*

## p. 155 | Lesson 25: Prefixes—Position, III

**A.**
1. introduction
2. permanently
3. peripheral
4. perimeter
5. persuaded
6. periodic
7. perfectly
8. circuit
9. introvert
10. circulation
11. intramural
12. perspective
13. intrastate
14. perception
15. circumstances
16. circumference

**B.** *(Answers will vary.)*

## p. 158 | Lesson 26: More Greek Word Parts

**A.** optic, optical, optometrist
archives, archaic, archaeologist
policy, politics, metropolitan
sophisticated, philosopher, sophomore
scholastic, scholarship
automobiles, automatically

**B.** *(Answers will vary.)*

## p. 161 | Lesson 27: Words from Other Languages, I

**A.** hickory
spaghetti, macaroni
chipmunk
opera
parakeet
monsoon
walrus
piano
yacht
(left to right) skeleton, cargo, heroic,
carnival, landscape, barbecue

**B.** *(Answers will vary.)*

## p. 164 | Lesson 28: More Related Words

**A.** seismometer
altimeter
odometer
asterisk
geology
cosmonauts

astronauts
navigation
geometry
altitude
geographic, supermarket, superpower,
alto, nautical, supervision

**B.** *(Answers will vary.)*

## p. 167 | Lesson 30: Words from Names

**A.**
1. tuxedo
2. hamburger
3. Braille
4. spoonerism
5. boycott
6. odyssey
7. sequoia
8. Fahrenheit
9. Celsius
10. mackintosh
11. zeppelin
12. malapropism
13. mercury
14. pasteurize
15. frankfurter
16. sandwich

**B.** *(Answers will vary.)*

## p. 170 | Lesson 31: Latin Roots, II

**A.**
1. attended
2. acceptance
3. sensation
4. conducted
5. perceived
6. adjust
7. justice
8. sensory
9. educate
10. acceptable
11. container
12. adjustments
13. productive
14. detained
15. deceived
16. sentimental

**B.** *(Answers will vary.)*

## p. 173 | Lesson 32: Noun Endings— Diminutives

**A.** ACROSS: 1. tablet 3. particle 4. bracelet
5. leaflet 6. yearling 10. statuette
11. cassette 12. luncheonette 13. banquet
14. pamphlet
DOWN: 2. booklet 3. packet 7. icicle
8. cabinet 9. diskette 10. sapling

**B.** *(Answers will vary.)*

## p. 176 | Lesson 33: Latin Roots, III

**A.**
1. complicated
2. terrace
3. applicable
4. conjunction
5. vocational
6. confined
7. territorial
8. financial

# Answer Key *(continued)*

9. infinite
10. refining
11. vocabulary
12. definitely
13. juncture
14. territories
15. vocal
16. duplicate

**B.** *(Answers will vary.)*

**p. 179 | Lesson 34: Words from Other Languages, II**

**A.**
1. igloo
2. kayak
3. parka
4. kimono
5. harpoon
6. caucus
7. haiku
8. kindergarten

9. mammoth
10. persimmon
11. tundra
12. waffle
13. toboggan
14. pretzel
15. hibachi
16. karate

**B.** *(Answers will vary.)*

**p. 182 | Lesson 35: Suffixes in Combination**

**A.** *Across, top to bottom:* naturalization, significantly, aimlessly, loneliness, sensationally, eventually, carelessly, economically, rhythmically; *down, left to right:* governmental, historically; *Up, left to right:* fortunately, architectural, mysteriously; *Diagonal:* favorably, peacefulness

**B.** *(Answers will vary.)*

# Teacher Resources

This section of the Teacher's Guide contains the following useful information.

**Cumulative Word List**
This section presents a comprehensive list of all words taught in *Spelling*. For each word, the grade level and the number of the lesson in which it is instructed are included.

**Scope and Sequence**
The chart in this section identifies the grade levels at which specific spelling strategies and skills are developed.

**Bibliography**
This bibliography includes informative professional articles and books about how students develop spelling proficiency as well as how they acquire related literacy skills. It also suggests a number of books for students.

**Index**
This index includes a useful list of major skills and activities.

# Cumulative Word List for Grades 6–8

This alphabetical list of 1,406 words includes all the spelling words that appear in Grades 6–8 of *Spelling*. Each word in the list is followed by two numbers. The first number indicates the grade in which the word appears. The second number indicates the lesson. Therefore, the listing "abrupt 6 33" indicates that the word *abrupt* appears in Grade 6, lesson 33.

| Word | Lesson | | Word | Lesson | | Word | Lesson | |
|---|---|---|---|---|---|---|---|---|
| abilities | 8 | 3 | agreeable | 8 | 6 | arrived | 7 | 10 |
| ability | 6 | 19 | agricultural | 7 | 33 | artist | 7 | 35 |
| abolished | 8 | 17 | aimlessly | 8 | 35 | aspirin | 7 | 29 |
| abrupt | 6 | 33 | allied | 6 | 12 | assembly | 6 | 20 |
| absence | 6 | 18 | alligator | 7 | 4 | assign | 6 | 20 |
| absent | 6 | 22 | allowance | 6 | 18 | assistance | 6 | 20 |
| absolute | 8 | 17 | alphabet | 8 | 11 | assistant | 6 | 22 |
| abstract | 8 | 17 | although | 6 | 6 | association | 6 | 20 |
| accelerate | 7 | 10 | altimeter | 8 | 28 | assurance | 6 | 18 |
| acceleration | 7 | 33 | altitude | 8 | 28 | asterisk | 8 | 28 |
| accent | 7 | 10 | alto | 8 | 28 | astronaut | 7 | 27 |
| accept | 6 | 10 | amateur | 8 | 8 | astronauts | 8 | 28 |
| acceptable | 8 | 31 | ambulance | 6 | 18 | astronomer | 7 | 27 |
| acceptance | 8 | 31 | American | 6 | 13 | astronomy | 7 | 27 |
| accepted | 7 | 10 | among | 6 | 6 | athletes | 7 | 29 |
| access | 8 | 5 | amount | 6 | 3 | atmosphere | 8 | 12 |
| accident | 6 | 20 | analogy | 7 | 32 | attendance | 7 | 21 |
| accidentally | 6 | 30 | analyze | 7 | 18 | attended | 8 | 31 |
| accommodate | 7 | 10 | anecdote | 8 | 5 | attitude | 7 | 15 |
| accompany | 6 | 20 | angel | 6 | 10 | attract | 7 | 22 |
| accompanying | 7 | 10 | angle | 6 | 10 | attractive | 6 | 27 |
| accomplish | 7 | 10 | announced | 7 | 10 | audience | 6 | 18 |
| accomplished | 8 | 6 | announcement | 8 | 6 | Australia | 7 | 9 |
| account | 6 | 3 | annoy | 7 | 10 | Australian | 7 | 9 |
| accumulation | 7 | 33 | answered | 6 | 16 | authority | 6 | 19 |
| accurate | 6 | 20 | antidote | 8 | 5 | autobiography | 7 | 33 |
| accuse | 6 | 20 | antique | 7 | 23 | autograph | 7 | 27 |
| accustomed | 6 | 20 | apart | 6 | 4 | automatically | 8 | 26 |
| achieve | 6 | 7 | apologizing | 7 | 32 | automobile | 7 | 30 |
| acquired | 8 | 3 | apparent | 6 | 20 | automobiles | 8 | 26 |
| actively | 6 | 30 | appearance | 6 | 18 | autumn | 7 | 25 |
| activities | 6 | 12 | applause | 6 | 20 | autumnal | 7 | 25 |
| activity | 6 | 19 | applicable | 8 | 33 | awe | 8 | 4 |
| adapt | 6 | 10 | applies | 6 | 12 | awesome | 7 | 11 |
| adjective | 7 | 29 | appoint | 7 | 10 | awful | 8 | 4 |
| adjust | 8 | 31 | appointed | 6 | 20 | awfully | 8 | 4 |
| adjustments | 8 | 31 | appreciate | 6 | 20 | awkward | 7 | 11 |
| administration | 7 | 33 | approach | 6 | 20 | backward | 7 | 11 |
| admire | 6 | 14 | approaching | 7 | 10 | bacteria | 6 | 26 |
| admit | 6 | 1 | approve | 7 | 10 | bait | 6 | 2 |
| admits | 7 | 22 | approved | 8 | 6 | bakery | 7 | 14 |
| admitted | 6 | 16 | apron | 6 | 15 | balance | 7 | 21 |
| adopt | 6 | 10 | archaeologist | 8 | 26 | ballet | 7 | 23 |
| advance | 6 | 1 | archaic | 8 | 26 | banjo | 7 | 5 |
| adventure | 7 | 34 | architectural | 8 | 35 | bankrupt | 6 | 33 |
| advertise | 7 | 18 | architecture | 8 | 11 | banner | 6 | 25 |
| advice | 8 | 6 | archives | 8 | 26 | banquet | 8 | 32 |
| advise | 7 | 20 | arctic | 7 | 12 | barbecue | 8 | 27 |
| advocate | 8 | 18 | argument | 6 | 19 | bard | 8 | 2 |
| affair | 6 | 20 | arithmetic | 8 | 11 | barefoot | 6 | 8 |
| affect | 6 | 10 | aroma | 8 | 11 | barefooted | 8 | 9 |
| affection | 6 | 20 | arrange | 7 | 10 | barometer | 7 | 27 |
| affectionate | 8 | 6 | arrangements | 7 | 10 | barred | 8 | 2 |
| Africa | 7 | 9 | array | 7 | 10 | barrier | 7 | 15 |
| African | 7 | 9 | arrest | 7 | 10 | basis | 6 | 15 |
| agent | 6 | 15 | arrested | 8 | 6 | bazaar | 8 | 5 |

| Word | | Lesson | Word | | Lesson | Word | | Lesson |
|---|---|---|---|---|---|---|---|---|
| beaten | 6 | 13 | cheating | 7 | 3 | contact | 6 | 1 |
| beautifully | 6 | 30 | cheetah | 6 | 15 | contained | 8 | 3 |
| bedtime | 6 | 8 | chemical | 8 | 12 | container | 8 | 31 |
| belief | 6 | 7 | childish | 7 | 11 | contented | 8 | 9 |
| berth | 7 | 2 | chili | 7 | 4 | continue | 8 | 4 |
| beverage | 7 | 12 | chipmunk | 8 | 27 | continued | 6 | 21 |
| bicycle | 7 | 28 | chocolate | 7 | 29 | continuous | 8 | 4 |
| binoculars | 7 | 28 | chorus | 8 | 11 | continuously | 8 | 4 |
| biography | 7 | 27 | chute | 7 | 2 | contract | 6 | 1 |
| biologist | 7 | 35 | cinnamon | 7 | 15 | contracted | 7 | 22 |
| biology | 7 | 32 | circles | 7 | 16 | controlling | 7 | 3 |
| birth | 7 | 2 | circuit | 8 | 25 | convention | 7 | 34 |
| biscuit | 6 | 6 | circular | 7 | 16 | conviction | 6 | 21 |
| bizarre | 8 | 5 | circulation | 8 | 25 | convince | 6 | 14 |
| blouse | 8 | 8 | circumference | 8 | 25 | cooling | 6 | 16 |
| boarder | 8 | 2 | circumstances | 8 | 25 | cooperate | 7 | 18 |
| bodyguard | 6 | 8 | cities | 6 | 12 | cooperation | 7 | 33 |
| booklet | 8 | 32 | civilian | 7 | 35 | corral | 7 | 4 |
| border | 8 | 2 | clarinet | 7 | 5 | corridor | 7 | 15 |
| bothering | 7 | 3 | classical | 7 | 5 | corrupt | 6 | 33 |
| boulder | 6 | 6 | clever | 6 | 25 | cosmonauts | 8 | 28 |
| boundary | 7 | 12 | climate | 6 | 24 | costume | 6 | 10 |
| bouquet | 7 | 23 | cocoa | 7 | 4 | count | 6 | 3 |
| boycott | 8 | 30 | colonial | 7 | 24 | county | 6 | 3 |
| boyfriend | 6 | 7 | colonies | 6 | 12 | coup | 8 | 8 |
| bracelet | 8 | 32 | colony | 7 | 24 | coupon | 7 | 23 |
| bragged | 6 | 16 | combination | 8 | 15 | courage | 6 | 6 |
| Braille | 8 | 30 | combine | 8 | 15 | coyote | 7 | 4 |
| breadth | 8 | 5 | comic | 6 | 24 | crawled | 6 | 3 |
| breath | 8 | 5 | commanded | 6 | 21 | creak | 6 | 9 |
| breathe | 6 | 2 | commander | 6 | 21 | creative | 6 | 27 |
| bride | 6 | 2 | commence | 6 | 21 | creek | 6 | 9 |
| brilliant | 7 | 21 | comment | 6 | 1 | criminal | 6 | 13 |
| buffalo | 7 | 15 | commercial | 6 | 21 | critical | 6 | 13 |
| buffet | 7 | 23 | commit | 6 | 21 | criticism | 8 | 22 |
| bugle | 7 | 5 | commitment | 7 | 22 | criticize | 7 | 18 |
| building | 6 | 6 | committed | 6 | 16 | crochet | 8 | 8 |
| burnt | 6 | 4 | committee | 6 | 21 | crooked | 8 | 9 |
| burro | 8 | 2 | commonly | 6 | 21 | croquet | 8 | 8 |
| burrow | 8 | 2 | commotion | 6 | 21 | cross | 6 | 3 |
| busy | 6 | 6 | communicate | 6 | 21 | cruelty | 8 | 22 |
| cabinet | 8 | 32 | communication | 6 | 21 | crystal | 6 | 25 |
| cactus | 6 | 26 | communities | 6 | 21 | cupboard | 6 | 8 |
| cafeteria | 7 | 4 | community | 6 | 19 | curb | 6 | 4 |
| calculate | 7 | 18 | companion | 7 | 24 | curiosity | 6 | 19 |
| camouflage | 7 | 23 | company | 7 | 24 | curious | 6 | 27 |
| capital | 8 | 2 | compelled | 7 | 3 | current | 6 | 22 |
| Capitol | 8 | 2 | complicated | 8 | 33 | custom | 6 | 10 |
| caravan | 7 | 30 | composer | 7 | 5 | cycle | 8 | 10 |
| carbohydrate | 7 | 32 | composition | 7 | 20 | cyclone | 8 | 10 |
| carefully | 6 | 30 | compromise | 7 | 18 | daylight | 7 | 1 |
| carelessly | 8 | 35 | concentrate | 8 | 18 | debate | 8 | 18 |
| cargo | 8 | 27 | concert | 7 | 5 | debris | 8 | 8 |
| carnival | 8 | 27 | conducted | 8 | 31 | decade | 7 | 28 |
| carrying | 7 | 3 | conductor | 7 | 5 | decay | 7 | 8 |
| cassette | 8 | 32 | confederate | 8 | 9 | deceived | 8 | 31 |
| catalog | 7 | 32 | conference | 6 | 18 | December | 7 | 28 |
| caucus | 8 | 34 | confidence | 7 | 21 | decent | 6 | 10 |
| celebrate | 7 | 18 | confident | 6 | 22 | decimal | 7 | 28 |
| Celsius | 8 | 30 | confined | 8 | 33 | declare | 6 | 4 |
| centimeters | 7 | 27 | confusing | 6 | 21 | decline | 7 | 8 |
| centuries | 6 | 12 | congratulate | 7 | 18 | decorate | 8 | 18 |
| century | 7 | 14 | conjunction | 8 | 33 | deduction | 7 | 8 |
| chairperson | 7 | 1 | conscience | 8 | 5 | defeat | 7 | 8 |
| champion | 7 | 30 | conscious | 8 | 5 | defects | 7 | 8 |
| championship | 6 | 19 | conservation | 8 | 14 | definitely | 8 | 33 |
| chaos | 6 | 25 | considered | 6 | 21 | dehydrated | 7 | 32 |
| characteristic | 7 | 33 | constant | 7 | 21 | delegate | 8 | 18 |
| chattering | 8 | 21 | constitution | 6 | 21 | delicious | 6 | 27 |
| chauffeur | 8 | 8 | constructing | 7 | 20 | democratic | 8 | 9 |

**190**    

| Word | Lesson | | Word | Lesson | | Word | Lesson | |
|------|--------|--|------|--------|--|------|--------|--|
| demonstrate | 8 | 18 | eighth | 6 | 6 | fabulous | 6 | 27 |
| denied | 6 | 12 | eject | 6 | 33 | factory | 7 | 14 |
| dependent | 7 | 8 | electrical | 8 | 12 | Fahrenheit | 8 | 30 |
| depends | 7 | 34 | electricity | 6 | 19 | fairy tales | 6 | 8 |
| depositing | 7 | 20 | electronic | 8 | 9 | faithfully | 6 | 30 |
| depot | 8 | 8 | elegant | 7 | 21 | familiar | 7 | 24 |
| depth | 6 | 1 | element | 6 | 22 | families | 6 | 12 |
| descent | 6 | 10 | elephant | 6 | 22 | family | 7 | 24 |
| description | 6 | 32 | eliminate | 8 | 18 | famous | 6 | 15 |
| descriptive | 6 | 32 | elite | 8 | 8 | fantastic | 7 | 24 |
| designated | 7 | 25 | embarrassed | 8 | 8 | fantasy | 7 | 24 |
| designed | 7 | 25 | embassy | 8 | 21 | fatal | 6 | 25 |
| despair | 8 | 4 | emigrate | 8 | 14 | fatigue | 7 | 23 |
| desperate | 7 | 29 | empty | 6 | 25 | favorably | 8 | 35 |
| desperately | 8 | 4 | enclose | 7 | 7 | February | 7 | 12 |
| destroyed | 7 | 8 | encourage | 7 | 7 | feminine | 7 | 11 |
| destruction | 7 | 20 | encyclopedia | 7 | 33 | feudal | 8 | 5 |
| detained | 8 | 31 | endurance | 7 | 21 | fiber | 6 | 15 |
| device | 6 | 10 | enemies | 6 | 12 | fiddle | 7 | 5 |
| devise | 6 | 10 | engine | 6 | 14 | fierce | 6 | 7 |
| dialogue | 7 | 23 | engineer | 7 | 35 | fifteen | 6 | 14 |
| diameter | 7 | 27 | England | 7 | 9 | finally | 8 | 5 |
| dictator | 8 | 14 | English | 7 | 9 | financial | 8 | 33 |
| dictionaries | 8 | 14 | enjoying | 7 | 7 | finely | 8 | 5 |
| dictionary | 7 | 14 | enormous | 6 | 27 | fireworks | 6 | 8 |
| difference | 6 | 18 | enough | 6 | 6 | following | 7 | 3 |
| different | 7 | 12 | enthusiasm | 7 | 7 | foolish | 7 | 11 |
| diplomacy | 7 | 24 | entrance | 6 | 18 | forbidding | 8 | 3 |
| diplomatic | 7 | 24 | envelope | 7 | 7 | foreign | 6 | 7 |
| disabled | 7 | 8 | environment | 8 | 12 | formation | 7 | 34 |
| disadvantages | 7 | 8 | episode | 8 | 11 | formula | 7 | 34 |
| disagreeable | 6 | 28 | equality | 8 | 20 | fortunate | 7 | 17 |
| disagreement | 6 | 28 | equation | 8 | 20 | fortunately | 8 | 35 |
| disappeared | 7 | 8 | equator | 8 | 20 | fortune | 7 | 17 |
| disappointment | 7 | 8 | equivalent | 8 | 20 | foul | 8 | 2 |
| disastrous | 7 | 29 | erupt | 6 | 33 | fowl | 8 | 2 |
| discovered | 7 | 8 | escape | 6 | 14 | France | 7 | 9 |
| discovery | 7 | 14 | especially | 7 | 17 | frankfurter | 8 | 30 |
| disguise | 7 | 8 | estimate | 8 | 18 | frantic | 6 | 14 |
| diskette | 8 | 32 | ethnic | 6 | 1 | freight | 6 | 7 |
| disliked | 7 | 8 | eventually | 8 | 35 | French | 7 | 9 |
| dismissed | 7 | 22 | evergreen | 8 | 1 | frequent | 7 | 21 |
| display | 6 | 25 | evil | 6 | 15 | Friday | 6 | 15 |
| dispose | 7 | 8 | exaggerated | 8 | 21 | friendship | 6 | 19 |
| disposed | 8 | 15 | examination | 7 | 30 | frigid | 6 | 24 |
| disposition | 8 | 15 | exceed | 7 | 7 | fungi | 6 | 26 |
| disrupting | 6 | 33 | excel | 7 | 7 | fun-loving | 6 | 8 |
| disruption | 6 | 33 | excellent | 6 | 22 | funnel | 6 | 25 |
| dissolved | 7 | 8 | except | 6 | 10 | further | 6 | 14 |
| distract | 7 | 22 | exceptionally | 7 | 33 | furthermore | 8 | 1 |
| distribute | 8 | 15 | excess | 8 | 5 | futile | 8 | 5 |
| distribution | 8 | 15 | exchange | 7 | 7 | gallery | 7 | 15 |
| documentary | 7 | 14 | excitement | 7 | 7 | gasoline | 7 | 30 |
| doubt | 7 | 17 | exclaim | 7 | 7 | gather | 6 | 25 |
| doubtful | 7 | 17 | exclude | 7 | 7 | gathered | 7 | 3 |
| doubtless | 7 | 17 | executive | 6 | 27 | generation | 8 | 10 |
| dough | 6 | 6 | exercise | 7 | 18 | generator | 8 | 10 |
| drama | 8 | 4 | existence | 7 | 21 | genes | 8 | 10 |
| dramatic | 8 | 4 | exit | 7 | 7 | genius | 8 | 10 |
| dramatically | 8 | 4 | expand | 7 | 7 | genuine | 7 | 11 |
| drowned | 7 | 29 | experience | 7 | 21 | geographic | 8 | 28 |
| duplicate | 8 | 33 | experiments | 8 | 12 | geography | 7 | 27 |
| eager | 6 | 15 | explode | 7 | 7 | geology | 8 | 28 |
| economically | 8 | 35 | explorer | 6 | 13 | geometry | 8 | 28 |
| ecstatic | 7 | 29 | exported | 8 | 14 | German | 6 | 13 |
| editor | 7 | 24 | express | 7 | 7 | gingerbread | 8 | 1 |
| editorial | 7 | 24 | extend | 7 | 7 | girlfriend | 6 | 7 |
| educate | 8 | 31 | extraordinary | 8 | 17 | glance | 6 | 1 |
| effect | 6 | 10 | extraterrestrial | 8 | 17 | globe | 6 | 2 |
| effective | 6 | 27 | extravagant | 8 | 17 | goalie | 7 | 35 |

**Teacher Resources**

191

| Word | Lesson | | Word | Lesson | | Word | Lesson | |
|---|---|---|---|---|---|---|---|---|
| goldfish | 6 | 26 | impolite | 6 | 31 | jaguar | 7 | 4 |
| good-natured | 8 | 1 | importance | 6 | 18 | Japan | 7 | 9 |
| gopher | 6 | 24 | important | 6 | 22 | Japanese | 7 | 9 |
| gorilla | 7 | 15 | imported | 8 | 14 | jazz | 7 | 5 |
| gotten | 6 | 14 | impossible | 6 | 31 | jewelry | 7 | 12 |
| governmental | 8 | 35 | impressed | 8 | 6 | joyfully | 6 | 30 |
| gracefully | 6 | 30 | improved | 8 | 6 | judges | 7 | 17 |
| grandparents | 7 | 1 | impulse | 6 | 1 | judgment | 7 | 17 |
| graph | 7 | 27 | impure | 6 | 31 | judicial | 7 | 17 |
| grayish | 7 | 11 | inability | 6 | 31 | juncture | 8 | 33 |
| Greece | 7 | 9 | inaugurate | 7 | 18 | justice | 8 | 31 |
| Greek | 7 | 9 | incident | 7 | 21 | justified | 8 | 3 |
| greenhouse | 6 | 8 | incidentally | 7 | 29 | karate | 8 | 34 |
| greenish | 7 | 11 | included | 8 | 6 | kayak | 8 | 34 |
| groan | 6 | 9 | incomplete | 6 | 31 | killer whale | 7 | 1 |
| groaned | 7 | 3 | incorrect | 6 | 31 | kilometers | 7 | 27 |
| gross | 6 | 2 | incredible | 6 | 31 | kimono | 8 | 34 |
| grove | 6 | 9 | indeed | 6 | 14 | kindergarten | 8 | 34 |
| guardian | 7 | 35 | indefinite | 6 | 31 | laboratory | 7 | 30 |
| guessed | 6 | 9 | independence | 6 | 18 | labored | 7 | 3 |
| guest | 6 | 9 | independent | 6 | 13 | labyrinth | 8 | 11 |
| guitar | 7 | 4 | index | 6 | 14 | landscape | 8 | 27 |
| gymnasium | 7 | 30 | Indian | 6 | 13 | large-scale | 8 | 1 |
| habit | 6 | 25 | indictment | 8 | 14 | larvae | 6 | 26 |
| haiku | 8 | 34 | indigestion | 6 | 31 | laser | 8 | 12 |
| hamburger | 8 | 30 | industries | 6 | 12 | later | 6 | 10 |
| hammered | 7 | 3 | inexpensive | 6 | 31 | latter | 6 | 10 |
| handkerchief | 8 | 1 | infinite | 8 | 33 | layer | 6 | 13 |
| handsome | 7 | 11 | influence | 8 | 21 | leadership | 6 | 19 |
| harmony | 7 | 5 | informal | 6 | 31 | leaflet | 8 | 32 |
| harp | 7 | 5 | inject | 6 | 33 | league | 7 | 23 |
| harpoon | 8 | 34 | injury | 7 | 14 | legislative | 6 | 27 |
| harvesting | 8 | 3 | innocent | 6 | 22 | length | 7 | 12 |
| haste | 7 | 25 | inscription | 6 | 32 | letting | 7 | 3 |
| hasten | 7 | 25 | inserts | 6 | 4 | librarian | 7 | 35 |
| headache | 7 | 1 | insist | 6 | 14 | library | 7 | 12 |
| headquarters | 8 | 1 | insisted | 8 | 16 | life jackets | 7 | 1 |
| healed | 6 | 16 | inspect | 6 | 32 | lifted | 6 | 16 |
| heart attack | 8 | 1 | inspection | 8 | 6 | lightning | 7 | 29 |
| heights | 6 | 7 | inspector | 8 | 32 | limousine | 7 | 30 |
| heir | 7 | 25 | inspiration | 7 | 34 | linen | 6 | 24 |
| hemisphere | 8 | 12 | inspired | 7 | 34 | liquid | 6 | 1 |
| heritage | 7 | 25 | instance | 6 | 18 | listening | 7 | 3 |
| heroes | 8 | 11 | instant | 6 | 22 | literature | 7 | 12 |
| heroic | 8 | 27 | instinct | 6 | 14 | local | 6 | 15 |
| hesitate | 8 | 18 | instructions | 7 | 20 | logic | 7 | 32 |
| hibachi | 8 | 34 | instruments | 8 | 12 | loneliness | 8 | 35 |
| hickory | 8 | 27 | insurance | 6 | 18 | lonesome | 7 | 11 |
| hippopotamus | 6 | 26 | intellectual | 8 | 21 | long-term | 8 | 1 |
| historian | 7 | 35 | intelligence | 6 | 18 | loudspeaker | 8 | 1 |
| historic | 8 | 9 | intense | 6 | 14 | loyalty | 8 | 22 |
| historical | 7 | 24 | intercept | 8 | 16 | luncheon | 7 | 30 |
| historically | 8 | 35 | intermediate | 8 | 16 | luncheonette | 8 | 32 |
| history | 7 | 24 | international | 8 | 16 | luxury | 7 | 14 |
| homemade | 8 | 1 | interrupt | 6 | 33 | macaroni | 8 | 27 |
| homesick | 8 | 1 | interrupted | 8 | 16 | machinery | 7 | 14 |
| horrid | 8 | 9 | interview | 8 | 16 | mackintosh | 8 | 30 |
| hotel | 6 | 25 | intramural | 8 | 25 | magnetic | 8 | 9 |
| hurricane | 7 | 15 | intrastate | 8 | 25 | magnificent | 7 | 21 |
| hydrant | 7 | 32 | introduction | 8 | 25 | magnificently | 8 | 20 |
| icicle | 8 | 32 | introvert | 8 | 25 | magnify | 8 | 20 |
| identification | 7 | 33 | invention | 7 | 34 | magnitude | 8 | 20 |
| identified | 6 | 12 | inventor | 7 | 34 | majority | 6 | 19 |
| identity | 7 | 29 | investigate | 8 | 18 | malapropism | 8 | 30 |
| igloo | 8 | 34 | investigated | 8 | 16 | mammoth | 8 | 34 |
| illegal | 6 | 31 | invisible | 6 | 31 | mandate | 8 | 18 |
| illustrate | 7 | 18 | irregular | 6 | 31 | marathon | 8 | 11 |
| illustrated | 8 | 6 | irresponsible | 8 | 6 | marine | 7 | 11 |
| immigration | 8 | 14 | irrigated | 8 | 6 | masculine | 7 | 11 |
| impatient | 6 | 31 | ivory | 7 | 29 | massacre | 7 | 15 |

ELEMENTS OF LANGUAGE | Second Course | *Spelling Teacher's Guide*

| Word | Lesson | | Word | Lesson | | Word | Lesson | |
|------|--------|---|------|--------|---|------|--------|---|
| mathematics | 7 | 30 | nuclei | 6 | 26 | pasteurize | 8 | 30 |
| matinee | 8 | 8 | nucleus | 6 | 26 | patio | 7 | 4 |
| mean-spirited | 6 | 8 | nursery | 7 | 14 | patriotic | 8 | 15 |
| mechanism | 8 | 22 | nutrients | 8 | 3 | patriotism | 8 | 22 |
| media | 6 | 26 | obedience | 6 | 18 | patriots | 8 | 15 |
| medicinal | 8 | 15 | objected | 6 | 33 | peacefully | 6 | 30 |
| medicine | 8 | 15 | objection | 8 | 23 | peacefulness | 8 | 35 |
| melancholy | 8 | 11 | objections | 6 | 33 | peach | 6 | 2 |
| memorandum | 7 | 30 | objective | 8 | 23 | pending | 7 | 34 |
| memorize | 7 | 18 | obligation | 8 | 15 | penetrate | 7 | 29 |
| mercury | 8 | 30 | oblige | 8 | 15 | penniless | 8 | 21 |
| metallic | 8 | 9 | oblong | 8 | 23 | perceived | 8 | 31 |
| meter | 6 | 15 | obscure | 8 | 23 | perception | 8 | 25 |
| meters | 7 | 27 | observation | 8 | 23 | perfectly | 8 | 25 |
| metropolitan | 8 | 26 | observatory | 8 | 14 | perform | 7 | 34 |
| microcomputer | 8 | 20 | obsessions | 8 | 23 | performance | 7 | 5 |
| microorganism | 8 | 20 | obstacle | 8 | 23 | perfume | 8 | 8 |
| microphone | 8 | 10 | obtained | 8 | 23 | perimeter | 8 | 25 |
| microscope | 7 | 32 | obvious | 6 | 27 | periodic | 8 | 25 |
| microscopic | 8 | 20 | obviously | 8 | 23 | peripheral | 8 | 25 |
| microwave | 8 | 20 | occasionally | 8 | 23 | periscope | 7 | 32 |
| middle-aged | 6 | 8 | occupant | 8 | 23 | permanent | 6 | 22 |
| migrate | 8 | 14 | occupation | 8 | 23 | permanently | 8 | 25 |
| mischief | 6 | 7 | occupied | 6 | 12 | permit | 7 | 22 |
| misfortune | 7 | 17 | October | 7 | 28 | permitting | 7 | 3 |
| missed | 7 | 2 | octopus | 7 | 28 | persecuted | 8 | 5 |
| missionary | 7 | 14 | odometer | 8 | 28 | persimmon | 8 | 34 |
| mist | 7 | 2 | odyssey | 8 | 30 | personality | 6 | 19 |
| moccasins | 7 | 15 | offensive | 8 | 23 | perspective | 8 | 25 |
| molecules | 8 | 12 | offered | 7 | 22 | persuaded | 8 | 25 |
| monologue | 7 | 32 | offering | 8 | 23 | petrified | 8 | 3 |
| monopoly | 7 | 28 | offshore | 7 | 1 | phenomenon | 8 | 11 |
| monotonous | 7 | 28 | omit | 7 | 22 | philosopher | 8 | 26 |
| monsoon | 8 | 27 | omitted | 8 | 3 | philosophy | 8 | 11 |
| monster | 6 | 14 | opera | 8 | 27 | phonograph | 8 | 10 |
| moonlight | 7 | 1 | opossum | 7 | 15 | phosphate | 8 | 18 |
| moose | 6 | 26 | opponent | 6 | 22 | photograph | 7 | 27 |
| mosquito | 7 | 4 | opportunity | 8 | 23 | photography | 7 | 27 |
| motive | 6 | 15 | opposite | 7 | 20 | physical | 8 | 11 |
| mountain | 6 | 3 | opposition | 8 | 23 | physician | 7 | 35 |
| multicolored | 8 | 20 | optic | 8 | 26 | pianist | 7 | 5 |
| multicultural | 8 | 20 | optical | 8 | 26 | piano | 8 | 27 |
| multimedia | 8 | 20 | optimism | 8 | 22 | picnic basket | 8 | 1 |
| multiplication | 8 | 20 | optometrist | 8 | 26 | pier | 6 | 7 |
| multitude | 8 | 20 | organization | 7 | 33 | pigeon | 8 | 8 |
| mummies | 6 | 12 | organize | 7 | 18 | pillow | 6 | 14 |
| muscle | 7 | 16 | original | 6 | 13 | pinnacle | 7 | 15 |
| muscular | 7 | 16 | orphan | 6 | 25 | pioneer | 7 | 35 |
| musical | 6 | 13 | oval | 6 | 25 | plaque | 7 | 23 |
| musician | 7 | 35 | overnight | 7 | 1 | plateau | 8 | 8 |
| mysterious | 6 | 27 | ownership | 6 | 30 | platform | 6 | 25 |
| mysteriously | 8 | 35 | packet | 8 | 32 | platinum | 7 | 29 |
| mythology | 7 | 32 | pain | 7 | 2 | pleasant | 6 | 24 |
| narrative | 8 | 21 | palace | 6 | 24 | pneumonia | 8 | 11 |
| naturalization | 8 | 35 | palette | 8 | 2 | poetic | 8 | 9 |
| naturally | 6 | 30 | pallet | 8 | 2 | pointed | 6 | 16 |
| nautical | 8 | 28 | pamphlet | 8 | 32 | policy | 8 | 26 |
| navigation | 8 | 28 | pane | 7 | 2 | political | 6 | 13 |
| necessary | 7 | 20 | parachute | 7 | 30 | politician | 7 | 35 |
| necessity | 6 | 19 | paragraph | 7 | 27 | politics | 8 | 26 |
| necktie | 7 | 30 | parakeet | 8 | 27 | polluted | 8 | 21 |
| negative | 6 | 27 | parallel | 8 | 21 | popular | 7 | 16 |
| negotiate | 8 | 18 | paralyze | 7 | 18 | population | 7 | 16 |
| nervous | 6 | 14 | parka | 8 | 34 | portable | 8 | 14 |
| nervously | 6 | 30 | participate | 8 | 18 | portrait | 7 | 23 |
| New Year | 6 | 8 | particle | 8 | 32 | position | 7 | 20 |
| nightmare | 6 | 4 | particles | 7 | 16 | positive | 6 | 27 |
| nonsense | 6 | 1 | particular | 7 | 16 | possibility | 7 | 33 |
| novel | 6 | 24 | partnership | 6 | 19 | potatoes | 8 | 3 |
| novelty | 8 | 22 | passionate | 8 | 9 | pounds | 6 | 3 |

**Teacher Resources**

193

| Word | Lesson | | Word | Lesson | | Word | Lesson | |
|---|---|---|---|---|---|---|---|---|
| poverty | 8 | 22 | refrigerator | 7 | 30 | scuba | 8 | 12 |
| prairie | 7 | 23 | refused | 8 | 3 | seashore | 6 | 8 |
| praise | 6 | 2 | regular | 7 | 16 | seaweed | 7 | 1 |
| predicting | 8 | 14 | regulate | 8 | 18 | seismometer | 8 | 28 |
| preferred | 6 | 16 | regulation | 7 | 16 | selfish | 7 | 11 |
| prejudice | 7 | 17 | rehabilitation | 7 | 33 | sensation | 8 | 31 |
| prescribed | 6 | 32 | rehearsal | 7 | 5 | sensationally | 8 | 35 |
| presence | 6 | 18 | reins | 6 | 7 | sensitive | 6 | 27 |
| preservation | 8 | 14 | reject | 6 | 33 | sensory | 8 | 31 |
| president | 6 | 22 | rejected | 6 | 33 | sentimental | 8 | 31 |
| pretzel | 8 | 34 | relationship | 6 | 30 | separate | 7 | 12 |
| prime | 6 | 2 | relief | 6 | 7 | separating | 8 | 3 |
| principal | 8 | 2 | reluctant | 7 | 21 | sequoia | 8 | 30 |
| principle | 8 | 2 | renewal | 6 | 28 | servant | 6 | 22 |
| prison | 6 | 24 | repayment | 6 | 28 | shone | 7 | 2 |
| probability | 8 | 12 | repeated | 8 | 15 | shoot | 7 | 2 |
| probably | 7 | 12 | repetition | 8 | 15 | shout | 6 | 3 |
| proceeds | 8 | 16 | replacement | 6 | 28 | shown | 7 | 2 |
| produced | 8 | 3 | reproduction | 6 | 28 | sign | 7 | 25 |
| productive | 8 | 31 | reservation | 8 | 14 | signature | 7 | 25 |
| profession | 8 | 4 | resign | 7 | 25 | significant | 6 | 22 |
| professionally | 8 | 4 | resignation | 7 | 25 | significantly | 8 | 35 |
| profit | 6 | 24 | resources | 8 | 3 | simulate | 8 | 18 |
| profitable | 8 | 16 | respectively | 6 | 30 | simultaneously | 7 | 33 |
| programming | 8 | 3 | respiration | 7 | 34 | siren | 6 | 24 |
| projected | 6 | 33 | responsibilities | 7 | 33 | skeleton | 8 | 27 |
| projections | 6 | 33 | responsibility | 6 | 19 | sketch | 6 | 1 |
| proof | 6 | 3 | restaurant | 7 | 29 | sleigh | 6 | 6 |
| propose | 8 | 15 | returned | 6 | 16 | slice | 6 | 2 |
| proposition | 8 | 15 | revised | 7 | 20 | slope | 6 | 2 |
| prosecuted | 8 | 5 | revolutionary | 7 | 14 | soar | 6 | 9 |
| prosperity | 8 | 16 | reward | 6 | 4 | so-called | 6 | 8 |
| protested | 8 | 16 | rhythm | 8 | 11 | softened | 7 | 25 |
| provisions | 8 | 16 | rhythmically | 8 | 35 | softly | 7 | 25 |
| psychiatrist | 7 | 35 | rigid | 8 | 9 | sonar | 8 | 12 |
| psychology | 7 | 32 | rival | 6 | 15 | sophisticated | 8 | 26 |
| purse | 6 | 4 | rivalry | 8 | 22 | sophomore | 8 | 26 |
| qualified | 6 | 12 | roar | 6 | 4 | sore | 6 | 9 |
| quart | 7 | 28 | roast | 6 | 2 | source | 6 | 4 |
| quarters | 7 | 28 | robbery | 8 | 22 | spaghetti | 8 | 27 |
| quartet | 7 | 28 | rodeo | 7 | 4 | Spain | 7 | 9 |
| radar | 8 | 12 | Roman | 6 | 13 | Spanish | 7 | 9 |
| radius | 6 | 26 | rotten | 6 | 13 | sparkling | 6 | 4 |
| ragged | 8 | 9 | rough | 6 | 6 | speaker | 6 | 13 |
| rapid | 6 | 1 | royalty | 8 | 22 | speaking | 6 | 16 |
| razor | 6 | 15 | ruined | 7 | 3 | specialist | 7 | 17 |
| reaction | 6 | 28 | rumors | 6 | 3 | specialty | 8 | 22 |
| reader | 6 | 13 | rupture | 6 | 33 | species | 6 | 26 |
| real | 7 | 2 | sack | 6 | 1 | specific | 7 | 17 |
| realism | 8 | 22 | sailboat | 7 | 1 | specifications | 7 | 17 |
| realize | 7 | 18 | salmon | 6 | 26 | spectacle | 6 | 32 |
| receipt | 7 | 25 | salt | 6 | 3 | spectacular | 6 | 32 |
| receive | 6 | 7 | sandwich | 8 | 30 | spectators | 6 | 32 |
| receiver | 6 | 7 | sapling | 8 | 32 | spectrum | 6 | 32 |
| reception | 7 | 25 | satellite | 8 | 21 | spelling | 6 | 16 |
| recess | 7 | 20 | Saturn | 6 | 25 | spike | 6 | 2 |
| recognize | 7 | 18 | saucer | 6 | 3 | spiral | 6 | 24 |
| recommendation | 7 | 33 | scarce | 6 | 4 | splendid | 6 | 1 |
| reconstruction | 6 | 28 | scattering | 8 | 21 | spoonerism | 8 | 30 |
| rectangle | 7 | 16 | scenery | 7 | 14 | squeeze | 6 | 2 |
| rectangular | 7 | 16 | scenic | 6 | 15 | stadium | 8 | 11 |
| recycle | 8 | 10 | scholarship | 8 | 26 | stagecoach | 8 | 1 |
| reddish | 7 | 11 | scholastic | 8 | 26 | stake | 6 | 9 |
| reel | 7 | 2 | scientist | 7 | 35 | stampede | 7 | 4 |
| refer | 7 | 22 | scientists | 8 | 12 | statement | 6 | 19 |
| reference | 7 | 12 | scope | 7 | 32 | stationary | 8 | 2 |
| references | 7 | 22 | scribbled | 6 | 32 | stationery | 8 | 2 |
| referring | 6 | 16 | scribe | 6 | 32 | statuette | 8 | 32 |
| refining | 8 | 33 | script | 6 | 32 | steak | 6 | 9 |
| reform | 7 | 34 | scrubbed | 6 | 16 | steal | 6 | 9 |

**194**

| Word | Lesson | | Word | Lesson | | Word | Lesson | |
|------|--------|---|------|--------|---|------|--------|---|
| steel | 6 | 9 | telegram | 8 | 16 | underlying | 8 | 16 |
| stimuli | 6 | 26 | telegraph | 8 | 16 | underneath | 8 | 16 |
| stimulus | 6 | 26 | telephones | 8 | 10 | undersized | 8 | 9 |
| straight | 6 | 6 | telescope | 7 | 32 | undertake | 8 | 16 |
| strain | 8 | 4 | telescopes | 8 | 16 | underwater | 7 | 1 |
| strategic | 7 | 24 | televised | 7 | 20 | undoubtedly | 7 | 17 |
| strategy | 7 | 24 | temperature | 7 | 12 | unemployment | 6 | 28 |
| strawberry | 7 | 1 | tentatively | 7 | 29 | unexpectedly | 6 | 28 |
| strength | 7 | 12 | terrace | 8 | 33 | unfortunate | 7 | 17 |
| strenuous | 8 | 4 | terrific | 8 | 21 | unfortunately | 6 | 28 |
| strenuously | 8 | 4 | territorial | 8 | 33 | uniform | 7 | 34 |
| stretcher | 6 | 13 | territories | 8 | 33 | unique | 7 | 23 |
| stroke | 6 | 2 | territory | 7 | 14 | universe | 8 | 12 |
| structures | 7 | 20 | thermometer | 7 | 27 | unlikely | 6 | 28 |
| studying | 7 | 9 | thieves | 6 | 7 | unpredictable | 6 | 28 |
| stupid | 8 | 17 | thigh | 6 | 2 | unsuccessful | 6 | 28 |
| subdued | 8 | 17 | though | 6 | 6 | unusually | 6 | 28 |
| subjected | 8 | 30 | thoughtfully | 6 | 30 | upright | 6 | 8 |
| submarine | 7 | 17 | thousands | 6 | 3 | uttered | 8 | 21 |
| submerged | 8 | 22 | threatened | 6 | 16 | vaccination | 8 | 21 |
| submit | 7 | 3 | thunderstorm | 6 | 8 | vague | 7 | 23 |
| submitted | 8 | 32 | tide | 7 | 2 | vanilla | 7 | 4 |
| subscription | 6 | 21 | tied | 7 | 2 | varied | 6 | 12 |
| substance | 7 | 17 | tobacco | 7 | 15 | various | 6 | 27 |
| subtracting | 8 | 22 | toboggan | 8 | 34 | vegetable | 7 | 12 |
| subway | 7 | 17 | token | 6 | 24 | vehicles | 7 | 16 |
| succeeded | 8 | 20 | tomato | 7 | 4 | vehicular | 7 | 16 |
| successfully | 7 | 30 | tomorrow | 7 | 15 | velvet | 6 | 14 |
| suede | 6 | 2 | tornado | 7 | 4 | verdict | 8 | 14 |
| suffer | 7 | 22 | torrential | 8 | 21 | victory | 7 | 14 |
| sufficient | 7 | 22 | tortillas | 7 | 4 | Vietnam | 7 | 9 |
| suite | 6 | 8 | tourism | 8 | 22 | Vietnamese | 7 | 9 |
| summit | 8 | 1 | transaction | 8 | 17 | violin | 7 | 5 |
| summoned | 6 | 21 | transcripts | 6 | 32 | vision | 7 | 20 |
| supermarket | 8 | 28 | transfer | 7 | 22 | visitors | 7 | 20 |
| superpower | 8 | 28 | transferred | 8 | 17 | vital | 6 | 15 |
| supervision | 8 | 28 | transformed | 7 | 34 | vocabulary | 8 | 33 |
| supplies | 8 | 12 | transient | 8 | 17 | vocal | 8 | 33 |
| supply | 6 | 20 | translation | 8 | 17 | vocational | 8 | 33 |
| supported | 8 | 14 | transmission | 7 | 22 | volunteer | 7 | 35 |
| surgeon | 8 | 8 | transportation | 8 | 17 | voyage | 7 | 23 |
| suspect | 8 | 32 | treason | 6 | 24 | waffle | 8 | 34 |
| suspended | 6 | 34 | treasury | 7 | 14 | walrus | 8 | 27 |
| suspense | 7 | 25 | tremendous | 6 | 27 | warrant | 6 | 4 |
| swallowed | 6 | 3 | triangle | 7 | 16 | watermelon | 7 | 1 |
| swayed | 7 | 2 | triangles | 7 | 28 | weak | 6 | 9 |
| syllable | 7 | 15 | triangular | 7 | 16 | weapon | 6 | 24 |
| symbolic | 7 | 10 | tricycle | 7 | 28 | weather | 6 | 9 |
| sympathetic | 8 | 10 | triggered | 8 | 21 | week | 6 | 9 |
| symphony | 8 | 10 | trio | 7 | 28 | weighed | 6 | 7 |
| symptoms | 8 | 10 | triple | 7 | 28 | well-wisher | 8 | 1 |
| synonyms | 8 | 10 | trout | 6 | 26 | whether | 6 | 9 |
| synthetic | 8 | 10 | trumpet | 7 | 5 | wholesome | 7 | 11 |
| system | 8 | 6 | tundra | 8 | 34 | wildlife | 7 | 1 |
| tablet | 8 | 32 | turtle | 6 | 4 | wondered | 6 | 16 |
| talent | 6 | 24 | tuxedo | 8 | 30 | wonderfully | 6 | 30 |
| technician | 7 | 35 | twelfth | 7 | 12 | worse | 6 | 4 |
| technique | 7 | 23 | typewriter | 7 | 1 | yacht | 8 | 27 |
| technological | 8 | 12 | umbrella | 7 | 15 | yearling | 8 | 32 |
| technology | 7 | 32 | uncertainty | 8 | 22 | young | 6 | 6 |
| teenager | 6 | 8 | uncomfortable | 6 | 28 | youth | 6 | 3 |
| teenagers | 7 | 30 | underground | 8 | 1 | zeppelin | 8 | 30 |

**Teacher Resources**

# Scope and Sequence

| | 6 | 7 | 8 |
|---|---|---|---|
| **SPELLING GENERALIZATIONS** | | | |
| **Sound-Letter Relationships** | | | |
| Consonants | ✓ | ✓ | ✓ |
| Consonant Digraphs | ✓ | ✓ | ✓ |
| Consonant Clusters | ✓ | ✓ | ✓ |
| Short Vowels | ✓ | ✓ | ✓ |
| Long Vowels | ✓ | ✓ | ✓ |
| Vowel Diphthongs/Vowel Digraphs/Variant Vowels | ✓ | ✓ | ✓ |
| R-Controlled Vowels | ✓ | ✓ | ✓ |
| Silent Letters | ✓ | ✓ | ✓ |
| Schwa | ✓ | ✓ | ✓ |
| Double Letters | ✓ | ✓ | ✓ |
| Spelling Patterns | ✓ | ✓ | ✓ |
| **Word Structure** | | | |
| Contractions | ✓ | ✓ | ✓ |
| Plurals/Possessives | ✓ | ✓ | ✓ |
| Inflected Forms/Comparatives/Superlatives | ✓ | ✓ | ✓ |
| Prefixes | ✓ | ✓ | ✓ |
| Suffixes | ✓ | ✓ | ✓ |
| Greek and Latin Word Parts | ✓ | ✓ | ✓ |
| **Word Analysis** | | | |
| Phonograms | ✓ | ✓ | ✓ |
| Compound Words | ✓ | ✓ | ✓ |
| Syllable Patterns | ✓ | ✓ | ✓ |
| Letter Patterns | ✓ | ✓ | ✓ |
| Pronunciation | ✓ | ✓ | ✓ |

# Scope and Sequence *(continued)*

| | 6 | 7 | 8 |
|---|:---:|:---:|:---:|
| **SPELLING STRATEGIES** | | | |
| Rhyming Words | ✓ | ✓ | ✓ |
| Word Shapes | ✓ | ✓ | ✓ |
| Word Families | ✓ | ✓ | ✓ |
| How to Study a Word | ✓ | ✓ | ✓ |
| Picture/Sound Out a Word | ✓ | ✓ | ✓ |
| Related Words | ✓ | ✓ | ✓ |
| Mnemonic Devices | ✓ | ✓ | ✓ |
| Spell/Proofread with a Partner | ✓ | ✓ | ✓ |
| Try Different Spellings/Beat Guess | ✓ | ✓ | ✓ |
| Dictionary/Definitions | ✓ | ✓ | ✓ |
| Proofread Twice | ✓ | ✓ | ✓ |
| Apply Spelling Rules | ✓ | ✓ | ✓ |
| **VOCABULARY DEVELOPMENT** | | | |
| Classify/Categorize Words | ✓ | ✓ | ✓ |
| Antonyms | ✓ | ✓ | ✓ |
| Content-Area Words | ✓ | ✓ | ✓ |
| Synonyms | ✓ | ✓ | ✓ |
| Homophones | ✓ | ✓ | ✓ |
| Multiple Meanings/Homographs | ✓ | ✓ | ✓ |
| Dictionary (for meaning) | ✓ | ✓ | ✓ |
| Word Origins | ✓ | ✓ | ✓ |
| Analogies | ✓ | ✓ | ✓ |
| Idioms | ✓ | ✓ | ✓ |
| Denotation/Connotation | ✓ | ✓ | ✓ |
| Parts of Speech | ✓ | ✓ | ✓ |
| Root Words | ✓ | ✓ | ✓ |
| **WRITING** | | | |
| Proofreading | ✓ | ✓ | ✓ |
| Frequently Misspelled Words | ✓ | ✓ | ✓ |

# Bibliography

## Professional List for Teachers

Bear, Donald R. "'Learning to Fasten the Seat of My Union Suit Without Looking Around': The Synchrony of Literacy Development." *Theory Into Practice* 30, No. 3 (Summer 1991): 149–157.

Bear, Donald R., and Diane Barone. "Using Children's Spelling to Group for Word Study and Directed Reading in the Primary Classroom." *Reading Psychology: An International Quarterly* 10 (1989): 275–292.

Bolton, Faye, and Diane Snowball. *Teaching Spelling: A Practical Resource.* Portsmouth: Heinemann, 1993.

Buchanan, Ethel. *Spelling for Whole-Language Classrooms.* Winnipeg, Canada: 1992.

Chomsky, Carol. "Invented Spelling in the Open Classroom." New England Kindergarten Conference (1973): 499–518. Portions of this article first appeared in "Beginning Reading Through Invented Spelling" in *Quality Education Makes a Difference (1–8)* and are reprinted by permission of Lesley College.

Cunningham, Patricia M., and James W. Cunningham. "Making Words: Enhancing the Invented Spelling-Decoding Connection." *The Reading Teacher* 46 No. 2 (October 1992): 106–115.

Farr, Roger, Cheryl Kelleher, Katherine Lee, and Caroline Beverstock. "An Analysis of the Spelling Patterns of Children in Grades Two Through Eight: Study of a National Sample of Children's Writing." Center for Reading and Language Studies, Indiana University, 1990.

Fry, Edward, Ph.D. *Spelling Book: Words Most Needed Plus Phonics for Grades 1–6.* Laguna Beach, CA: Laguna Beach Educational Books, n.d.

Gentry, J. Richard. *SPEL . . . Is a Four-Letter Word.* Portsmouth: Heinemann, 1983.

Gill, J. Thomas Jr. "Focus on Research: Development of Word Knowledge as It Relates to Reading, Spelling, and Instruction." *Language Arts* 69 (October 1992): 444–453.

Goodman, Yetta M. "Language and the English Curriculum," *Education in the 80's: English.* Edited by R. Baird Shuman, n.p.: National Education Association, 1981.

Graves, Donald H. *Writing: Teachers and Children at Work.* Portsmouth: Heinemann, 1983.

Hillerich, Robert L. *Teaching Children to Write, K–8: A Complete Guide to Developing Writing Skills.* New York: Prentice-Hall, Inc., 1985. (excerpts)

Hodges, Richard E. *Learning to Spell.* Urbana, Illinois: ERIC Clearinghouse on Reading and Communication Skills and National Council of Teachers of English, 1981.

---. "The Conventions of Writing" in *Handbook of Research on Teaching the English Language Arts,* 775–786. n.p., 1991.

Holdaway, Don. "Shared Book Experience: Teaching Reading Using Favorite Books." *In Early Literacy: A Constructivist Foundation for Whole Language.* Edited by Constance Kamiij, Maryann Manning, and Gary Manning, 91–109. n.p. National Education Association, 1991.

Jongsma, Kathleen Stumpf. "Reading-Spelling Links." *The Reading Teacher* (April 1990): 608–610.

---. "Editorial Comment: Developmental Spelling Theory Revisited." *Reading Psychology: An International Quarterly* 10 (1989): iii–x.

Loomer, Bradley M. *Spelling Research: The Most Commonly Asked Questions About Spelling . . . And What the Research Says.* Mt. Vernon, Iowa: Useful Learning, 1990.

McAlexander, Patricia J., Ann B. Dobie, and Noel Gregg. *Beyond the "SP" Label: Improving the Spelling of Learning Disabled and Basic Writers.* National Council of Teachers of English, 1992.

Morris, Darrell. "The Relationship Between Children's Concept of Word in Text and Phoneme Awareness in Learning to Read: A Longitudinal Study." *Research in the Teaching of English* 27, No. 2 (May 1993): 132–154.

---. "'Word Sort': A Categorization Strategy for Improving Word Recognition Ability." *Reading Psychology: An International Quarterly* 3: (1982): 247–259.

Routman, Regie. *Invitations: Changing as Teachers and Learners K–12.* Portsmouth: Heinemann, 1991. (excerpts)

---. "'The Uses and Abuses of Invented Spelling." *Instructor* (May/June 1992): 418–424.

Schlagal, Robert C., and Joy Harris Schlagal. "The Integral Character of Spelling." *Language Arts* 69 (October 1992): 418–424.

Strickland, Dorothy S. "Emergent Literacy: How Young Children Learn to Read." *Educational Leadership* (March 1990): 18–23.

Swisher, Karen. "An Action Model for Research in the Classroom: Developmental Spelling K–2." Paper presented at the annual meeting of the College Reading Association, Crystal City, VA, October 31, 1991 to November 3, 1991.

Templeton, Shane. "New Trends in an Historical Perspective: Old Story, New Resolution—Sound and Meaning in Spelling." *Language Arts* 69 (October 1992): 454–466.

---. "' Teaching and Learning the English Spelling System: Reconceptualizing Method and Purpose." *The Elementary School Journal* 92, No. 2 (1991): 185–201.

Texas Education Agency. *Spelling Instruction: A Proper Perspective.* n.p.: Texas Education Agency, Spring, 1991.

Tompkins, Gail E., and David B. Yaden, Jr. *Answering Students' Questions About Words.* Urbana, Illinois. ERIC Clearinghouse on Reading and Communication Skills and National Council of Teachers of English, 1986.

Wilde, Sandra. "An Analysis of the Development of Spelling and Punctuation in Selected Third and Fourth Grade Children": 1–47. Department of Language, Reading, and Culture, College of Education, University of Arizona, n.d.

---. "A Proposal for a New Spelling Curriculum." *The Elementary School Journal* 90, No. 3 (1990): 275–289.

---. "'Spelling Textbooks: A Critical Review." *Linguistics and Education* 2 (1990): 259–280.

---. *You Kan Red This!* Portsmouth: Heinemann, 1992.

Zutell, Jerry, and Timothy Rasinski. "Children's Spelling Strategies and Their Cognitive Development." *In Developmental and Cognitive Aspects of Learning to Spell: A Reflection of Word Knowledge.* Edited by Edmund H. Henderson and James W. Beers, 52–73. n.p.: International Reading Association, 1980.

---. "Reading and Spelling Connections in Third and Fifth Grade Students." *Reading Psychology: An International Quarterly* 10 (1989): 137–155.

**Word Play and Language-Related List for Students**

Agee, Jon. *Go Hang a Salami! I'm a Lasagna Hog! And Other Palindromes.* New York: Farrar, Straus, & Giroux, 1992.

Albert, Burton. *Code Busters!* Niles, IL: Albert Whitman, 1985.

Barrett, Judi. *A Snake Is Totally Tail.* New York: Atheneum, 1983.

Carroll, Lewis. *Jabberwocky.* Honsdale, PA: Caroline House, 1992.

Ciardi, John. *The Hopeful Trout & Other Limericks.* Boston: Houghton Mifflin, 1989, 1992.

Cole, William. *Poem Stew.* New York: HarperCollins, 1981, 1983.

Gackenbach, Dick. *Timid Timothy's Tongue Twister.* New York: Holiday House, 1986.

Hepworth, Cathi. *Antics! An Alphabetical Anthology.* New York: Putnam, 1992.

Hunt, Bernice K. *The Whatchmacallit Book.* New York: Putnam, 1976.

Kaye, Catherine Berger. *Word Works: Why the Alphabet Is a Kid's Best Friend.* Boston: Little, Brown and Company, 1985.

Keller, Charles. *Daffynitions.* Treehouse, 1978.

Kellogg, Steven. *Aster Aardvark's Alphabet Adventures.* New York: Morrow, 1987, 1992.

Lee, Dennis. *Alligator Pie.* Macmillan Canada, 1974.

Maestro, Guilio. *What's a Frank Frank? Tasty Homograph Riddles.* New York: Clarion, 1984.

---. *What's Mite Might? Homophone Riddles to Boost Your Word Power!* New York: Clarion, 1986.

Musgrove, Margaret. *Ashanti to Zulu: African Traditions.* New York: Clarion, 1988.

Terban, Marvin. *The Dove Dove: Funny Homograph Riddles.* New York: Clarion, 1988.

---. *Too Hot to Hoot: Funny Palindrome Riddles.* New York: Clarion, 1985.

# Index

# Index *(continued)*

**Greek word parts** *[continued]*
*gen-*, 20–21
*opt-*, 58–59
*-phon-*, 20–21
*poli-*, 58–59
*schol-*, 58–59
*soph-*, 58–59
*sym-*, 20–21
*syn-*, 20–21

**Home activities,** (xxii), 2, 4, 6, 8, 10, 16, 18, 20, 22, 24, 30, 32, 34, 36, 38, 44, 46, 48, 50, 56, 58, 60, 62, 68, 70, 72, 74, 76, 78, 94, 97, 100, 103, 106, 109, 112, 115, 118, 121, 124, 127, 130, 133, 136, 139, 142, 145, 148, 151, 154, 157, 160, 163, 166, 169, 172, 175, 178, 181
**Homophones,** 2, 3

**Identifying endings,** 4, 5, 18, 19, 38, 39
**Identifying vowel sounds ,** 32

**Journal entries,** 37

**Kinesthetic modalities,** 21, 35, 73, 75

**Latin Roots**
*-ceive-*, 70–71
*-cept-*, 70–71
*-dict-*, 30–31
*-duc-*, 70–71
*-duct-*, 70–71

*-fin-*, 74–75
*-junct-*, 74–75
*-jus-*, 70–71
*-migr-*, 30–31
*-plex-*, 74–75
*-plic-*, 74–75
*-port-*, 30–31
*-sens-*, 70–71
*-sent-*, 70–71
*-serv-*, 30–31
*-tain-*, 70–71
*-ten-*, 70–71
*-ten(d)-*, 70–71
*-terr-*, 74–75
*-voc-*, 74–75
*-vok-*, 74–75
**Learning differences,** 1, 3, 5, 7, 9, 15, 17, 19, 21, 23, 25, 31, 33, 35, 37, 39, 45, 47, 49, 51, 57, 59, 61, 63, 69, 71, 73, 75, 77, 79
**Limited-English-proficient students**
*See* Meeting individual needs; Second-language support.
**Listening and pronouncing,** 37
**Listening for roots,** 74

**Meeting individual needs**
*See* Second-language support.
**Modalities**
*See* Auditory modalities; Kinesthetic modalities; Visual modalities.
**Modeling,** (xxii), 2, 4, 6, 8, 10, 16, 18, 20, 22, 24, 30, 32, 34, 36, 38, 44, 46, 48, 50, 56, 58, 60, 62, 68, 70, 72, 74, 76, 78

**Nouns,** 38, 39, 48, 49

**Paragraphs,** 7, 11, 19, 21, 23, 33, 37, 39, 59, 79
**Practice activities,** 1, 3, 5, 7, 9, 11, 17, 19, 21, 23, 25, 31, 33, 35, 37, 39, 45, 47, 49, 51, 57,

# Index *(continued)*

**Practice activities,** *[continued]*
59, 61, 63, 69, 71, 73, 75, 77, 79, 95, 98, 101,
104, 107, 110, 113, 116, 119, 122, 125, 128,
131, 134, 137, 140, 143, 146, 149, 152, 155,
158, 161, 164, 167, 170, 173, 176, 179, 182

**Practice test,** 13, 27, 41, 53, 65, 81

**Prefixes**
  *ab-,* 36–37
  *ad-,* 10–11
  *circu(m)-,* 56–57
  *equ(i)-,* 44–45
  *extra-,* 36–37
  *in-,* 10–11
  *inter-,* 34–35
  *intra-,* 56–57
  *intro-,* 56–57
  *magni-,* 44–45
  *micro-,* 44–45
  *multi-,* 44–45
  *ob-,* 50–51
  *per-,* 56–57
  *peri-,* 56–57
  *pro-,* 34–35
  *sub-,* 36–37
  *tele-,* 34–35
  *trans-,* 36–37
  *under-,* 34–35

**Pretests/Posttests,** (xxii), 2, 4, 6, 8, 10, 16, 18,
20, 22, 24, 30, 32, 34, 36, 38, 44, 46, 48, 50,
56, 58, 60, 62, 68, 70, 72, 74, 76, 78

**Proofreading,** 1, 3, 5, 7, 9, 11, 17, 19, 21, 23,
25, 31, 33, 35, 37, 39, 45, 47, 49, 51, 57, 59,
61, 63, 69, 71, 73, 75, 77, 79
  advertisement, 47
  diary entry, 17, 51
  fact file, 35
  journal entry, 37
  letter, 1, 31, 57, 69, 73, 77
  newspaper report, 59
  note, 63
  paragraphs, 7, 11, 19, 21, 23, 33, 37, 39, 59,
    79
  poster, 71
  questions, 49
  report, 3
  sentences, 7, 9, 25, 45, 75
  story, 5

**Pronunciation,** 9, 33

**Recognizing plural endings,** 4
**Recognizing related words,** 6, 22
**Recognizing easily confused words,** 8
**Recognizing patterns,** 46
**Recognizing similarities in words,** 20, 48
**Recognizing specialized vocabulary,** 24
**Recognizing spelling changes,** 70
**Recognizing word parts,** 20, 34

**Resources**
  home activities, (xxii), 2, 4, 6, 8, 10, 16, 18,
    20, 22, 24, 30, 32, 34, 36, 38, 44, 46, 48, 50,
    56, 58, 60, 62, 68, 70, 72, 74, 76, 78, 94, 97,
    100, 103, 106, 109, 112, 115, 118, 121, 124,
    127, 130, 133, 136, 139, 142, 145, 148, 151,
    154, 157, 160, 163, 166, 169, 172, 175, 178,
    181
  practice activities, 1, 3, 5, 7, 15, 17, 19, 21,
    23, 25, 31, 33, 35, 37, 39, 45, 47, 49, 51, 53,
    55, 61, 63, 65, 67, 73, 75, 77, 79, 95, 98,
    101, 104, 107, 110, 113, 116, 119, 122, 125,
    128, 131, 134, 137, 140, 143, 146, 149, 152,
    155, 158, 161, 164, 167, 170, 173, 176, 179,
    182
  word cards, (xxii), 2, 4, 6, 8, 10, 16, 18, 20,
    22, 24, 30, 32, 34, 36, 38, 44, 46, 48, 50, 56,
    58, 60, 62, 68, 70, 72, 74, 76, 78, 93, 96, 99,
    102, 105, 108, 111, 114, 117, 120, 123, 126,
    129, 132, 135, 138, 141, 144, 147, 150, 153,
    156, 159, 162, 165, 168, 171, 174, 177, 180

**Reteaching,** 1, 3, 5, 7, 9, 11, 17, 19, 21, 23, 25,
31, 33, 35, 37, 39, 45, 47, 49, 51, 57, 59, 61,
63, 69, 71, 73, 75, 77, 79

**Roots,** 22, 23, 30, 31, 70, 71, 74, 75

**Scope and sequence,** 196–197

**Second-language support,** (xxii), 2, 4, 6, 7, 8,
14, 16, 18, 20, 21, 22, 23, 24, 30, 31, 32, 34,
36, 38, 44, 46, 48, 49, 51, 56, 58, 60, 62, 63,
68, 70, 71, 72, 73, 74, 76, 78

**Self-check,** (xxii), 2, 4, 6, 8, 14, 16, 18, 20, 22,
24, 30, 32, 34, 36, 38, 44, 46, 48, 50, 52, 54,
60, 62, 64, 66, 72, 74, 76, 78

# Index *(continued)*

**Sorting**
 closed sort, (xxii), 2, 4, 6, 8, 10, 16, 18, 20, 22, 24, 30, 32, 34, 36, 38, 44, 46, 48, 50, 56, 58, 60, 62, 68, 72, 74, 76, 78
 open sort, (xxii), 2, 4, 6, 8, 10, 16, 18, 20, 22, 24, 30, 32, 34, 36, 38, 44, 46, 48, 50, 56, 58, 60, 62, 68, 72, 74, 76, 78
**Spelling clues,** 1, 3, 5, 7, 9, 11, 12, 17, 19, 21, 23, 25, 26, 31, 33, 35, 37, 39, 40, 45, 47, 49, 51, 52, 57, 59, 61, 63, 64, 69, 71, 73, 75, 77, 79, 80
 adding endings to a word, 12
 adjective endings, 19
 analyzing word parts, 64
 base words, 7, 79
 checking base words, 26
 checking base words and suffixes, 80
 checking roots, 31
 checking short vowel sounds, 39, 40
 checking spelling of base words, 12
 checking syllables, 37, 77, 80
 comparing possible spellings, 35, 40, 64
 comparing spelling patterns, 26
 compound words, 1
 correct pronunciation, 9
 double consonants, 12, 47, 52
 finding base words and roots, 80
 French spelling patterns, 17
 Greek words, 23, 59
 Greek word parts, 21
 homophones, 3
 identifying the base word, 49, 52
 Latin roots, 71, 75
 listening to sounds, 69, 80
 prefixes *ad-, in-,* 11, 51, 57
 pronouncing clearly, 40
 pronouncing other forms, 33, 40
 pronouncing words correctly, 12
 proofreading in pairs, 26
 recognizing roots, 40
 suffixes, 79
 trying alternative spellings, 80
 using mnemonic devices, 12
 using pronunciation as a guide, 64
 visualization, 45, 52, 64
 word endings 5
 word parts, 63
 word shapes, 61, 73, 80
 working together, 25
 writing a word two ways, 52

**Spelling strategies,** 1, 3, 5, 7, 9, 11, 12, 17, 19, 21, 23, 25, 26, 31, 33, 35, 37, 39, 40, 45, 47, 49, 51, 52, 57, 59, 61, 63, 64, 69, 71, 73, 75, 77, 79, 80
**Spelling words, (**xxii), 2, 4, 6, 8, 10, 16, 18, 20, 22, 24, 30, 32, 34, 36, 38, 44, 46, 48, 50, 52, 54, 60, 62, 64, 66, 72, 74, 76, 78
**Student self-assessment**
 *See* Self-check.
**Students acquiring English**
 *See* Second-language support.
**Suffixes**
 *-ate,* 38–39
 *-cle,* 72–73
 *-et,* 72–73
 *-ette,* 72–73
 in combination, 78–79
 *-ism,* 48–49
 *-let,* 72–73
 *-ling,* 72–73
 *-ry/-ery,* 48–49
 *-ty,* 48–49
**Summarizing,** 1, 3, 5, 7, 9, 11, 17, 19, 21, 23, 25, 31, 33, 35, 37, 39, 45, 47, 49, 51, 57, 59, 61, 63, 69, 71, 73, 75, 77, 79

**Testing**
 pretest, (xxii), 2, 4, 6, 8, 10, 16, 18, 20, 22, 24, 30, 32, 34, 36, 38, 44, 46, 48, 50, 56, 58, 60, 62, 68, 70, 72, 74, 76, 78
 posttest, 1, 3, 5, 7, 9, 11, 17, 19, 21, 23, 25, 31, 33, 35, 37, 39, 45, 47, 49, 51, 57, 59, 61, 63, 69, 73, 75, 77, 79
 practice test, 13, 27, 41, 53, 65, 81
**Transitional spellers,** 2, 21, 23, 25, 31, 39, 45, 51, 57, 59, 61, 63, 69, 75

**Unit activity options,** 14, 28, 42, 54, 66, 82
**Using context clues,** 63, 78
**Using picture clues,** 23, 31
**Using visual clues,** 36

# Index (continued)